ABANDONED SHIP

SHIP

AN INTIMATE ACCOUNT OF THE
COSTA CONCORDIA SHIPWRECK

BENJI SMITH

ABANDONED SHIP

—

AN INTIMATE ACCOUNT OF THE
COSTA CONCORDIA SHIPWRECK

copyright © 2013 by Benji Smith

First Edition: January 13, 2013
(revision 1; with some minor edits)
(revision 2; fixed lots of typos)
(revision 3; reformatted with smaller type & fewer pages)

published by Benji Smith via CreateSpace
ISBN-13: 978-1481285933
ISBN-10: 1481285939

This is a memoir.
The events described in this book truly happened.
But in the interest of good storytelling,
I've invented lots of dialogue
and changed a few names.

ABANDONED SHIP

PART ONE

I

The stars were beautiful that night.

Though, of course, we didn't notice the stars at all until much later.

On January 13, 2012, at about 9:45 in the evening, the Costa Concordia cruise ship crashed into a reef and sank just off the coast of Giglio, a tiny island in the Mediterranean Sea.

Emily and I were passengers on that ship. It was our honeymoon.

Both of us wore lightweight jackets — much too thin for the coldness of the winter wind blowing across the hull of the ship — and neither of us had any socks. It hadn't occurred to us at the beginning of the disaster that the ship would really sink, or that we'd have to wait five hours to be rescued. In our minds, it was probably just a drill, or maybe a temporary glitch, so we didn't dress for the occasion or gather up any of our belongings. We thought we'd spend fifteen minutes at our emergency "muster station" and then return to our cabin to enjoy the rest of our voyage.

But this was no drill. It was the real thing.

And we didn't escape on the lifeboats.

The ship had listed too severely to one side, and our own lifeboat couldn't be lowered to the water without getting stuck, or flipping over, or crashing into the side of the cruiseliner.

Or maybe the crew just didn't know how to deploy it. We couldn't tell the difference, and it didn't really matter anyhow. They seemed just as scared and confused as the rest of us. Eventually they gave up trying, and we all got back on the ship.

We had been abandoned. Left behind to die.

By that point, all the working lifeboats had long-since gone, and with them most of the passengers and crew.

The ship was sinking. Fast.

We could feel it moving beneath us, being sucked into the sea at an accelerating pace, as though pulled toward its doom by some enormous undersea monster with ten thousand tentacles and a voracious appetite.

The starboard side flooded first, and the ship leaned hard to the right. Tables and chairs overturned, leaving broken glass everywhere, and the walls became floors. As the staircases flooded with water, we stayed on the outside of the ship along the perimeter, searching for safety.

Ultimately, we climbed over the railing and used a sequence of ropes to lower ourselves down the outer hull of the ship. The windows of the cabins on the lower decks gave us footholds until we got down to the lowest part of the hull, the part that would usually be underwater if the ship had been upright.

It was at this point, with nowhere further to go, that we waited for the ship to finally finish sinking.

I told Emily that I loved her. She kissed me. I sang her a song. We cried a little. With one hand each, we held onto the rope. And with the other hand, we held each other.

And then we waited.

We didn't know whether the ship would finish sinking before we could be rescued, but we felt in our hearts that either our rescue or our demise was imminent. Beneath us, the ship lurched and moaned, collapsing into the gaping mouth of the sea. Things were moving so quickly, there was so much adrenaline, so much movement, and water all around us...

And then nothing happened.

An hour passed. Then another hour.

The ship stopped sinking. The rescue boats didn't rescue anyone.

We waited.

And while we waited, we noticed the stars. The cloudless nighttime sky was bright with starlight, and under that illumination, we looked into each other's faces and saw some measure of hope. We sang songs in the moonlight. We cried a little, out of relief and hope and exhaustion and despair.

We told jokes. Crazy morbid jokes.

And we held onto the rope.

This book tells the story of our escape from that sinking ship.

But I'm also going to tell the story of the institutions that failed us. The cruise company. The Italian police. The U.S. and Chinese Embassies. The major news networks. The United States Congress.

In every case, they ignored and dismissed us. One after another, they shrugged their shoulders at our safety and turned their backs on our well-being. We entrusted them with our lives and with our stories and with the pursuit of justice, and one after another, they broke that trust and left us to fend for ourselves.

And we *did* fend for ourselves.

Not just Emily and me, but also our family and friends, and the four thousand strangers who became our brothers and sisters in the midst of this tragedy. We fought hard to escape, and now we're fighting hard to tell our story. When the news media edited our story into sound bites and ignored the institutional failures, we vowed to take the story back from them and tell it ourselves. This book is my humble attempt.

But this is also a spiritual book. Not because it's a religious book — we're not religious people — but because the characters and events in this story represent a microcosm of humanity. A morality play on the sea. Probably more than anything else, this is a book about islands of compassion in a sea of indifference.

Finally, this is a story about an astonishing journey. A journey that took us someplace unexpected — like all important journeys do — and then changed our lives forever.

Sometimes a physical journey becomes a spiritual journey. Sometimes you visit a place, and it changes you.

But *all* spiritual journeys are physical journeys, because you can't get outside yourself unless you leave the house first.

Sometimes you embark upon a journey deliberately, but most of the time, the journey is thrust upon you.

This is our journey.

2

This story began in June 2011, about six months before the cruise. I had just come home from work. Emily sat on the couch with a laptop computer in front of her and a gigantic smile on her face.

"Hey sweetheart," I kissed her. "How was your day?"

"It was good. Really good." she replied breathlessly. "I talked to my aunt Apple this afternoon and she had an idea about going on a cruise together this January from Barcelona to Sicily and then to Rome and the south of France and Tunisia, and she said that she would pay for the whole cost of our cruise which includes meals and lodging, of course, if we just pay for the airfare, because she and John and their friends Erik and Chui Lin want to see Europe but they don't speak any European languages, and even their English isn't good enough, so I can be their tour guide on the trip and book all the hotels and translate for them, and in exchange for being the tour guide, you and I can go on this really cheap trip to Europe, and I think it'll be really *really* fun. What do you think?"

I blinked my eyes.

"What?"

Emily repeated herself.

This is one of the first things you should know about Emily: she throws her whole self into everything she does. You can call it "obsession" if you want, or perhaps even "compulsion," but there's no question that she radiates enthusiasm. It's one of the reasons I love her. But sometimes, if I'm not expecting it, her enthusiasm hits me in the face like a cannonball, and I have to ask her to slow down a little bit.

I had always known about Emily's lust for travel. She was born in Hong Kong — where all of her extended family mem-

14

bers still live — but she started traveling the world when she was still very young. As a middle-school student, she enrolled in a foreign exchange program for a few weeks in California. And then she spent her last two years of high school studying music at a boarding school in England before going to college in Miami and grad school in Boston.

Now, she's the founder and artistic director of a classical music ensemble, but she also does a lot of touring on her own — three weeks out of four during the busy season — so she's an expert travel planner with plenty of practice planning complicated trips for big groups of people. She's been all over Europe and Asia, and now she wanted to bring me along on her world travels.

"Yeah sure," I said. I'm usually up for adventure, though I'm not very impulsive myself. "Sounds like fun."

For the next six months, Emily and Apple planned the details of the trip.

* * *

Apple is Emily's favorite aunt, and Emily is Apple's favorite niece.

The first time you hear her name, you might think it's a little weird. But for someone from Hong Kong, with a Chinese name given at birth and an English name chosen sometime later, it's actually a perfectly normal name. We also know a girl named "Oscar" and a friend of a friend named "Yogurt."

Apple is forty years old and works as an officer in the Hong Kong Police Department.

Since Hong Kong is so dense and so urban, most cops don't drive cars. Officers on patrol generally walk through a neighborhood in uniform, mingling and getting to know the people and the business owners, keeping the peace, responding to reports of disorderly conduct or minor street crime. Driving a car has become something of a symbol of achievement in the Hong Kong police force, reserved for the most skilled and versatile drivers. Apple was one of the first women ever to pass the driving exam.

On some days, she might drive a government official from one police station to another and then take a long lunch. But on other days, she transports criminals between prison buildings or gets into high-speed chases to catch escaping fugitives. The work suits her well. She's equally content cruising around the city all afternoon, or engaging in a high-stakes adventure full of hot speed and adrenaline.

In her spare time, she plays professional baseball with the Hong Kong national team. And when she's not doing that, she cultivates live coral. It's a slow, solitary, meticulous hobby. It's actually a lot like growing bonsai trees, but underwater. She's been doing it for more than ten years now, and just a few weeks ago, she sold her living room couch to make room for a new hundred-gallon tank.

Of course, it's impossible to introduce Apple without simultaneously introducing her husband John. Throughout this book, anytime you hear Apple's voice, you can pretty much always imagine John standing by her side nodding his head and smiling contentedly, both of them dressed in hiking boots and neon-colored ski jackets from The North Face. They go everywhere together, and they always get along.

Curiously, she never refers to him by name. She always just says "my husband."

John works for the Hong Kong police too, managing the fleet of vehicles. He's not a mechanic, but there are mechanics that work for him, or in his department at least; he's not exactly an officer or a manager, though he works alongside those kinds of cops too.

The way I understand it, when some other police officer says "There's something wrong with my police car," John's job is to say, "Okay, I'll make sure somebody takes care of that for you."

Because the Hong Kong P.D. is so generous with giving vacation days to its employees, John and Apple spend most of their free time travelling the world, trekking in Nepal, riding motorcycles through Thailand and crisscrossing Europe.

Anyhow, Apple is the reason we went on this trip. The whole cruise was her idea.

* * *

Emily and I originally met online. Not on a dating site, but on *craigslist*.

I was living in Cambridge, Massachusetts and looking for a new housemate, so I put up an ad online, and Emily replied. She moved in a few weeks later.

We became fast friends, but nothing romantic developed between us for the first six months or so. After that, things moved very quickly. We saw each other every day — and shared a home together — so once we started dating, the relationship quickly developed into something serious. But let me tell you… It can be very awkward trying to foster a budding new relationship with a housemate, going out on a first date with somebody who already keeps her toothbrush right next to yours.

We had been dating for about nine months at this point, but we weren't even engaged when we started making our Costa Concordia plans, so it wasn't originally supposed to be our honeymoon.

After a spontaneous proposal and a six-week engagement, we eloped on December 30th, a few days before leaving for Europe and a week or so before boarding the cruise ship.

It was a tiny wedding. Instead of inviting our family and friends from all of the United States, Asia, and Europe, we had a private ceremony at the Cambridge Town Hall with just the two of us (and a few friends we enlisted to capture the event in photos and videos). The day after the wedding, we sent this video to everyone we knew:

http://bit.ly/benjiandemily

A silly video for a spur-of-the-moment wedding, between two ridiculous people.

The next morning, December 31st, I woke up and looked at Emily lying next to me.

"Happy anniversary," I said.

"Mmmmmmm… Happy anniversary." she replied groggily, rolling over and putting her arm around me. "Sing me a song…"

Without a moment's thought, I opened my mouth and hoped something coherent would come out:

Today is the…
second-most special day…
in the his-to-ry…
of our marriage.
It's the anniversary…
of YESTERDAY!
Happy one-day anniversary!

Okay, so maybe it wasn't coherent. I'm not much of a song-writer. Still though, for the first few weeks of our marriage, I sang a new anniversary song every day.

3

When Chloe and Owen were born, their bodies were like kittens. Owen weighed two pounds five ounces, and Chloe weighed one pound, fifteen ounces.

These are my twins, and I'd like to take a moment to introduce them too, as well as my youngest daughter Macy. They didn't sail with us on the Costa Concordia, but they're always on my mind, so their roles in this story are important too.

But before I introduce the kids, I actually need to go way back in time and tell you something about my own upbringing. I grew up as the middle child — the second of three boys — in a devout Mormon family. We went to church together every single week (my dad was the volunteer Bishop of our congregation for a few years), and there was never any coffee or alcohol in my house. We weren't even allowed to watch TV on Sundays. We were hardcore.

Both of my brothers served as missionaries for two years in the jungles of Guatemala, but by the time I was old enough to go on a mission, I already knew I wasn't interested.

I didn't believe.

After high school, I moved to Salt Lake City and attended Brigham Young University. At first, I was nervous about going to a Mormon school, but I made lots of friends and got involved in the theater program — I majored in playwriting — and after a few semesters I stopped daydreaming about transferring to some other school.

One semester, I fell in love with a Mormon girl named Julie who I met in my Shakespeare class. We were sure that our love was strong enough to bridge our differences in faith, and our different ideas about the world, and our different goals in life. We were so sure it would all work out. I was twenty-one and she was twenty-four when we got married, and after four years together, we had kids.

Chloe and Owen were born three months early — at 27 weeks gestation — and they spent the next four months under constant medical care in the Newborn ICU of the Utah Valley Regional Medical Center.

They had feeding tubes up their noses and oxygen tubes down their throats. EKG pads had been glued to their chests, and the glowing red light of an oxygen sensor had been taped to the bottoms of their feet. Their eyes were still closed (again, like kittens), and a protective mask shaded their faces from the bright hospital lights. All day and all night, their bodies trembled with the mechanical rhythmic breathing of the high-frequency respiratory ventilators, delivering an unnerving 150 breaths per minute.

Their skin was covered with a thin, wispy coat of fur. With their rose-and-honey-colored skin, it made them look like peaches.

Julie and I stayed by their bedside, singing them songs and kissing the tops of their heads and holding their hands, which were still too tiny to even clasp around my thumb. We unbuttoned our shirts and held the babies against our bare chests, so that they could feel our warmth and hear our heartbeats.

Owen developed some minor problems with his lungs, and he fought off pneumonia during his first few weeks of life. But for the most part, he thrived.

Chloe, on the other hand, battled through an onslaught of injuries and tribulations.

First of all, she suffered from high blood pressure. The beeping and buzzing of the machines can be very stressful to premature infants, who ought to still be swaddled in the warmth and quiet of the womb. So the doctors gave her medication to keep her blood pressure down.

But with all the poking and prodding, and all the needles and tubes, her blood pressure kept climbing, eventually causing a capillary in her brain to burst.

When we got the news, Julie and I could hardly breathe. For days and days, we did nothing but cry.

The hemorrhage caused a blood clot to form in her ventricles, clogging their normal drainage and leading to an excess buildup of cerebrospinal fluid. A team of neurologists performed brain surgery on her, implanting a thin tube — looking almost like a strand of spaghetti — deep into her brain. This tube would let the fluids drain, relieving the pressure and preventing additional swelling around the muscular-control centers of her cerebral cortex.

The damage already done in those brain regions would eventually lead to cerebral palsy. But there seemed to be some damage to her pituitary gland as well, triggering the onset of premature puberty. Chloe would need annual shots of powerful hormones to keep adolescence at bay.

At the same time, an over-saturation of oxygen in her bloodstream caused runaway growth of new capillaries in her eyes. Without surgery, her retinas would detach, and she would be blinded for life. A pediatric ophthalmologist clamped her eyes open for an hour and a half, shooting more than two thousand bursts of laser light to burn away the excess capillary tissue from the back of her eyes.

I stood there in the operating room and watched.

Meanwhile, the muscle at the top of her stomach — the muscle responsible for maintaining a tight seal between her stomach and esophagus — was too weak to do its job, and Chloe suffered intense burning pains of acid reflux, especially when she ate.

To cope with that pain, she suppressed her sucking reflex and stopped eating.

A team of neonatal gastroenterologists performed a *nissen fundoplication* surgery, cinching up some of her stomach tissue (like a drawstring at the top of a pair of sweatpants) and implanting a feeding tube directly into Chloe's stomach.

To this day, there's a little plastic nozzle on her tummy, like a beach ball, and we learned to feed her by squeezing a syringe of breast-milk through a tube and into that nozzle.

And then, just when we thought all of Chloe's medical issues had all been taken care of, the drainage tube in her brain got clogged and needed to be replaced.

So she needed brain surgery.

Again.

All the while, Julie and I sat at her bedside and cried and wondered why.

Why was this happening to us?

Why was this happening to our daughter?

21

Julie wrestled with crippling guilt, plagued with the notion that she might have done something wrong in managing her pregnancy. Maybe she shouldn't have gone for all those long walks with me. Maybe she should have been more diligent about bed-rest during the riskiest parts of the pregnancy. Maybe there was something she could have *done* to prevent the premature birth.

But even more than that, she wondered what this disaster was supposed to *mean* in our lives? Was this misery brought upon us as a punishment from God? What lesson was our Heavenly Father trying to convey? Was he trying to teach us humility through sacrifice? Was he trying to teach us patience and kindness? She bent her knees to the ground and raised her eyes toward the heavens and asked why. Over and over again, *why?*

Sometimes she would wipe the tears from her eyes and smile at me, saying "God never gives us more than we can handle. Whenever things get really bad in our lives — whenever we're really sad and struggling to get by — we should remember to feel flattered, because God thinks we're strong enough to pull through."

She looked to me for strength and stability. In our Mormon household, I was the priesthood holder and she turned to me as the conduit to God's power, asking me to give Chloe a healing blessing.

Mormons believe that when men are ordained as stewards of the priesthood, they literally wield the power of God in their hands. And when they keep their hearts and minds aligned with the voice of the Holy Ghost, they can righteously command the elements of the earth to obey. They can persuade winds to change their course and wounds to be healed in accordance with God's mighty will.

During my time as a Mormon, I was ordained an Elder of the priesthood. I had been entrusted with this power and authority.

With my tiny daughter in the hospital, her body so badly broken and our hearts so heavy with her suffering, Julie turned to me and asked me to perform the laying-on-of-hands and say a prayer of blessing for Chloe.

My heart pounded.

Was I worthy to hold God's priesthood power?

Did I even believe in God?

I had become an atheist many years before — when my high school science classes started teaching me about evolution and DNA and dinosaurs, and when my social studies classes taught me about the bloodthirsty history of religious wars throughout the ages — and I had always felt comfortable and happy with my atheism.

But after Julie and I got married, I had started coming back to church again. Usually I sat next to her and read a paperback novel while she participated in the weekly service. But over the past few years, I had also gradually returned to the faith, and I was now teaching Sunday School classes and participating in the church community.

I had friends in that community, and we all took comfort in the network of kind-hearted people we could rely upon to help us out during tough times. Being a part of that community was nourishing and wonderful.

But did I actually believe in any of this stuff?

Julie looked at me and repeated her question.

"Will you give Chloe a blessing?"

I looked down at my hands, these hands that had been authorized by God to wield his mighty power.

"Yes," I replied. "Of course."

The next day, I stood at Chloe's bedside and put my hands on her tiny head.

"Chloe Madison Smith," I closed my eyes and spoke these words I knew by heart. "By the power of the Melchizedek Priesthood which I hold, I lay my hands upon your head and confer upon you a healing blessing from the Lord."

And then I stopped.

This was the part of the blessing where I could speak by inspiration, saying whatever words came into my mind. I bit my lower lip and squeezed my eyes more tightly shut, tears streaming down my cheeks, as I tried to quiet my thoughts and focus my mind to listen for the promptings of the Holy Ghost, a character I was pretty sure didn't even exist.

I had heard other people offer these kinds of blessings before. I had heard them say "In the name of Jesus Christ, I command you to be healed." And I had heard their confidant booming voices as they ordered cancer cells to remiss and diseases to abate. I knew all the words to say.

23

But I couldn't bring myself to say them.

"Chloe, your Heavenly Father loves you very much." I wept as I spoke. "He has important plans for you in this life, as a member of your Earthly family and as one of His children. Your story will be an inspiration, and your presence will bring joy into many people's hearts."

I couldn't do it.

I couldn't speak the words that would make her whole, because I didn't believe it would work. I knew it was a fantasy — a dream — and I was just as ashamed to indulge in that fantasy as I was to abstain from it.

I opened my eyes and wiped the tears from my face. As much as I wanted to, I couldn't perform a miracle. As much as my heart broke from yearning for it, I couldn't command the impossible.

I looked down at my wiggly little daughter smiling up at me, and I wondered why.

Why should I look for meaning somewhere else? Why should I close my eyes and ask for answers from the heavens when I could open them instead, and look at the world right in front of me, accepting it without explanation or miraculous intervention?

Why search and struggle and yearn for the threads of God's great plan, when I could instead turn my face downward to the earth and appreciate the grit and texture of the universe's grand improvisation?

The heavens are empty, but the earth is full of life.

* * *

I felt a crushing burden lift from my shoulders.

The trauma of Chloe and Owen's premature birth felt so much more manageable without having to also worry about interpreting God's inscrutable plans. And talking to doctors about the potential outcomes of various procedures felt much more comforting to my heart than pleading with God for a miracle.

It took me a few months to muster up the courage to tell Julie about my collapsing faith. It was especially hard to communicate with her, since she had learned to take so much comfort and solace from her belief in God, and the two of us had begun to speak different languages.

From her vulnerable vantage point, my words were like poison; hopeless and sterile. Likewise, her increasing devotion had become oppressive and burdensome to me.

Over the next year, we tried to figure out what to do. We loved each other very much and wanted to stay together. But we couldn't figure out how to navigate our shared life anymore, with two different North Stars leading toward two different horizons.

We tried befriending other mixed-faith couples and asking them how they kept their marriages functioning, but none of them seemed happy.

Mormon doctrine makes it pretty much impossible for a Mormon and a non-Mormon to stay happily married for a lifetime, and we eventually figured out that we too would be happier apart.

* * *

Nine years have passed since the twins' premature birth. Over the course of those years, Chloe has overcome a mountain of obstacles, learning to talk and walk and eat and read and write. She still gets most of her nourishment through that little nozzle in her tummy, and she still walks with a limp. And yes, her vision is pretty bad.

Her mind operates on a slightly different plane than the rest of us, but she smiles and laughs and asks questions and gives people hugs and rides the bus to school and plays with her toys. She knows her multiplication tables, and her spelling is impeccable. All things considered, she has a pretty good life.

Owen watches out for Chloe. He holds her hand and whispers quiet words to comfort her. He hangs out with her, and he cares for her, and when she gets left behind or teased by other kids, sometimes he cries for her. I've never seen another kid with so much sincerity and kindness and warmth and sensitivity.

But worry is the companion of sensitivity, and Owen is a chronic worrier. I know he worries about my faith. He's not quite sure what to think about a dad who doesn't go to church, and I'm not quite sure what to do about that either.

* * *

Five months after our divorce, Macy was born.

Macy is a bright, delightful child with basically no fear of anything. She's fiercely independent, too. Taking her to the mall or the aquarium or any crowded place is a recipe for losing her. At any moment, Macy might decide she'd rather be out exploring by herself than under the supervision of any adult, so she'll disappear around a corner and head off in her own direction.

She has a wickedly off-kilter sense of humor too. Once, when she was just four years old, she asked if she could tell me a story.

"Sure, sweetheart," I said. "I'd love to hear a story."

"Once upon a time, there was a momma and a baby" she said, her voice singsongy with storybook nostalgia. "At bedtime, the momma said, 'night night, baby,' and put the baby down in the crib. Then she turned off the lights and shut the door."

"But then," Macy said, her voice suddenly lowering to a whisper. "a bunch of ants walked under the door and into the room. They climbed up the crib and under the covers. And they ate the baby, until there was nothing left but *bones*!"

For a moment, I could say nothing. I was stunned silent. When the blood returned to my face, I laughed and congratulated Macy on telling such a good story.

More recently, Macy accidentally swallowed a handful of magnets — those super-powerful little round magnets, each about the size of a pea. She had been trying to determine whether they were strong enough to attract each other through her teeth, and then somehow, she swallowed five of them.

As it turns out, those magnets can be deadly if swallowed. They can get stuck inside a person's digestive system, potentially even ripping holes in the intestinal walls.

As soon as Julie realized the danger, she called 911. Macy was excited to ride in the ambulance, but she got *really* excited when she found out that she might even need surgery.

When she pooped out the magnets later that night, averting the worst potential outcomes, Macy was especially disappointed that nobody was going to cut her open, which would have been "so *cool*."

So anyhow, those are my kids:

Chloe the Special.

Owen the Kindhearted.

Macy the Brave.

At the time of the shipwreck, Chloe and Owen had just turned nine. Macy was seven. I think about them all the time, and even if they weren't physically with us on the Costa Concordia, they were always on my mind.

4

"Someday, we should take your kids on a cruise like this," said Emily, as we dragged our suitcases along the sidewalk next to the pier, our necks bent backwards and our faces turned upward in awe. The ship was so big as to strain our imaginations.

"Yeah," I replied, squinting up at the great looming girth beside us. "This ship would blow their minds."

At almost a thousand feet long, the Costa Concordia stretched further than three football fields from stem to stern. That's about two tenths of a mile, making it the biggest Italian ship ever built, and twice the size of the Titanic. And with its seventeen decks — including thirteen passenger decks and four decks of offices and engine rooms and infirmaries and kitchens, and then of course all the cabins for the thousand-plus crew members — well, this was really more of a floating city than a cruise ship.

A boat is a mere vehicle… This was a behemoth, a civilization cast upon the waters.

It was January 9th, and we were in Spain. We had spent the past four days in Barcelona, in a fourth floor walk-up apartment on *Passeig de Gràcia*, near the *Avinguda Diagonal*. We ate tremendous food and drank tiny cups of excellent coffee, and we visited our friends in their cute little retirement bungalow nearby.

We saw the stunning, impossible architecture of Gaudí as we walked through his masterwork, the *Sagrada Família* — an absolutely mammoth cathedral in the heart of Barcelona with an architectural style I had never seen before.

Unlike the gothic cathedrals I had seen elsewhere in Europe, this building had no straight lines or right angles anywhere. The walls and pillars and towers and lofts were all designed with organic curves and spirals, the spires reaching up into the sky like stalks of asparagus. The façade was festooned with stone foliage, adorned with carvings of palm fronds and ivy and cypress trees and flowers. Great stone turtles sat beneath the bases of the massive spiral columns, and hundreds of tiny bird statues — of pelicans and doves and geese — perched upon the exterior structures of the building. All of this lushness carved from stone.

The interior was somehow even more breathtaking than the exterior. Row after row of monolithic stone columns rose up from the ground like tree trunks, tapering as they climbed skyward and branching into hundreds of smaller stone limbs, this massive scaffolding supporting a leafy stone canopy above us. And at the center of that canopy, nearly 250 feet overhead, an intoxicating ray of sunshine shone down through a circular skylight, illuminating an orange-and-gold spiral, radiating outward from the center and looking exactly like the sun shining through the treetops.

Construction of this fantastical basilica had begun in 1883 and continued until Gaudí died in 1926. There were a few decades of interruption, but construction picked back up again in the 1950s and continues to this day. Although the doors opened to the public just a few years ago, in 2010, it's still not even finished. The current architectural team estimates a completion date sometime in 2026 or 2028.

When the people of Barcelona asked Gaudí if he was worried about the project timeline — a project that wouldn't be completed until more than a hundred years after his death — he famously said "My client is not in a hurry."

I thought about Gaudí as Emily and I walked along the pier, craning our necks to gape at the enormous cruise ship floating in the water next to us. I felt almost the same feeling of smallness looking up at the ship as I had felt a few days before, staring up into the stonework canopy of the *Sagrada Família*. Both structures took my breath away, drawing my gaze with an uncanny magnetism as I whispered to myself: *How is this possible? How could human beings possibly have built such a thing?*

"Welcome to the Costa Concordia!" said the woman at the desk, a sunny smile spread across her cheeks. "Tickets and passports, please."

We gave her our tickets and showed her our passports,

though we were surprised to learn that the cruise company would keep our passports for the whole duration of the cruise.

"It actually makes things much easier for you," said the woman, with a delightful Italian accent. "As long as we stay within the European Union, there's no need for you to show your passport when we go from Spain to Italy or from Italy to France. We've already taken care of everything for you. So you can go ashore sooner and see more of the local attractions. And when you come back here to Barcelona, we give you your passport back."

"That makes sense," said Emily, as the agent tucked our passports into a box behind the counter.

"Aboard the ship, you need only to carry your Costa Card," the agent continued, as she lead us in front of a screen and snapped our pictures with a digital camera. "The Costa Card is your identification and your room key. It's linked to your credit card, so you can also use it to buy food and drinks, or in the slot machines in the casino; you can use it to pay for spa treatments or massages or to enroll in our guided off-ship excursions. Whenever you leave the ship to visit a port, a crew member will scan your Costa Card. And then in the evenings, before we head back out to sea, we won't leave port until every person has returned to the ship and scanned their Costa Cards at the door."

Two plastic cards slid from a slot in a machine on the counter — our smiling faces printed on the back of the card next to the magnetic strip — and the woman behind the counter handed them to Emily and me. They were still warm, like cookies.

"And then here are your emergency cards," added the desk agent, giving us a second set of plastic cards, these ones bright red. "We ask you to please attend a safety presentation at five o'clock, in the London Lounge, at the far end of deck five. At the end of the presentation, we will collect your red safety cards, so please do make sure to attend."

We handed over our luggage and walked up the gangplank into the ship, scanning our brand new cards with a crew member at the door.

"Welcome aboard," he said, gesturing toward the lobby through the doors behind him. "Your cabin will be number 2265, on the second deck. You can find stairs and elevators through the doorway and down the hall to your left."

We thanked him and stepped through the main entrance into the Europa Atrium, a vast entrance hall with fifty-foot ceilings and every surface adorned with a smorgasbord of lush, lickable ornamentation in a rainbow of colors and textures. Everything looked like it was made of candy.

From the ceiling, a garden of blown-glass sea anemones hung upside down into the room. Illuminated from within by an ever-changing spectrum of vivid color combinations — first pink-and-green, then crimson-and-orange or blue-and-red — they cast an otherworldly glow down into the foyer.

At the other end of the room, a bank of four glass elevators cars climbed up and down the height of the room — each one clear and crystalline with emerald green glass details and brass-trimmed fixtures around cherry wood panels — hauling new passengers up to their rooms on the upper decks. Some other passengers walked up and down the grand staircase, poking their heads into the jewelry shops and art galleries on the upper levels or peering over the bannisters and down into the hall where we stood.

At the customer service desk in the far corner, men and women stood behind the counter wearing white shirts and navy-blue blazers. Flag-pins on their lapels indicated the different languages they could each speak, and in front of their desk, a buzzing, chattering group of new passengers checked in and asked questions about the ship, or about their cabins, or their new Costa Cards. Across from the customer service desk, a dozen or so passengers sat laughing and mingling and sipping drinks at a long, curving bar with an obsidian countertop. The rich red leather pedestal of each barstool sat perched atop a gleaming column of freshly-polished chrome. The bartender — dressed in a black vest and bowtie — rattled a silver shaker over his shoulder and poured a bright blue concoction into a row of sultry glass goblets.

The floor in front of the bar was checkered with tiny black and white tiles arranged in a herringbone pattern. And in the center of the huge room, there was a wide circular dance floor made from pale hardwood and inlaid with walnut panels, cut into the shape of a sea anemone. Just like the ceiling.

A glossy black grand piano sat on the other side of the dance floor, though it was still early in the afternoon, so there was no pianist at the keyboard.

We climbed downstairs one level and found our cabin. There were two hallways running lengthwise through the ship, and a row of cabins on each side of both hallways. So there were two rows of cabins on the exterior of the ship — with windows and balconies overlooking the sea — but there were also two rows of cabins on the ship's interior, with no windows at all.

That's where we found our cabin: on the starboard side, in an interior room with no windows. John and Apple had splurged for cabin on deck 7, with a big balcony overlooking the water. Erik and Chui Lin (pronounced "choy-lin") were in the room next door. But Emily and I opted for the cheaper, simpler room without a view. It was comfortable, and we didn't need anything fancy anyhow.

It looked pretty much like any ordinary motel room — though perhaps a bit smaller — with a seamless injection-molded plastic bathroom in the corner, almost exactly like an airplane lavatory, but with a built-in shower stall.

Our luggage had already arrived — the two suitcases lined up next to the foot of the bed — so we unpacked our clothes into the closets and drawers, and then we left our cabin to explore the rest of the ship. We checked out the four different swimming pools, five restaurants, thirteen bars, and three dance floors. Plus the library, theater, casino, art gallery, chapel, video arcade, and tennis courts.

"Look, they even have a daycare center," said Emily, "with activities for kids of all different ages."

"Very interesting," I said, nodding my head. "Maybe we really should bring my kids on a cruise like this someday."

"I think they would love it here," she replied.

* * *

By the time we finished our tour and made our way down to the fifth deck London Lounge, we were five minutes late for the safety presentation.

"There's a world-class chocolatier directly behind us in the Budapest Piano Bar, and a full casino-style gambling experience — with video poker machines and an assortment of table games — in the Barcelona Casino, just past the piano bar."

Emily and I sat in the back of the room and watched the

English-speaking host — a guy named Sean — narrating a PowerPoint presentation about the ship.

"He's still talking about the layout of the ship," whispered Emily. "Maybe he hasn't gotten to the safety information yet."

For the next twenty minutes, Sean told us about all the ship's amenities. He told us where to go for breakfast and how to order an unlimited-drinks package using our Costa Card. He told us about onboard spa — the biggest spa on any cruise ship in the world — and the different kinds of face and body services it offered. His PowerPoint slides featured an exhaustive grid of data explaining the different pricing tiers for the various spa packages and different kinds of discounts we might qualify for.

"They have a two hour 'couple's massage,'" Emily whispered, snickering at the screen. "It's only 200 euros."

"You really can't go wrong with the excursions," continued Sean. "These are *guided* bus tours, taking you to all of the most beautiful sites, so that you can save time going from place to place, tasting all the local flavors without missing a thing. And of course, you can also charge the excursions to your Costa Card."

Finally, he finished his presentation, turning the slideshow off and the lights on, and saying, "If you have any questions whatsoever, please feel free to ask. My name is Sean, and I'm here to help you make the most of your cruise."

We got up from our seats and approached the podium at the front of the room.

"Hi Sean," said Emily. "Are you the one who collects our red safety cards?"

"Yes actually, I am," he said, taking the cards and putting them into his pocket.

"We walked in a few minutes late," Emily continued. "Did we miss anything important? Is there going to be a drill?"

"There's no drill today," said Sean, "but you can find all the safety information you need in your cabin. There'll be a red binder on the desk, with information about ship's emergency procedures. And on the back of your cabin doors, there's a map of the ship with an escape route."

"Oh, okay," said Emily. "Thanks for your help."

"No problem," Sean smiled. "If you have any questions, please feel free to find me anytime and ask."

5

Dinner on the Costa Concordia is served in two massive shifts. At six o'clock, 1500 people file into the two main restaurants. Every place setting has a two-page paper menu providing at least three different choices for each course of a six-course meal. By six fifteen, a fleet of Filipino waiters wearing black tuxedos sweep through both restaurants, taking everyone's orders and start delivering drinks.

Over the next two hours, the waiters deliver all six courses — passengers wolfing down cheese platters and duck confits and raspberry sorbets — until eight o'clock, when the kitchen staff start to cleanup and prepare for the next round. At nine o'clock, they do the whole thing over again with the other 1500 passengers.

"Welcome aboard the Costa Concordia, ladies and gentlemen," said our waiter, "My name is Ronald del Mundo, and I'll be your dinner waiter for the next seven days."

Ronald spoke softly. He was tall and thick, built like a tree trunk with a big smile and bright eyes, and he always addressed us as "sir" and "ma'am."

Over the next four days, Ronald tended to all of our fussy AmerAsian whims without complaint, bringing ice water for the Americans and hot water for the Chinese and breaking all the rules of the prix fixe menu on our behalf, bringing us an extra appetizer or letting us trade a dessert for another piece of fish. He brought us extra napkins and extra plates and he waited patiently while Emily translated back and forth between English and Cantonese to place everyone else's orders.

"What does asterisk mean on menu?" asked Apple, pointing to a tiny star in the margin next to the chicken piccata.

"Ah yes, ma'am" said Ronald, glancing down at the menu.

"Those items are prepared ashore and frozen fresh in our facility; we defrost them and finish them here in the ship's kitchen before serving them to you."

"Frozen food?" asked Apple, scanning through the menu and looking at all the asterisks in the margins. Two thirds of the menu items were essentially TV dinners.

"Yes, ma'am," replied Ronald with a warm understanding smile. "If you prefer, you can always choose one of the other items from the menu — the items without an asterisk — and you can rest assured that those items will have been freshly prepared."

We ate our meal and drank our wine and laughed about the ridiculous immensity of the ship. Emily was always at the center of the conversation, since she was the only one who could speak fluently in both English and Cantonese to translate for the group.

As we came to the end of our meal, Apple asked, "How old are you, Ronald? How long you work on cruise ship?"

"I'm forty years old, ma'am," he replied. "And I work sixteen hours every day. Seven days a week."

All of us gasped.

"Sixteen hours?" I asked. "With no weekends?"

Ronald smiled and nodded gently, "People need to eat every day."

"But that's not what I asking," interjected Apple. "I mean... how many *years* you work on cruise ships?"

"I've been aboard the Costa Concordia ever since she set sail in 2006. And then I was aboard another ship before this one for ten years."

"Sixteen years? You've been working on a cruise ship the past sixteen years?" asked Emily. "Seven days a week for sixteen hours a day?"

"Sometimes I take a week to go back ashore and visit my family," said Ronald. "But, yes ma'am, that's basically true."

"Where is your family?" asked John.

"In the Philippines, sir," he replied. "Would you like to see a picture of my daughter?"

"Yes, please," we all replied.

Ronald looked over his shoulder — probably to make sure his supervisors were out of sight — and then he reached into his wallet for a dog-eared photo of a teenage girl.

"She's going to college in the fall," he said. "That's why I work all these long days, over all these long years."

Gently, he placed the picture back into his wallet and then said, "Time for dessert, ladies and gentlemen. Have you all made your selections?"

6

Over the next few days, we visited Palma de Mallorca, and then Cagliari and Palermo.

Originally, Tunisia had also been on the itinerary, and I had been excited to visit northern Africa for the first time. But ever since the Arab Spring — started by the Tunisian fruit vendor who lit himself on fire to protest harassment by the corrupt local government officials — Tunisia had been embroiled in revolution, and our cruise ship was not going to stop there.

In Sardinia, we rode a rickety bus up a precarious road, to the top of a cactus-covered bluff, where we visited a medieval church built into a cave in the side of the mountain. I bought my kids lots of little trinkets and souvenirs from street vendors — marionettes and figurines and picture books and a necklace with a purple pendant — and Emily and I took hundreds (yes, hundreds!) of pictures together. In Sicily, we bought boxes of fresh sun-dried tomatoes and salted capers at an outdoor produce market. Then, Emily and Apple each bought a bowl of steamed octopi and ate them like candy.

Every morning, when we left the ship, we scanned our Costa Cards at the door. And every evening, when we returned, we scanned them again to signify our arrival.

On most days, we had seven or eight hours of shore time between our arrival and our next departure. But those intervals usually overlapped with the local siesta hours — when all the local businesses closed and all the employees took afternoon naps — so mostly we just looked into the shop windows and walked the city sidewalks enjoying the architecture and the street entertainers.

When we came back to the ship each evening, our room had been tidied up for us: the bed made and the towels hung, of course. But we were surprised to see that our dirty laundry had all been picked up off the floor, folded, and stacked at the foot of the bed. All of our loose papers had likewise been gathered up and stacked on the desk.

We never saw any crew member enter or exit our room, but every time we left for a few moments, somebody would come into our room and straighten things up. Whether we went to eat breakfast or dinner, or if we spent a few hours dancing or having drinks, the room was always tidier when we returned than it had been when we left. The only explanation I could conceive of was: elves.

"There's a card by the door," said Emily. "It says our cabin steward is named 'Jonathan,' and that he's pleased to be of service."

We never saw Jonathan work his elvish magic, but we appreciated his willingness to serve.

* * *

As the days passed, the novelty of the ship's lush interior design had grown a bit stale. Where before we had seen glassy surfaces and wood paneling and leather upholstery, now that we looked more closely, we saw plasticky materials and plywood veneers and vinyl chairs.

The ostentatious ornamentation in every direction started to look dusty and tacky and gaudy, like Las Vegas. Not the sleek new parts of Vegas with the Bellagio and the Venetian, and a different Cirque du Soleil show on every street corner. I'm talking about Liberace in a velvet tuxedo playing a rhinestone piano. Old Vegas.

This feeling of gold-plated faux luxury was reinforced every evening when we returned to the restaurant and placed our dinner orders from a fancy-sounding menu of defrosted items.

And then every evening between dinner courses, the wait staff would perform a brief, painfully cheesy, musical number. For example, after our first day in Italy, while we waited for our main entree to be served, the loudspeakers crackled to life and a recorded voice said — first in Italian and then Spanish and French before finally English — "Attention, passengers and crewmembers. The wait staff of the Ristorante Roma would like to dedicate this next song to all of you."

The members of the wait staff — each of them now wearing a floppy Italian chef's hat in red, white, or green — took their positions on the upper balcony of the two-story restaurant, or lined up along the banister of the grand staircase or down in the lower-level where we sat. After a few moments, the loud-speakers played a crackly recording of an accordion, and the waiters sang:

> *When the moon hits your eye*
> *like a big pizza pie,*
> *that's amore!*

I felt bad for them. Although this was technically an Italian cruise ship, most of the crew members were from the Philippines or India or South America, so they probably weren't bubbling with Italian national pride. And most of them had probably been singing this song once a week for the past sixteen years. They didn't look like they enjoyed it much anymore. Somewhere along the line, they had lost their passion for this piece of classic Italian culture.

* * *

After dinner that night, the six of us went to the Budapest Piano Bar on the fifth deck and found a big round table with a wrap-around booth near the chocolatier. Once we got ourselves all situated, we waved to a passing cocktail waitress with tiny flags of Britain and Spain pinned to her lapel. In theory, those pins meant she should be a fluent speaker of English and Spanish.

"Excuse me," Emily said, "We'd like to order a few bottles of wine."

The waitress swiped my Costa Card through a handheld scanner and printed a receipt, which I signed. Then she disappeared through a doorway toward the kitchen.

We sat and waited for her to return, but almost an hour passed by with no sign of her. Finally, we saw her again — at another table taking orders, and completely oblivious of our presence — so we waved our arms to get her attention.

I looked at her name tag: *Erika Soriamolina (Peru)*

"Erika! Come here…" I called. "Where is our wine? It's been

an hour."

She wrinkled her forehead, confused. "You want bottle of wine?" she asked, reaching for her handheld scanner.

"No no no. We already *paid* for two bottles," I said. "An hour ago. And now we're still waiting for them."

"Ah yes, of course," she said, suddenly gasping and nodding her head as she rushed out of the room. "I come back soon."

Ten minutes later, she reappeared with two bottles of wine and a kitchen boy carrying a tray of six wine glasses. While the boy arranged the glassware, she reached for her handheld scanner and printed me a new receipt.

"Did you just charge us for this again?" asked Emily.

"Again?" asked Erika, confused.

I reached into my pocket and pulled out the other receipt. The one from an hour ago.

"Oh no!" she put her hand to her mouth. "I am so sorry! I charge you one time, and then I charge you again."

"That's okay," I muttered. "It was an accident. Can we get a refund though, please?"

"Yes yes yes," she stammered. "First thing in morning, I will make a refund."

"In the morning?" I asked. "Why do we have to wait until morning? Can you just do the refund now?"

"No, I cannot make refund now," she struggled to find the English words to explain. "Only when office is open, in the morning."

"Can we talk to a manager?" Emily asked.

Erika hung her head. "Yes, just a minute. I come back with manager."

A few minutes passed, and she returned with a wiry, bald-headed Indian man in a black suit. "Yes, hello. I am a manager."

We showed him our receipts and told him what had happened, and he tried explaining why the refund couldn't be processed until morning. It didn't make any sense, but he offered to give us his name, and we could check up with him tomorrow to get a receipt for the refund.

Meanwhile, Erika stood in the background, shuffling her feet and looking down at her hands. I felt bad for her. She was probably going to get in trouble.

* * *

The next morning, the ship stopped in Sardinia.

After we walked down the gangplank and up along the pier, we found ourselves on the main boulevard running along the coast.

This side of the street was lined with piers, hundreds upon hundreds of small and medium-sized sailboats tied to a labyrinth of old wooden docks. On the other side of the street there were shops and cafes and sidewalks filled with pedestrians, strolling down the avenue and admiring the boats.

We crossed the street and joined that river of people, winding down the walkway and holding each other's hands and turning our faces upward to enjoy the unseasonable sunshine on that crisp winter morning.

After a few minutes, we noticed a group of people up ahead of us had started gathering in a circle. When we caught up to them, we saw a man in the middle of the group dressed in a black top hat and a coat with tails. He stood there in the center of an ever-widening circle, twisting his moustache like a matador while the crowd gathered round.

"What's going on here?" Emily whispered to me.

"I don't know," I replied. "But I think it's gonna be good!"

Just then, the man with the moustache raised his white-gloved hands into the air for a moment of silent fanfare before gesturing one hand down toward the ground.

That's when we noticed the tiny wooden platform on the sidewalk in front of him. It was painted crimson, with black and gold trim, about six inches long and ten inches wide. And perched on top of the platform were two tiny kittens, maybe twelve weeks old, curled up in a ball together and sleeping.

The man reached out with a black wooden cane and tapped the side of the platform.

Knock knock knock.

One after the other, the two kittens opened their eyes, yawned, and stretched out their little paws. As they stood up and arched their backs, we noticed a pair of itty-bitty white mice curled up together and sleeping between where the cats had been lying a moment ago.

41

As the sunlight shone down between the still-groggy cats, the mice woke up too, yawning and looking around at their surroundings.

"Is this supposed to be some kind of *show*?" Emily whispered at me.

"I don't know," I said. I had never seen anything quite like this before. "Maybe this is some kind of circus act. Maybe the cats and mice are all going to ride little bicycles or something."

The man with the moustache looked down at the miniature platform with all the sleepy animals and tapped his wooden cane again.

Knock knock knock.

The cats looked up him and yawned again. Then they turned around and pounced on the mice, sinking their teeth into the white fur and shaking their bodies back and forth, tearing into their flesh and smearing blood up into their whiskers.

The crowd gasped, and the man with the moustache stood there smiling and nodding his head. After a few moments, he took off his top hat and held it out toward the crowd. A few reluctant hands dropped coins into the hat as the man said, "Grazie! Grazie mille!!"

Emily and I blinked our eyes.

"Did that really just happen?" Emily asked, as we walked away.

* * *

The crazy thing is that Emily and I remember that little story very differently.

When I originally wrote this chapter, Emily read it and said "That's not how it happened! The cats didn't actually kill the mice. They just tormented them with their paws and picked them up in their teeth, carrying them around then dropping them and batting them around. But they didn't *kill* them."

I'm sure of it, though. I remember the blood.

In my memory, the cats killed the mice.

But Emily is absolutely sure about it too: In her memory, the mice live.

"If there had been blood," she says, "I would remember it."

42

We've discussed this difference many times, and neither of us is willing to budge from our story, but we both recognize that both versions can't possibly be true. One of us must have misremembered.

Over the next week, we would learn not to trust our memories, which can be chaotic and unreliable and deceptive. In fact, many of the events in this book actually have slightly different versions in my mind and in Emily's mind. She and I don't remember everything the same way.

Sometimes she jogs my memory, and I immediately see that my original version was wrong. But sometimes we can't reconcile the differences in our recollections, and we have to just agree to each hang onto our own independent memories, with no notion of which one is closer to the actual truth.

This book is flawed.

But it's the best story I can tell.

Someday, I'd love to read a book from the captain's perspective, with unpublished details about the events on the night of shipwreck. Or a well-researched book about the internal politics of corruption at a company like Costa. I'd be very intrigued to learn more about the allegations of hardcore drug use and sexual assault aboard this and other Costa cruise ships, not to mention the personal experiences of the four-thousand-plus people who experienced this tragedy. I'm interested in the legal battles that will continue for years to come, and I'm very interested in the criminal investigations and corporate politics that will unfold.

Please, somebody, write that book!

But I'm not an investigative reporter or a maritime historian, so that's not what this book is going to be.

This is a more personal story.

I'll try my best to get the facts straight, though I can't promise I won't make mistakes.

Obviously, anything that appears in quotation marks is not really a direct quote. Except in a few rare cases where there are real transcripts, I'm just reconstructing conversations from memory for the sake of telling a story that's true to my heart.

And as for me, I'm sticking with my version: I say the cats killed the mice.

* * *

That night, Emily and I were both tired, so we each grabbed a book and rode the green glass elevators up to the Prague Lounge, a wine room on the fourth deck where a classical music trio would play for us while we read.

The room was empty when we went in, except for the three musicians — a pianist, a violinist and an upright bassist — whose heads turned toward the door as we entered. Now that there was somebody in their room, they would need to start playing something.

When our bottle of wine was delivered, Emily took a moment to say hello to the musicians and chitchat about their instruments and to tell them that she was also a professional musician, so they should just play whatever music they wanted. They didn't have to play the same old stuff for us if they didn't want to.

We sat and sipped our wine and read our books, while the musicians played *The Girl from Ipanema* and then *The Wind Beneath My Wings*.

This was a goofy sort of cruise, but we were having fun.

I kissed Emily and sang her another anniversary song:

Some people say that the number thirteen
is an unlucky number, but from what I have seen,
it's the luckiest number; there's no need to be blue,
cuz today I've been married thirteen days to you!

I had been making up these songs and singing them to Emily every day for the past two weeks, and it had become a game to see how long I could keep coming up with original lyrics.

7

We woke up early on the morning of January 13th. The ship would be arriving in Civitavecchia at 7:30. From there, we'd take a train for an hour and arrive in the heart of Rome. This was going to be a big day.

Rome.

We woke up at 6:45 and ate an early breakfast in the ship's cafeteria before meeting the rest of the family at the bottom of the gangplank.

Once in Rome, we started our day out in front of St. Peter's Basilica, standing in middle of the *Piazza San Pietro*, an elliptical courtyard six hundred feet across and encircled by 284 massive Doric columns hewn from travertine marble.

Erik tapped Emily on the shoulder and spoke to her in Cantonese for a few minutes. Chui Lin stood by his side, nodding her head and smiling, a fur coat pulled around her shoulders against the chilly morning wind.

"He wants to go shopping," Emily said. "I told him we'll buy tickets for the bus tour, and then he and Chui Lin can get on and off the bus whenever they want. So if they'd rather spend more time shopping and less time seeing the sites, that's up to them."

The *Roma Cristiana* bus tour follows an eight-mile loop around the city, with a dozen or so stops near all the major attractions and a fleet of buses departing from each location every half hour. It would be a perfect way for everybody to see whichever parts of Rome they wanted to see.

"We can just walk around ourselves, though, right?" I asked. Emily and I always prefer to travel on foot once we get into a new city. Just like our trips to Shanghai or Hong Kong, we might walk ten miles in the course of a typical day, zigzagging around between the ancient ruins and the street markets and the art galleries.

So far though, we had spent every day on this trip on our feet, and Erik and Chui Lin were getting tired of walking around all the time. They had never traveled like this before, usually preferring to sign up for a carefully orchestrated group tour package and then staying with the crowd.

"Absolutely," she said. "These guys can handle being on their own for a few hours."

Before putting them on the bus and heading our separate ways, we all bought tickets to see the inside of St. Peter's Basilica and rented headsets at the door so that we could hear the audio tour.

But this one was different than any other audio tour I had ever heard before. Rather than talking about the artistic and historical and architectural facts about the building, the narrator instead focused on the religious meanings of everything. Not the way an academic or a museum curator would tell you about a subject, but the way a true believer would.

Which makes sense. This was the Vatican, after all.

It was interesting to see these objects in front of us and hear how a devout Catholic might interpret their meaning — and there was a part of me that really wanted to hear more — but there was an even bigger part of me that found the whole thing kind of annoying and distracting. So I turned off the audio and put the headphones in my pocket, figuring I could just look around on my own instead.

Eventually, I made my way toward the tomb of St. Peter at the center of the cross-shaped room.

According to the placard, the earthly remains of St. Peter himself were entombed here, inside a wooden box in a secret room, through a hidden door behind a wall in an underground altar, beneath another massive altar meant only for the Pope, made from the largest piece of bronze in the world, below a hundred-foot dome at the very spot where the apostle had been crucified upside down almost two thousand years ago.

Catholics love this stuff.

When we finished looking around at St. Peters, we put the rest of the family on a tour bus and then made our way to the Sistine Chapel. There had been only two things on my absolute must-see list in Rome: One of them was the Colosseum, and the other was the ceiling of the Sistine Chapel.

We followed the signs through a long and winding corridor, through hallways hung with maps and tapestries, until finally we found ourselves in the Sistine Chapel beneath Michelangelo's legendary frescoes. We turned our faces upward toward the *Creation of Adam* and watched the figure of God reach his right hand toward the outstretched lifeless fingers of Adam.

I had never noticed it before, but the figure of God rests, with his angels, upon a pillowy red pedestal in the exact shape of the human brain.

The image reminded me of the story Athena's birth. She had been conceived inside Zeus's skull and could only be born when the blacksmith Hephaestus swung his axe to crack Zeus's head open and relieve his mounting headache.

* * *

We left the Vatican and took the bus a few stops, heading toward the *Piazza Navona*. But within a few minutes of getting off the bus, we were lost.

Of course, we *adore* getting lost in a new city. So we walked aimlessly through the narrow cobblestone streets for a while, winding through an outdoor market and admiring the crimson color of the tomatoes shining in the noontime sun or the emerald-green of the artichoke leaves. A statue of a hooded monk stood in the center of the market — between the fruit vendors and the fishmongers and the florists with their huge tables full of bright blooms.

"Excuse me," I asked a woman passing by, "Can you tell me how to get to the *Piazza Navona*."

"No," she replied, without turning her face or slowing her pace.

We tried asking a few other people for directions, but the result was the same. We were surprised but amused. These people definitely understood what we were asking. They certainly knew how to get around town, and they absolutely knew the locations of the major landmarks. They just weren't willing to help us.

"What a funny culture!" Emily exclaimed.

Contrast this with Shanghai where people *always* give directions to strangers, even when they don't know how to get where you're going, or what you're even talking about. In China, it's rude to refuse to give directions. Most Chinese people would prefer to wave their arms vaguely in the air and mumble a few minutes of worthless nonsense, rather than suffer the humiliation of refusing to help. Italian culture — it seemed — was exactly the opposite.

So we got out our map and tried figuring it out for ourselves.

"I think this is the *Piazza Campo de' Fiori*" said Emily, pointing to our map. "The outdoor market is here, and if we walk down this way, it will lead us toward the Pantheon. It's huge, so it shouldn't be hard to find.

Every few blocks, we made wrong turns and had to backtrack, but eventually we found the Pantheon. I had been very interested in seeing this relic from the Roman Empire. The whole idea of the Pantheon is that it was a temple to *all* of the Roman gods. Unlike other smaller temples to specific gods, the Pantheon was dedicated to all of them. The whole family of deities.

But evidently, they changed all that. When we got there and walked in the massive front doors, I discovered that the whole thing had been converted into a Christian monument.

"Excuse me," I waved my hand to a woman standing nearby with a name tag pinned to her blouse. "I thought the Pantheon was a Roman temple, not a Christian monument."

"Yes yes," she replied, nodding her head and smiling. "That is true, originally. But they changed it."

"Really?" I asked. "When did that happen?"

"Thirteen hundred years ago," she replied. "In the year 609."

Well, I guess that's why they didn't ask my permission.

* * *

There are thousands of tiny archaeological dig sites throughout Rome. Everywhere you look, around every corner, there's another roped-off rectangle of open earth where researchers have excavated an ancient road or the crumbled corner of a building or the ruins of a plaza.

Remnants of viaducts can be seen overhead, and green grassy patches — like parks, but fenced-off and forbidden to passersby — are dotted with circular slabs of marble from where some ancient column toppled over, leaving its sections like links of sausage on the lawn.

We found lunch — a couple of big flaky pastries filled with ham and cheese — at a bakery near the Pantheon, and we ate them while walked the streets and absorbed the colors and textures of the city.

Next, we stopped at the *Fontana di Trevi*, a huge bank of fountains with a statuesque façade of water and stone, bubbling and frothing with energy and motion and life. At the center of the iconography stood Oceanus, one of the great Titans — predecessors of the gods — and ruler of the oceans.

"He personifies the oceans, which the Romans imagined as an immense river flowing round the earth," I read aloud from a sign nearby, "and from which all streams of water derive."

Emily reached into her pocket. "Legend says that if you throw a coin into the fountain, you'll return to Rome again someday."

"Really?" I asked.

"Yep," she replied, turning her back toward the fountain and tossing a coin over her left shoulder. "I was here five years ago, and I tossed a coin into the fountain, just like I'm doing right now."

She gave me a coin and watched as I turned around to throw it over my own shoulder.

"Well, I guess it worked then, right?" I said. "Because here you are."

"Yes, of course it worked!" she said, flashing me a big smile. "Here I am!"

* * *

We had only one thing left to see: the Colosseum. For me, this was the main attraction. I had been looking forward to this all day.

The walk from the fountains to the Colosseum was about a mile long, but we walked slowly, strolling down the *Via dei Fori Imperiali* and holding hands until the massive shape of the ancient building climbed up over the horizon and loomed above everything else.

"Let's take a picture!" exclaimed Emily.

We tried pointing the camera ourselves, holding it at arms-length while we positioned the Colosseum behind us. But every time we snapped a picture and then looked at the image on the LCD screen, our heads were blocking the view.

We looked like we were standing on some ordinary street, without a single Colosseum anywhere.

"Maybe we just need to move closer," I said, frowning down at the viewfinder.

So we walked a little bit closer and tried again, but every time with the same result.

"You have a gigantic head!" said Emily, giggling as she looked at the latest failed attempt.

I laughed and put my hands on her cheeks, "No, you have a gigantic head!"

We kept walking toward the Colosseum, and every few blocks, we tried again, snapping more pictures of our gigantic heads blotting out one of Europe's most colossal antiquities.

"You know, I heard it's possible to see the Colosseum from space," I said, looking down at yet another failed snapshot.

Emily's face erupted with laughter. By now, we both had tears streaming down our cheeks.

I wiped my eyes and looked back up at the rows of columns encircling each level of the massive stone structure. With my eyes pointed off in the distance, Emily raised the camera to her face and took a spontaneous picture of me, this time without the two of us both blindly trying to cram ourselves into the frame.

"Mmmmmmm… very cute." Emily looked down at the LCD screen and smiled. "I don't know what's going on, but you're very photogenic today."

She lifted the camera again and snapped a few more shots. "Yes yes yes. Very nice."

"Can I see?" I asked, trying to sneak a peek at the screen.

"Nope," she said with a grin. "I'll show you later. Right now I don't want to spoil the moment. So you just keep standing there looking adorable, and I'll keep taking pictures."

As we walked the last few blocks and paid our admission fee at the gate, Emily kept taking more pictures.

Snap snap snap.

Me standing in front of the Colosseum floor. Me looking thoughtfully at the gate where the ancient gladiators would have confronted the ancient lions and had their ancient heads bitten off. Me laughing and smiling at my new bride and basking in the glow of her affection.

Snap snap snap snap snap.

"Can I take some pictures of you?" I asked.

"No way," she replied, capturing a few sneaky shots of me trying to chase her down and take the camera back. "You can take pictures of me tomorrow. Right now, I'm in the middle of a project. Say cheese!" And she took my picture again.

It was a love-attack.

When someone loves you, and takes your photo like you're a movie star, it makes you smile. Like a movie star. Then, when they see you smiling like a movie star, it makes them want to take your photo again and again. And when someone is so excited to take your photo, it makes you smile even more, like a big ridiculous puppy dog. And when your smile is so big and happy and silly, and you're smiling at the person you love, it makes that person want to capture the moment on camera and preserve it forever. It's a big happy sappy feedback loop.

(Like when you give a mouse a cookie.)

* * *

By the time we left the Colosseum, the sky had begun to turn pink and orange; dusk was setting in, and we took a bus back to the colonnaded plaza in front of St. Peters where our day had begun.

John and Apple showed up a few minutes later, but it took another fifteen minutes for Erik and Chui Lin arrive. When we finally saw them, dragging their feet with exhaustion and looking at us with weary frustration, we knew something had gone wrong.

They had spent the entire day on the bus, never getting off to walk around or see any of the sites. They never even went shopping.

Each tour bus takes about three hours to circumnavigate the city, but most of that time is spent sitting for fifteen or twenty minutes at each stop and waiting for new passengers to board. Between stops, the bus stays on the major roads, so it doesn't actually drive right up to the interesting buildings. To see the Trevi fountains or the Pantheon or the inside of the Colosseum, you have to walk at least a few blocks.

By staying on the bus, they had missed all that.

We took the train back to Civitavecchia, where the cruise ship was moored, and climbed the gangplank back up into the ship.

* * *

All of us were exhausted.

Rome had been our longest day spent in port so far.

Plus, we had spent the previous three nights drinking and dancing, and it was starting to catch up with us. Or at least, it was starting to catch up with me. I had a bit of a headache and a general sense of weariness.

At dinner, I had only a half glass of wine, and I stayed quiet throughout most of the meal. Emily and her family laughed and talked in Cantonese, but I sat quietly off to the side and read while I ate, only occasionally looking up to say a few words. Emily was glad to have a break from translating everything, and I was glad to have some quasi-alone time while I read my book.

We finished eating at around eight o'clock, and my headache started getting worse. I wasn't sure if I wanted to go straight to bed or if I wanted to keep reading until I drifted off to sleep, but I was sure I didn't want to roam the ship and party with everyone else. Emily went upstairs with the rest of the family to discuss the next day. They would probably get a bottle of wine and maybe go see the magic show.

I excused myself to our cabin, where I stripped to my tee shirt and boxer shorts and slid into bed. I read for an hour or so, until my eyes started to get heavy.

It was about nine thirty.

At about that time, Emily came back into the room and sat next to me on the bed. Apple had sent her back to check on me.

"Hey there sweetheart," she whispered as she tiptoed into the room. "Want to see the pictures from the Colosseum?"

"Yeah sure," I replied, rolling over next to her while she tinkered with the camera and set up a slideshow.

Looking through the pictures she had taken of me that afternoon, I felt like a movie star all over again.

PART TWO

8

But then we heard a noise.

It was almost nothing.

A slow soft scratching sound came from behind us, like a pencil tip drifting across a page.

Emily and I turned toward the source of the sound, just in time to see a small plastic box slide off the edge of the dresser and topple to the floor. When it hit the ground, the lid popped open, and a thousand tiny green capers — bought yesterday at an outdoor market in Sicily — bounced and rolled in every direction. A spray of salty dust rained down into my open suitcase.

"Oh no!" cried Emily. "Not the capers! I was going to cook something really nice with them when we…"

But she didn't finish her sentence.

We were both sitting up in bed now, and with that change in posture, I felt a spooky otherworldly feeling in my inner ear. Something about my equilibrium was off balance. I looked Emily in the eyes and could see that she felt the same thing.

Something very strange was happening.

"That must have been a really big wave." whispered Emily.

"I don't know," I whispered back. "It doesn't feel like a wave. Or else… wouldn't we rock back the other way eventually?

"I think I can feel the ship moving," said Emily. "Just sit for a second and close your eyes, and see if you can feel it too."

I closed my eyes and tried to expand my senses out into the ship, feeling for some kind of movement. And after a second, I felt it too.

We waited for a few moments, frozen in a heightened state of perception.

Throughout the past five days, we had felt the gentle — almost imperceptible — motion of the ship. It was like a slight squishiness more than anything else.

Nothing like this.

Then, an empty wine bottle started to move, creeping inch by inch toward the edge of the table as though possessed by a tiny, timid ghost. When it reached the precipice, it hesitated for a moment of contemplation and then tipped over the edge, thumping down on the carpet and rolling under the bed.

"What's happening?" gasped Emily.

And then, as though electrified, the whole room came to life. Books and papers slid off the desk. A paper-mache marionette I had bought in Sicily as a gift for my kids jumped from its shelf with wild eyes and flailing arms.

We watched the chaos unfolding around us for another five seconds, so disoriented and confused that we just sat motionless and watched.

But then a heavy scraping noise from overhead caught our attention.

There was a TV set on a shelf at shoulder-level. It was an old tube-style TV with a heavy glass face, weighing probably 50 pounds, and it was about to tumble off its shelf. Without thinking, I jumped off the bed and caught the TV just before it launched into the air, shoving it back into its cabinet.

Then the lights flickered off and on again.

It was only dark for a moment, a second or two at the most, but the change was like a lightning strike to us.

"We've gotta get out of here," Emily said. "Something is very *very* wrong. We should get our life jackets and go to the muster station."

"The mustard station?" I asked. "What's that?"

Emily opened drawers and cabinets, looking for life jackets. "The *muster* station. It's up on the fourth deck, where all the lifeboats are kept. Anytime there's an emergency, we're supposed to muster ourselves up to the muster station."

Emily found the life jackets in the closet by the front door. "Here, take this," she said, handing me a life jacket and keeping one for herself. "And don't forget your Costa Card. We might need it at the muster station, but I don't know where mine is, and I don't want to spend any time looking for it."

I slipped the Costa Card into my back pocket and glanced around the room one final time. My cell phone was on the floor next to the nightstand, so I grabbed it: if the power went out again, the phone might make a handy flashlight.

"When we get back here later," I said, "we're going to have one hell of a mess to clean up."

9

With our life jackets in hand, we left the cabin. Out in the hallway, chaos had already begun to erupt. Before we even got out into the corridor, a cluster of people ran by. Parents pulled their young children along by the hand and carried their babies in their arms.

We pulled our life jackets around our necks and wrapped the straps around our backs. We clicked the buckles and pulled them tight.

Next to me, a man called out to his family members down the hall. A woman shouted back at him, but I didn't know what they were saying. The same babel of languages that had previously been such an exhilarating presence now became fuel for the fire of chaos. Italian, Spanish, and French overwhelmed most of the other communication, but we still occasionally heard desperate cries of English and German.

Walking down the hallway felt like stepping onto a crooked sidewalk panel. We could feel the tug of gravity beneath us, and it was pulling in the wrong direction; not directly downward, but at a slight angle. We held our arms out to our sides to keep our balance.

Out in the hallway, one of the members of the crew tried to calm the passengers, gently reassuring us that "everything is under control. Please stay calm and go to your muster station to await further instructions."

He didn't look calm. He looked scared. But he also looked like he cared that *we* believed that things were under control.

Emily noticed his name tag: Jonathan. This was the mysterious Jonathan, who had been hiding quietly behind the scenes, bringing us fresh towels and making our bed and folding our dirty laundry. It was nice to finally see his face, though we wished there hadn't been so much worry in his eyes.

Our cabin was just ten or twenty yards from the main staircase, so we didn't have very far to go.

When we stepped out into the open air of deck four, we saw that hundreds of other people had already managed to make their way up to their own muster stations. Hordes of be-lifejacketed passengers huddled around the step-ladders leading up to the lifeboats, every desperate individual trying his best to squeeze into a place at the front of each line.

All along both sides of the ship, twenty-six giant oblong boats with dusty white hulls and mustard-yellow canopies were neatly tucked into place like eggs in a carton, their doors sealed and their canopies tied down.

Each lifeboat was hung from a system of pulleys, on a pair of retractable railings. Before lowering the boats to water-level, those railings would first need to extend ten or fifteen feet outward. Only then, with the railings in that fully-extended position, the ropes could be slowly fed through the pulleys and the lifeboats would safely descend to the water. But right now, none of the railings had been extended, and the lifeboats were all still tucked beneath the overhang in their resting positions.

The ship was so long — more than three football fields from stem to stern — that it was hard to get a good idea of what was going on, except in our own direct vicinity. But from where we were standing on the port side of the ship, about halfway between the bow and stern, we could see three lifeboats in either direction. At each boat, a crowd of about 150 people stood.

Nearby, I saw a woman holding a crying baby — maybe one year old — but wearing a full-size adult life jacket.

"He can't wear this. He'll drown!" The woman was shouting to a man nearby, her husband probably.

We didn't stand still long enough to hear the rest of their conversation, but I imagined a whole scenario about them. I imagined the two of them in their cabin, just like we had been, lying on the bed and playing with the baby. Just like us, when the ship slumped to one side, they rummaged through their closet looking for life jackets. Just like us, they probably found two adult-sized life jackets but nothing for their baby.

"It's a good thing we didn't bring my kids on this trip," I said to Emily.

"Yeah," she replied. "Good thing."

Just then, a man approached us. He was tall and handsome, like a fire fighter from Paris or Normandy, with rough grey stubble on his cheeks and a swoosh of salt-and-pepper hair. Without a word, he checked the buckles of Emily's life jacket and pulled her straps tight, with an intensity that bordered on anger. And when he finished with Emily's life jacket, he did the same for me. He didn't say anything to us (and probably didn't speak a word of English), but when he was done, he looked each of us in the eye and nodded his head.

After about 30 minutes, there was an announcement. First in Italian. Then Spanish and French, and finally in English.

"Attention passengers and crew," the loudspeaker crackled and popped. "On behalf of the captain, I'd like to thank for you for your patience and apologize for the inconvenience. There has been an electrical fault in one of the generators. Our technicians have the issue under control and should have power restored shortly. Thank you for your patience."

"Who is this other guy, speaking 'on behalf of the captain?' Why can't the captain just talk to us himself?" asked Emily.

"He's probably too drunk," I said. "They don't want him slurring his speech over the intercom."

"You think so? You think the captain was drunk?" Emily asked.

I shrugged. "I wouldn't be surprised."

"Maybe it really is a power failure," said Emily.

"Really?" I asked.

"Well, I don't know anything about boats, but what if there are two giant propellers at the back of the ship, but only one of those propellers is spinning?" With her hands, Emily drew a picture in the air. "Or maybe the rudder is turned all the way over to one side, and it got stuck there. So maybe we're doing a really sharp turn, and that's why the ship is tilting over to one side."

I considered this possibility for a second. "You mean like how a motorcycle leans way over into a turn?"

"Yeah. Something like that," said Emily. "What do you think?"

"Hmmm… Maybe."

"Yeah. Maybe."

We stood silently for a few minutes, leaning our backs against the outer wall of ship and watching the people all around us. They held each other's hands and looked anxiously around, waiting for some signal. We all waited to see what would happen next.

"Do you think the ship is sinking?" Emily asked.

"I don't know…" I don't usually worry about things. I'm not the kind of person who expects the worst. But my spidey-senses were all thrown out of whack, and this new surreal universe had confounded my ability to make rational judgments. "Yeah, maybe… Maybe the ship is really sinking."

"This is so weird," said Emily. "Do ships really sink? Is that really possible?"

"I guess maybe they do."

"This is definitely not an electrical failure."

I laughed.

"Definitely not."

Emily pretended to speak on the loudspeaker. "Attention passengers. We have lost electrical power to our anti-ship-sinking-machine. Please stand by for sinking, and thank you for cruising with Costa."

I laughed along with her. "We apologize for the inconvenience!"

As we waited for something to happen, the people around us began to get restless.

Some people shouted for the crew to let us board the lifeboats. Without any information about what was really happening, the initial feeling of panicked anxiety was putrefying, turning rancid and sour from neglect. We could smell the despair.

The loudspeaker crackled back to life, and the same sequence of voices repeated the same message and languages as before. We knew before we heard the English voice that the message was the same.

"Attention passengers. We thank you for your patience and apologize for the inconvenience. Blah blah blah blah blah. There has been an electrical fault in the ship's generators. Our technicians have the matter under control, and we should have power restored shortly. Yada yada yada. Please remain calm and stand by for further instructions."

Bullshit.

We all knew this was bullshit.

The ship had been leaning, no… *sinking*, for over an hour

now. And we were getting impatient to hear what was really happening and what they were planning on doing about it.

"What about my family?" Emily wondered. "They won't understand these announcements."

She had a good point. There we no Chinese voices on the loudspeaker. Nobody was translating for them. Wherever they were right now, we could be sure they knew even less than we knew about what was going on.

"John and Apple will be fine." I said. "And if Erik and Chui Lin are with them, then they'll be fine too."

But I could imagine their disorientation. What if this had been a Chinese cruise, with all the announcements in Mandarin? What would I have done? How would I have figured out what to do?

By this time, the absence of the captain's voice was starting to seem weird. We had been at the muster station for over an hour. Why wasn't he talking to us directly? And when would someone finally tell us what was really happening?

Emily was getting cold, and so was I.

"I forgot to put on socks."

"Me too. And I'm not wearing a bra."

We were both wearing lightweight zipper jackets from Old Navy. The kind of thing you wear on a September afternoon in Boston for walk through Harvard Square. Not the kind of jacket you wear on the deck of a ship in the middle of January.

"Attention! Attention!"

This new voice hadn't come from the loudspeaker. One of the nearby crew members had cupped his hands around his mouth and was shouting instructions at us directly.

"Everyone, please go back to your cabins and await further instructions."

This seemed insane.

"Go back to your cabins now, and make sure you have your life jackets. Please wait in your cabin and listen for further instructions."

Everyone around us looked dumbfounded.

Go back to our rooms? Could that really be the best idea?

But we had been hungry for some sense of direction. Some sense of what to do next. And even if this seemed like an insane idea, it was an idea. It was something. So we all started moving, shuffling as a mass toward the doors and into the ship, down the hallway and toward the stairs.

When we finally made it to the main staircase, another member of the crew stood on the steps and blocked our progress.

"No. Everybody stop!" he shouted. "Nobody is going back to their cabins. Get back to your muster station and wait for further instruction from the captain."

10

"Let's walk around and check stuff out," Emily said.

"Okay, I'm game for that," I replied.

Walking around and checking stuff out is perhaps what Emily and I do best.

Whenever we travel, we almost never make a concrete itinerary. Last year, we just showed up in Shanghai without any finalized plans. We walked into a hotel to ask if they had any vacancies, and then we roamed all over the city, just walking around and checking stuff out.

So we went for a walk — a field trip — exploring a little further down the deck. We passed by two… three… four other lifeboats. In front of each one, a different crowd of characters enacted basically the same play: a few crew members pleaded with the people in the crowd to stay calm and be patient. The passengers increasingly shouted back at the crew members, asking why nobody was doing anything and why they wouldn't let us start boarding the lifeboats. If something didn't happen soon, things might get ugly.

"Do you want to see if we can go back down to our room?" asked Emily. "I'm really cold, and I just want to get a jacket."

"Well, I wouldn't mind putting on a pair of socks, to tell you the truth. My feet are getting pretty cold." I looked back down the deck toward the double-doors leading back inside the ship. "But I don't think they're going to let us go downstairs. There's a guy stationed at the stairwell, sending everybody back to the muster station."

Emily paused and thought for a moment. "Isn't there a staircase in the restaurant?"

"You're right!" I said. "We can go through the restaurant and down the stairs, and maybe from there we can sneak back down to our cabin."

The staircase connects two huge dining rooms on the lower and upper levels. At dinner, just a few days ago, the waiters and busboys had all sung to us (*That's Amore!*) while climbing up and down those stairs.

The back wall of the restaurant was oriented toward the front of the ship, and we entered the upper dining room on the fourth floor through those back doors. But after a few steps, we stopped moving altogether.

All across the dining room, tables had toppled over onto their sides. The floor was covered with spoons and forks and knives and broken glass. Enough food and wine to feed fifteen hundred people was now strewn all over the floor and mashed into the carpet, with puddles of water and wine creating slippery patches between the overturned tables.

With the ship tilting so far over to one side now, it would be too easy to slip and fall down into a minefield of sharp objects and broken furniture.

This room was a death trap. The world's worst slip-and-slide.

"Oh my god. Why did we come in here?" I asked.

"Umm…" Emily's face had frozen, her eyes wide with astonishment as she surveyed the scene and took in the devastation. "The stairs. We were going to climb down the stairs."

We found the stairs, but they too were covered in broken glass and wet food scraps. And with the ship now tilting at an increasingly extreme angle, the stairs looked much too dangerous.

But as we looked down into the lower deck of the dining room, we saw something unusual.

Along the side of the dining room, a group of people had set up a few tables and chairs. The tables wouldn't normally have been of much use, though, since anything placed atop one of these tables would immediately slide off or roll away.

Except elbows. And chins. And foreheads.

Amid all the other chaos surrounding us, these people had taken the time to create a place to sit and cry for a few minutes, with their heads in their hands and their elbows on the crooked tables, their faces hidden and their shoulders trembling with sobs.

And unlike almost everyone else we had seen, these people

weren't wearing life jackets.

"Maybe they left their life jackets in their cabins," Emily suggested.

"Yeah."

"Maybe they tried to go back to get them but weren't allowed back on the stairs."

"Yeah, maybe so." Another table overturned nearby, sending its contents crashing to the floor. "We've got to get out of here."

We took the nearest exit back onto the outer deck. We were still on deck four, though now we had moved from the starboard side of the ship to the port side.

11

The port side deck looked almost exactly like the starboard deck, with crowds of increasingly panicked passengers congregating around the entrance to every lifeboat, their bodies smashed shoulder-to-shoulder against each other. Although now at least we were on the uphill side of the sinking ship, which seemed like an improvement.

Nearby, a cute young Colombian crew member put her hand on the shoulder of a little old woman with tears in her eyes.

"No no, of course not. This is no big deal." She smiled and shrugged, scoffing at the idea that anything serious might be happening. "Sometimes we forget that we're all on a big boat. These kinds of things just happen sometimes."

My breath caught in my throat. I could see what she was trying to do, and I admired her very much at that moment. She could see that people were really *really* scared. Completely terrified. And instead of using the sterile language of officialness that provides such a convenient hiding place for cowardly authority figures, this young woman was staying perfectly calm and using kindness to help keep other people calm too.

She created that sense of calm not as a hiding place for herself but as a blanket to share with others. She took her responsibilities seriously.

At the same time, I could see that she herself knew that this was definitely *not* the kind of thing that "just happens" on a boat. I looked into her eyes, and I could see that she was terrified too, way back behind all the kindness and caring and responsibility.

But she was doing a remarkable job of hiding it.

"Hello," said Emily, after the little old lady walked away, her emotions much more under control. "What's your name?"

She smiled at us. "Hi. I'm Karledys Lopez."

"Thanks, Karledys." said Emily. "You're doing a really fantastic job, and we just want to say thank you."

She looked at us and shrugged. "It's okay. I'm not doing anything special. This is just what things are like sometimes on a boat! Everything will be back to normal soon."

But she could see that Emily and I didn't need her reassurance as much as some of the other more desperate passengers. So she flashed us a smile and turned her eyes back toward the crowd, scanning for someone else who might need a hug or a smile.

* * *

Over the next fifteen or twenty minutes, the energy of the crowd intensified. People started shouting and pleading with the crew members.

"Let us onto the lifeboats!"

"We have children! Please, let us get off this ship!"

"What are you waiting for?"

Karledys Lopez now stood at the top of a stepladder, her body the only thing between the lifeboat and the angry mob below.

"Please, everyone!" she shouted, her hands cupped around her mouth. "Please stand back and form a line. We must stay organized."

But her voice hardly carried over the noise of the crowd, and every effort to form an orderly line failed immediately.

Behind her, a few crew members climbed onto the lifeboats. For the most part, they seemed to be attending to their emergency duties, opening doors and preparing various ropes and pulleys. But several of them weren't doing anything at all, except claiming a seat.

"Look at that guy!" Emily pointed at one of the stowaway crew members, a wiry Indian man with a pencil-thin mustache. "I recognize him from breakfast. He's one of the egg chefs. I guess he thinks he's more important than everybody else."

The loudspeaker crackled again, and the multilingual voices started to make another announcement.

In Italian, we heard them say *abandonar il barco*.

I don't know any Italian, and not very much Spanish, but I heard that word *abandonar*, and I was sure it must mean *abandon*. I could taste the word. I could see it hanging in the air up above us. Floating, like smoke.

Abandon.

Abandon ship.

The chaos had subsided and for a moment, there was only stillness. All the passengers and crew stood statuesque, their heads tilted in concentration as we all listened.

The English voice finally spoke. He did not apologize for the inconvenience. He didn't thank us for our patience. Everything was not under control.

"Attention passengers, the captain has issued the abandon ship order. Please proceed to the nearest lifeboat and board in orderly fashion."

But why?

"They still didn't say what happened," said Emily. "They still didn't tell us *why* we're abandoning ship. Did we hit an iceberg or something?"

"I don't know." I said. "I… I don't know. Maybe this is just temporary. Like… maybe we'll all get in the lifeboats and they'll take us to shore until they can fix the ship, and then we'll come back tomorrow and everything will be back to normal."

"Yeah, maybe…" replied Emily.

When the announcements stopped, all of the people unfroze from their positions and the chaos resumed, though now with a new intensity and fervor.

"I need everyone to line up." Karledys shouted, her hands still cupped around her mouth. The smile had gone from her face. The tranquil façade had fallen away. "We cannot board the lifeboat until everyone gets in a line."

Emily and I tried to line up, but there was no line. Just an unruly mob, with each person sliding a shoulder in front of us or wedging a foot into position or scooting their children between us and the lifeboat. Nobody *pushed* us, per se. But unless we pushed *back*, we would definitely wind up at the back of the line.

"Everyone is cutting in front of us," said Emily.

"I know," I replied.

"I think we're going to end up at the back of the line."

I nodded my head. "Yeah… probably…"

"I don't want to push anybody." A single teardrop rolled down her cheek.

I put my arm around her shoulders. "Neither do I."

"If we don't push anybody, then we might not get onto a lifeboat, and then we might die…" she continued.

I took a deep breath. "I know."

We tried to keep our place in line, but without getting aggressive, it wasn't working. Without pushing anyone it was impossible to move forward, and we found ourselves at the back of the mob holding tightly onto each other's hands.

Just then, someone in the crowd shouted, "Women and children first!"

It took a moment for the implications of this to sink in.

Someone was suggesting, no… *demanding*, that we let go of each other. Our fates so far had been intertwined, and we had stayed relatively calm. But the idea that we would separate was horrible.

Nevertheless, the crowd shifted and churned with movement as the men fell back and made way for the women. In this turmoil, Emily was swept away from me. I could feel my heart pounding as I watched her move forward, into the herd of people being escorted onto the boat.

Until I couldn't see her anymore.

She was on the lifeboat, but I was still on the sinking ship.

She was only a few feet away, but I felt like she was gone.

Then, I heard her voice calling out to me from within the lifeboat.

"Benji! Benji!"

A sense of overwhelming loneliness flooded into my system, like rat poison dissolving into my bloodstream.

Most of the men stayed in the back of the line and waited. But some others refused to separate from their loved ones, pushing their way ahead with defiant looks on their faces. And among the men who actually did stay at the back, most were also now pushing their way to the front of the men's group, to be the first on the lifeboat after all the women had gotten aboard. In this turbulent maelstrom of faces and arms and life jackets, for the first time, I pushed back.

"*Benji!*"

When Emily was with me, I could deal with catastrophe. With her hand in mine, we could walk across the deck of a sinking ship and still laugh. But with her taken away from me, I could feel a tidal wave of panic starting to wash in from deeper seas of despair.

When I reached the stepladder, I peered into the lifeboat and saw Emily inside, holding hands and comforting two women who were both crying uncontrollably. She saw me at the doorway, looking in.

"Oh my god… *Benji!*"

"Emily!"

Karledys Lopez still stood at her post in the entryway of the lifeboat.

"I'm sorry." she said. "This boat is full."

"Full? But…"

How could the boat be full?

"You can try going to the next boat. Maybe they'll still have room for you there."

I looked to my left and right, down the length of the deck. From where we stood, I could see three lifeboats in either direction. In front of each boat, an increasingly intensifying crowd of passengers buzzed like angry bees.

At this exact moment, all across the decks of the ship, I imagined other people just like me being told to find somewhere else to go; the lifeboats were full. I imagined being turned away from this boat only to struggle for some other seat on some other boat and being turned away again and again. But most importantly, I imagined doing all that alone. I imagined trying to find my escape route without Emily.

"No. I'm getting onto this boat. My wife is here."

12

I made my way toward Emily, down the center aisle and past row after row of wooden benches.

She was sitting near the back of the lifeboat, between two German women, comforting and calming them. For a moment they held hands, then Emily put their heads on her shoulders, stroking their hair and patting them on the back. As they cried, their faces contorted and their shoulders shook.

"Benji, this is Sielke and Anna."

The two women wiped tears from their faces. In spite of their misery, they looked like they were getting better rather than worse. They seemed to be slowly regaining their composure.

Emily has this kind of effect on people. Wherever we go, people fall in love with her. She's so generous with herself. These people had just barely met her, but already she had made a difference in their lives. That's just what Emily does. It's one of the reasons I love her.

I sat down with the three of them. Our knees touched across the small aisle.

"Hello Sielke. Hello Anna."

I gave them each a big hug and a kiss on the cheek.

Emily put her hands on Anna's knee and gave it a gentle squeeze before crossing the aisle to sit with me. She wrapped her arms around my shoulders and whispered in my ear.

"I was afraid you weren't going to make it."

"Me too."

"The girl at the door said the lifeboat was full. She told me to go onto the next boat."

Emily wiped a tear from her eye. "Oh my god… I don't know what I would have done if you had gone onto a different boat."

"Me neither. I was really scared we weren't going to be able to find each other."

"How did you get onto this boat then, if she said it was full."

"I just told her my wife was here, and she let me in."

She nuzzled her head into the crook of my neck.

"I'm starting to get really scared."

Just then, Karledys Lopez raised her voice.

"Please, everyone, we need to count how many people are on this boat, to see if we have room for any more people."

The two German women cast their eyes hopefully toward the door. They were looking for their own husbands.

"Please everybody, we're going to count everyone, row by row. When it's your turn, say the next number out loud. Like this…"

She pointed at herself and said "one". Then she pointed at the first passenger, in the first row. For a moment, this man stared blankly at her, not knowing what she wanted. Then it clicked: with a thick, syrupy, Spanish voice, he said "dos".

Tres… Quattro… Cinque… Sei… Seven… Huit… Neuf… Dieci…

The count moved slowly throughout the lifeboat, in a pidgin blend of Spanish, Italian, English, French, and German. Each person spoke his or her own language, but we all kept count together.

Ventisei… Ventisette… Ventotto…

There was a small window next to our seat, like a window on an airplane. Looking through that window, I could see back to the deck of the ship, where the crowds were thinning. But the people who remained were becoming increasingly desperate. They were lined up waiting for us to finish counting, to see if we had enough room amongst ourselves to save their lives.

Quarante-deux… Quarante-trois… Forty-four… Forty-five… Cuarenta y seis…

Next to the German women and directly across the aisle from us sat a young couple holding hands. They were tall and lean. The life jackets made them look sportsmanlike, as though they were just on their way to an exciting whitewater rafting trip or something.

"Hey guys." Emily flashed a big smile at them "Pretty good cruise, huh?"

They returned the smile.

"Yes yes. Very much fun. Perhaps we will do some swimming a little later."

Emily laughed. "Sounds like fun. Maybe we'll join you! My name is Emily, and this is my husband Benji."

"My name is Miljo," said the boy.

"And I'm Bilja," said the girl.

"Where are you from?" Emily continued. "We're from Boston."

"Very nice. We are here from Montenegro."

They could see the look of confusion on our faces. Montenegro... Montenegro... We had both heard of it, but had no idea where it was.

"You have heard of Yugoslavia?"

"Yes!"

"Now it is called Montenegro."

"Okay, I know where that is." I replied. "I hope you are having fun. This is actually our honeymoon."

They both laughed and threw their hands up in the air. "It is also our honeymoon! Very exciting! "

The head count finally made its way to our part of the boat.

Emily was "Sixty-four."

I was "Sixty-five."

Miljo and Bilja were "sixty-six" and "sixty-seven".

A few moments later, and the count was complete. We had seventy-five people on our lifeboat. Karledys Lopez breathed a sigh of relief. "There's room for one hundred and fifteen people, so we can take another forty."

Karledys Lopez and the Indian egg chef opened the door again and let a few more people onto the boat. Sielke and Anna were overcome with relief when their husbands finally climbed through the doorway, and they showered them with wet tearful kisses.

It didn't take long to fill up the lifeboat, though, and after a few minutes, the door closed again. There were five crew members aboard this lifeboat: Karledys Lopez and four Filipino men, plus the egg chef. As soon as the doors closed, the men started trying to lower the lifeboat down to the water.

They spoke in Tagalog, so we couldn't understand what they were saying, but they sounded confused. They sounded scared.

They shook their heads and shouted.

Two of them came to the back of the boat, near where Emily and I were sitting, looking over some of the ropes and pulleys and other equipment and then shouting back to their friends at the front of the boat. Then the guys from the front of the boat came back to look at whatever our guys were looking at.

Then more shouting.

After a few minutes, two of the crewmen went back to the front of the ship.

More shouting. More confusion.

"What's the hold up?" I asked Emily. "Why aren't we going down to the water?"

And then, suddenly, the boat moved.

The world dropped out from beneath us. Like a trap-door had been opened, we felt ourselves falling, weightless for a moment before plunging into the void.

And then just as suddenly, we stopped, each of us landing with a thud on the same wooden benches that had disappeared from beneath us just half a second before. We had fallen only a foot or two.

But in those few feet, we all realized the horrible situation of our precarious perch.

In their ordinary resting positions, the lifeboats were nestled tightly against the ship's deck on a retractable scaffolding. Directly beneath us were the walkways of deck three. In order to lower safely to the sea, we first needed to push ten or fifteen feet further away from the cruise ship. But since we were on the uphill side of the sinking ship, the crewmen would need to fight against gravity to push the lifeboat out to the full extent of the scaffolding.

If they botched the operation, our lifeboat full of one hundred fifteen people would crash onto the surface of deck three.

One of the crewmen found a long pole with a hook on one end. He held the hook side with both hands and lodged the flat side against one of the supporting beams on the exterior of the ship. He pushed with all his strength, the tendons in his neck tightening. A few drops of sweat dripped down his forehead and into his eyes.

He pushed hard for five or ten seconds, and when he was satisfied that we had pushed far enough away from the ship, he nodded his head and put down the pole, joining his coworkers at their posts again. They conferred for a few minutes and then tried again to lower the boat.

This time, it was only the front side of the boat that dropped, but the falling sensation was just as dramatic as it had been before.

And this time, there was screaming.

Because now it wasn't the third deck beneath us. Now we were at least forty or fifty feet above the water. Now if we dropped, we would almost certainly die.

The Filipino guys were shouting at each other. The guy at the front of the lifeboat — the one who had pushed us out from the ship with the big pole — he seemed to be in charge, and he was especially angry.

But then the ship dropped again, this time from the front, and everyone screamed again. The guy at the front of the ship shouted at everyone else, and they all shouted back at him.

We could feel the lifeboat swaying at the end of its ropes, as we dangled high above the water.

Emily and I held hands more tightly than ever. I leaned my head in toward her ear and whispered "These guys are going to kill us."

Emily braced herself for another jarring fall. "Is our lifeboat broken?"

"I don't know. Maybe it's broken or maybe these guys just don't know how to work it. Doesn't make much difference though, does it?"

We had only descended seven or eight feet, entirely by falling suddenly a foot or two at a time. The Filipino guys shouted at each other again for a few minutes.

And then, with no idea what else to do, they pulled us back up to our starting position, opened the door, and ushered all of the passengers back out onto the deck of the cruise ship again.

When it was our turn, we followed everyone else off the lifeboat.

13

A palpable sense of silent doom hung in air among the passengers of our lifeboat, as we climbed down the step ladder and struggled back onto the ever-more slanting surface of deck four.

The ship was leaning so severely now that it was difficult to stand up straight or walk along the deck. Instead, we all stood in a single-file line, with our backs leaning up against the outer wall of the cruise ship. One hundred and fifteen of us.

We had been on a lifeboat, but now we weren't. *We were back on the ship.*

BACK ON A SINKING SHIP!

I looked down the deck, trying to figure out who was in charge. Who could help us? Somebody somewhere had to have some idea what we should do. Where was the captain? Or the first officer? Or *any* of the officers?

The only person I could see who might be any help was the tall strong Filipino man from our lifeboat. He stood with his back against the wall, his eyes casting all about, as though in search of some place to hide.

"What do we do now?" I asked.

"Everything is under control," he mumbled back at me.

"No, you don't understand. Where do we go? All these people" I pointed to the scores of people now standing motionless against the ship. "What do we do."

He looked at me again, then silently shifted his gaze down the length of the deck. "Everything is okay."

And with that, he walked off, floating away like a ghost toward the bow of the giant vessel.

I returned to Emily and shrugged my shoulders.

"What did he say?" she asked.

"Nothing. He said everything is under control."

Emily's eyes narrowed. "We're on our own."

14

In hindsight now, it seems like we stood in that spot for a long long time, looking around, and trying to assess the situation. But it must have just been a minute or two.

Emily took the lead.

"Okay let's think about our options." She tugged on the zipper of her hoodie, her eyes trained on some distant focal point in her imagination. "I think all of lifeboats are gone. Except maybe ones like ours that are broken. So we're going to have to think of something else. At some point, we might have to jump in the water... What do you think?"

I looked out into the sea.

We didn't know where we were or how far from shore the ship was sailing. The air was chilly, and it was January after all, so the water would surely be bitter cold.

"We might have to swim eventually," I agreed. "So we should prepare ourselves for that possibility, but I think we should wait until it's clear that we have no other choice."

She nodded her head. "I agree."

Just then, a man approached us. He wore a polo shirt with the cruise line's logo. He had a short, rough beard and loud Italian voice. "You must go across to the other side of the ship!"

"The other side?" I was confused. "But the other side of the ship is sinking!"

"Yes," shouted the man. He had no patience for this explanation, "You fool! The other side is low to the water, so that is where you will go to jump onto a raft."

"And if we don't get onto a raft?" I asked. "If there is no such raft? What do we do then?"

"There will be a raft!" He looked at me like I was crazy.

I looked quickly at Emily, confirming our agreement with

a glance. She nodded her head, and I looked back at the man.

"No, we will not go to the sinking side of the ship."

He snorted indignantly and hurried past us, trying to convince others to follow him.

And then, out of nowhere, we heard a familiar voice.

"Emily! Benji!"

John and Apple had just come through the door, with Erik and Chui Lin right behind them. All of us stared at each other for a moment, astonished to cross paths like this.

Emily and Apple threw her arms around each other and squeezed tight.

"Oh my god, you're still here! You're okay! Where have you been?" asked Emily.

"We went to our rooms." Apple said.

"You were in your rooms? This whole time?" Emily was amazed.

"Yes yes" replied Apple. "We were in magic show when there was a very big crash. Everything fall over. We get very scared, but they say 'is only electrical problem. Everything okay. Go to your room.' So we go to our room and we wait for announcement. Then we have some whisky and we eat some food."

Emily's eyes grew wider and wider as she heard the story and realized what it meant.

"And then, the ship keeps falling over more and more and *more*." Apple pantomimed as she spoke, reaching her arms out as though to steady herself in the collapsing ship. "And we think to ourselves 'where is announcement?' So we go outside to hallway, and is nobody there. And we go to stairs. Nobody there too. We think 'where is everybody?'"

She shrugged her shoulders.

"But everybody is gone. We go outside, and the lifeboats is all gone too. Nobody left."

They had been forgotten too. Left behind just like us. All of us abandoned.

"The whole time, we keep thinking about you," said Apple, her voice slow and sad now. Soft and nostalgic. "All the time I keep saying 'Please, let Benji and Emily be okay. Please let them be safe.'"

"Well, at least we're all together now," I said. "I can't believe you guys found us. What are the chances of *that*?"

The six of us working together would stand a much better chance of making it, if we could just figure out what to do next and all help each other survive. At some point, we might all have to jump in the water together, and it would be important to stick together and work as a team.

At this point, the boat was tipped over so sharply, the slope was steeper than any driveway I've ever driven on (even in San Francisco or Park City, which both have ridiculous driveways). It was almost impossible to stand up without holding onto the wall. And as we walked, we only did so in the v-shaped corner where the wall met the floor.

Almost like the floor was *becoming* a wall.

And if the floor turned into a wall... then the outer deck railing would soon turn into a *ceiling*.

And if that happened, if the ship kept sinking, and if it kept tilting as it sank, then we would be trapped. We wouldn't be able to climb up to the railing, and we definitely wouldn't be able to climb *over* it. We wouldn't be able to jump, and when the ship finally sank, we would be trapped in the canyon between the upturned floor and ceiling. When the ship finally sank, it would create a vacuum and suck us down with it.

If we didn't get off the ship before that point, we would be in big trouble. Big serious crazy trouble. So, if we had no other choice, we should try swimming away from the wreck before getting sucked into its wake. But there was no sense jumping into the water until we could be absolutely sure we wouldn't be rescued beforehand.

(Comically, almost all of our ideas about how to safely escape a sinking ship had been somehow inspired by scenes from the movie *Titanic*, and this whole idea of the ship creating suction on its way to the bottom of the sea was a particularly terrifying concept that we all remembered clearly from the film.)

I was thinking this through when Emily spoke.

"We can't stay here," she said.

"Yeah..." I said, a little startled. "I was just thinking the same thing."

The six of us looked over the railing, peering over the edge and down onto the third deck, fifteen feet below.

The third level was much like the fourth, with an open-air deck and waist-high railing. But below that point, the first and second decks were strictly indoors with no external deck. If we

83

could get down to deck three, we could perch on the railing there and take a wait-and-see approach. If we needed to jump, we would jump. But not until then.

If we could get down to deck three, we would have *options*. If we stayed here on deck four, we would be trapped.

Erik heaved open one of the heavy double-doors leading into the ship's stairwell, and the six of us crawled back inside.

These stairs led all the way down the lowest decks of the vessel. Down to the machine rooms and the crewmember cabins. Somewhere in this stairwell, if we climbed down far enough, we would eventually find the floodwaters creeping up the stairs. Maybe it would be two flights down, or three. Or maybe four. But it was down there somewhere, cold and black, and it was definitely rising.

I could *feel* the water down there, lurking like a poltergeist beneath the basement floorboards.

And the stairs themselves were almost impossible to climb. With the increasingly severe angle of the ship, the staircase descended at a precarious angle. One by one, we inched our way down the stairs for the next ten minutes, grappling hand over hand and clasping each other's wrists as we descended together to the next level.

When we finally reached the third level, we found ourselves on the inside of the same kinds of double-doors we had come down through on the fourth deck. But this time, the doors were up above us, as though at the top of a steep hill. And they were very heavy.

"I will count to three," said Apple, "and then everybody must push. Very *very* hard."

She gave the signal.

And we all pushed. We pushed with all the strength we could muster. But we couldn't find the right angle. Our feet kept sliding down the floor, and we couldn't get the right kind of leverage. Or maybe it was locked or stuck or something, or maybe there was something on the other side of the door, blocking it from opening. But whatever it was, the door wouldn't budge.

John took a deep breath and closed his eyes. "We must… go back up."

I wiped the sweat off my forehead and looked back up the stairs. This was *wrong*. We weren't supposed to go *back*.

But back we went anyhow, hoisting ourselves up with the railing and then reaching down to help pull one another up.

Fifteen minutes later, we found ourselves back on deck four. Right back where we started.

"We need to find a rope," said Emily.

On the face of it, it seemed like finding a rope would be easy. There were ropes all around us. More than twenty lifeboats had already been lowered to the sea by a system of ropes and pulleys. But those ropes had been coated with a thick oily lubricant, and we wouldn't be able to grip them well enough to climb.

"Maybe we look up here," said John, gesturing up one of the step-ladders to the platform where a lifeboat had been so recently nestled. We climbed up the steps, pulling ourselves up through the railings and bars like kids on a jungle-gym.

When we reached the platform, we found a solitary man in a pea-coat with long brown hair hanging in curls around his ears.

"Please go away," said the man, without looking at us.

John looked at me and shrugged. I approached the man. "Excuse me. We're trying to find a rope."

He stared out at the blackness. "Go somewhere else."

"We need a rope." I said, trying to make eye contact. "We're going to look around here for something."

He scoffed but didn't say any more. He wasn't interested. He just kept staring out into the midnight sea.

"Over here!" called John.

He had found a rope.

It was bright orange and made of a wiry, plasticky nylon-like material. It was at least 40 feet long and about a half-inch in diameter. I'm no expert on ropes, but this one seemed good.

John pulled the rope into a series of loops and tied a sequence of knots, one every foot or two down along the length of the rope. Then he tied the end of the rope to the deck railing and tossed the dangling end over the ledge.

"When you go down, hold very tight like this." John demonstrated holding onto one of the knotted loops of the rope. "Has very easy grip."

Erik nodded his head and took the lead, grasping the rope in his hands and climbing up over the railing. Without pause or hesitation, he vanished down to the deck below.

When he reached the bottom, he called back up the Chui Lin. She pursed her lips and took the rope in her hands. I could see a twinkle of fear in her eyes, but there was no hesitation in her actions. Just like her husband before her, she shimmied up over the railing and down the fifteen feet to the deck below. John and Apple followed.

Emily took the rope in her hands and swung around into rappelling position — her feet flat against the ship and her back toward the sea — and I couldn't help but think she looked like a Navy Seal, or maybe a mountaineer climbing down into the gaping mouth of a dormant volcano.

As I took my own turn at the rope, I looked down at the five others now below me, and I felt a swelling of pride. What an incredible family!

And yet, at the same time, I couldn't help thinking about my own kids. What if we had brought them along on a trip like this? In spite of her cerebral palsy, Chloe *has* learned to walk, albeit with a pronounced limp. But she wouldn't be able to walk on these slanted floors, and she certainly wouldn't be able to climb down a rope. What would I do?

I suppose I would have carried her. I would have held her in my arms and carried her down the rope. That's exactly what I would have done.

But as I took the rope in my hands and climbed over the railing — lowering myself hand-over-hand down the rope and finding footholds among the electrical boxes and conduits welded to the side of the ship — I was grateful that I didn't have to.

When my feet touched the third deck, I looked up and saw all the people up above us still on the fourth deck.

Emily and the rest of our group had started moving further down the deck, a little closer to the back of the ship. They wanted to check things out and look for ideas about where to go next.

I touched Emily on the shoulder. "I'll be with you guys in a minute. I'm just going to stay here by the rope and see if I can help some of the people from up there get down here."

"Okay. Be safe." She kissed me on the cheek.

"I will."

"And stay within my eyesight. I don't want to lose you."

"I'll just be right here."

She joined back up with Apple and John, looking for good places to continue climbing.

"Where is Benji?" asked Apple. "We wait for him."

"No," said Emily. "He'll be here in a minute. He has to go help those people."

I held onto the outer railing of the third deck, leaning way out and waving my free arm, shouting to get the attention of the people still searching for escape from the fourth deck.

"Hello! Hello!!"

Someone looked down at me. I spoke using the simplest English I could, hoping the other people would understand. "You must climb down."

He looked at me quizzically.

"Here is a rope! You must come down here!"

They didn't understand.

I couldn't think of what else to do. So I climbed halfway back up the rope and then back down again. I pointed to a person nearby.

"You..." I said.

Then I pointed down toward the third deck. "You must come *down!*"

I completed the gesture by climbing back down to the third deck and pointing to my feet. "You must climb down here!"

A look of comprehension lighted up in his eyes. "Ah ah. Sì sì sì. Grazie! Grazie mille!"

The man reached for the rope and started clambering up over the railing.

"No, wait!" I called back up to him. He stopped and looked back at me, confused.

I didn't know how to say it in Italian...

"Tell the other people..."

No, that wasn't working.

Maybe he would understand it in Spanish. "Todas las personas."

All the people.

I said it again.

"Todas..."

"...las..."

"...personas!"

He nodded his head and turned back to the other people on deck four. He was calling for their attention and starting to show them the rope.

Good enough for me.

I turned to catch up with Emily and the others.

15

The ship was almost at a forty-five degree angle now. If we waited much longer, we wouldn't be able to climb over the railing. The deck beneath our feet would soon turn into a wall, and we would be trapped at the bottom of a ten-foot-deep canyon, with no chance of escaping before the sea-water rushed in.

A few dozen people had come down our rope ladder now, and it looked like nobody was using that rope anymore. The people still on the fourth deck had stayed there because they didn't want to move, and we couldn't change their minds. So I climbed up the wall and untied the rope from the railing where we had secured it earlier.

Erik tied the rope to the third-deck railing and heaved his body up over the top of it. Then he stopped for a moment to help Chui Lin over the bar, and then the two of them disappeared down onto the other hull of the ship, holding the rope and slowly scooting their way toward the waterline.

The boat kept sinking, and the railing kept leaning further and further inward. Climbing over even a short bar had become almost impossible. Next to me, Emily tried unsuccessfully three times to get one of her feet up and over the top bar of the railing.

Looking over at her, I put one knee on the ground and held the other one up in a right-angle like a stepladder.

"Here, climb up this way. Step on me. Then you can pull yourself up."

Emily looked at me. Her eyes shone with a gloss of new-formed tears. Then she stepped on my leg and climbed over the railing.

"Benji, is this a dream?" she asked me.

I had to stop for a moment to wonder. She made a good point.

"I'm pretty sure this is a video game," I replied.

And with that, she gave me her hand and pulled me up over to the other side of the railing.

16

"What if we die?" Emily asked.

She didn't look scared. Her voice was strong. And there was no panic in her eyes.

"If we die, then we die," I said. The air was cold, and I could see my breath forming plumes of fog as I spoke. "I honestly don't know. We might not make it… But in the meantime, at least we're here together. At least we can enjoy each other's company for the rest of our lives."

Emily nodded. "I want to spend the rest of my life with you."

All around us, other people were climbing over the railing too. Nobody had gone down yet. It was steep and scary, and nobody wanted to go first.

Emily sat next to me, on my left. Next to her were Chui Lin and Erik. Next to Erik were Apple and John. And just a little way beyond John, maybe twenty feet away from where I sat, a heavy, disheveled-looking man was trying desperately to clamber over the railing. But the ship was leaning so severely now — almost forty-five degrees — he couldn't do it on his own.

"John!" I called out. He didn't hear me. "John! John!"

Finally, he heard my voice and turned his head.

I pointed at the guy struggling to hoist himself over the rail. "Help that man!"

John turned his head, finally noticing the man's struggle. Together, John and Apple helped pull him over the railing. And when they had gotten him up over the edge, the three of them helped a few more passengers with the maneuver. And then a few more.

But there were others who didn't climb up with us.

We couldn't convince everyone, and we couldn't stay behind waiting to convince everyone to overcome their fear and reluctance.

Throughout the whole escape, we helped everyone we could, all those who were willing to accept our help. Erik and John helped with their strength, lifting and pulling and guiding those who needed a hand. Apple and Emily helped with their cunning, by seeing opportunities to escape and making quick decisive plans. Chui Lin helped with her bravery, showing that anyone with the physical capability could grab onto a rope and climb down over the edge, overcoming the most basic panic and fear.

I was so proud to be with these extraordinary people.

At this point, the ship (still sinking) had leaned far enough over so that it was at an almost 45 degree angle, and we finally felt okay about climbing down.

"We go." Erik pointed down toward the water. This was the most English I had ever heard him speak. He smiled a dutiful smile and nodded his head. We watched him shrink into the distance as he scrambled down the hull of the ship and toward the water line.

"He's always the first one down the rope," said Emily. "Or the first one into the stairwell."

"Yeah." I said. "He's brave."

"That's not how I operate," Emily explained. "I don't ever want to be the first one to do anything. Too risky."

Chui Lin followed Erik, and then John and Apple after her.

"On the other hand, I don't want to be the last one either." she continued. "That's also too risky. I don't want to get left behind, do I?

"Well, then I guess it's your turn," I said, gesturing toward the rope, "if you want to keep your second-to-last spot."

I moved toward the rope and got ready to follow Emily down next. "Wait…" she said. "Hang on a second…"

I stopped and turned toward her.

"I want to say goodbye." Her voice quavered imperceptibly. "Just in case we have to jump in the water and there isn't enough time to say anything later. Just in case something happens and we both die out here, or even worse if only one of us dies… If something awful happens, and I don't ever see you again, I don't want to ever *ever* regret that we didn't take the time to say goodbye."

"You're right. You're totally right." I put my arms around her and felt the tears welling up in my eyes. We had been so busy saving our lives and overcoming our fears and solving problems with ropes and stairs and ladders that we had forgotten to be sad. "Goodbye. I love you and I'll miss you, and I hope more than anything not to lose you. But just in case… Goodbye. Goodbye, sweetheart."

"Goodbye." Emily put her head on my shoulder and took a deep breath. "I'm glad we got married before this trip."

"Yeah, me too." I said. "In fact, I think today is our fourteen-day anniversary."

"Oh yeah?" said Emily, lifting her head up and smiling at me. "Do you have a present for me?"

"Well, I didn't have time to go to the jewelry store. Partly because of the ship sinking and everything — and I'm really sorry about that; there's no excuse — but I did write you a song. So there's that."

"You wrote me a song?" gasped Emily.

"Yes, I did."

"Will you sing it for me?"

"I will."

"Right now?"

"Yes, right now."

"I'm ready whenever you are."

"Don't rush me. I'm preparing… *artistically*."

I looked straight into Emily's eyes — eyes so dark you can't see where her pupil ends and her iris begins; eyes so black, she looks like her pupils are *always* dilated, which gives you this subconscious feeling like she's in love with everyone, all the time — and I made up another anniversary song.

I held an imaginary microphone to my lips and imagined Harry Connick, Jr. singing a sad slow soft jazz melody.

Fourteen days
might not seem
like a long time
for a marriage.
But what if those fourteen days
could last the rest of your life?
Fourteen days!
Fourteen days!!

93

Then, silently, Emily took hold of the rope and climbed down to where John and Apple had perched. I followed right behind her. We kept climbing until we were about fifteen or twenty feet above the water.

And then we looked up at the sky.

The moon was full and bright, high in the sky above us, and the stars were shining more brightly than I can ever remember seeing them. Somehow, I felt lucky. It didn't make any sense, but I felt lucky to be here with Emily, here in this bizarre setting, at this one pivotal moment, with the two of us holding onto a rope on the side of a sinking ship, under a tremendous luminescent glittering sea of stars.

For a while, we didn't say anything else. We just listened to each other breathe. We held onto the rope and looked up at the night sky.

All the while, the ship kept sinking.

17

For a few minutes, everything stopped. Like the universe taking a breath between cries.

I looked up at the stars and suddenly remembered another starry night, sixteen years ago.

I had gone up into the mountains with some friends — all of us were freshmen at BYU — to sit around a campfire toasting marshmallows and telling stories.

It was the beginning of springtime, so we hadn't gone very far into the foothills for this trip. Further up the mountains, there was still snow.

By around midnight, we were about ready to drive back to the dorms. No one had been drinking (remember that BYU is a Mormon school), so we there were no worries about whether we could drive safely. We put out the fire and gathered up our trash and stuffed ourselves back into the car.

The guy driving the car was tall and skinny with a mop of curly blonde hair and buggy eyes. And some-times he got a little over-excited about things. None of us knew him very well, but then again none of the rest of us had a car.

As we drove back down the winding mountain road, whipping around the curves, I told him I thought he was driving a little too fast around some of the corners.

He smiled a devious little smile.

"Oh yeah? You think that's fast? Check this out…"

Instead of braking into the next corner, he put on the gas. He threw his head back and laughed a kind of mad-scientist laugh as he pulled the steering wheel hard left and whipped us around the next curve.

And then we all felt something go wrong.

We were sliding.

It was late March or early April, and although the coming of spring had melted almost all of the snow, it left behind a sprinkling of gravel and small rocks on all of the roads. By late summer, the regular car traffic on all of these roads would eventually brush the gravel to the side. But that hadn't happened yet, so the roads were still dotted with thousands of tiny rocks and pebbles. For us, driving on the gravel was like driving across a field of soapy marbles.

As our momentum overcame the friction of the tires on the pavement, we lost our grip and slid diagonally toward the edge of the road, a steep drop-off with no guard rail.

I remember hearing everyone in the car simultaneously gasp. No one screamed. And then...

time
slowed
to
a
crawl
...

I could feel the texture of the individual pebbles sliding and rolling beneath the tires as vividly as if I was walking on a rocky beach, wearing only a thin-soled pair of sandals. Like stones beneath my toes.

Those physical sensations were so detailed and so peculiar, it captured my attention for a moment and distracted me from what was happening. And then I realized.

We're sliding on the gravel. We're going to go over the edge. We're going to die.

I had heard stories like this before and seen news photos of mangled automotive wreckage, where the passengers had perished after some foolish maneuver on a treacherous road. But I had never expected to be in such a circumstance myself. I never thought it'd happen to me.

And I was fascinated by the whole experience. I felt like an external observer, watching this accident on a movie screen or through a telescope, or maybe a microscope. Something about the scale felt very surreal; everything seemed much bigger and slower than in real life. Or maybe smaller and faster. I couldn't tell which.

As we slid toward the edge of the precipice, I realized that all such car accidents in the past had unfolded just like this, but that the human experience is fleeting and that such knowledge is rare and transitory. People in fatal car accidents only taste that knowledge for a moment, and then their comprehension disappears with them like smoke.

When we reached the edge, I felt the tires let go of the earth. The small rocks between our toes disappeared, and we floated into the air with a kiss.

We hung there in the sky for an endless moment, suspended as though by a delicate scaffolding of invisible fibers. Without the sound of tires skidding or of anyone breathing, I felt strangely enveloped in peaceful repose.

I thought about the poem "Fire and Ice," by Robert Frost:

Some say the world will end in fire,
Some say in ice.
From what I've tasted of desire
I hold with those who favor fire.
But if it had to perish twice,
I think I know enough of hate
To know that for destruction ice
Is also great
And would suffice.

It occurred to me that even when the world ends in fire, it also ends in ice. Even in the midst of a cataclysmic external experience, with destruction and chaos all around, our minds have the ability to focus and hone in on that pinpoint of light inside ourselves. Within the fire, there is always ice.

And then my mind turned to the topic of religion. I remembered the old saying "there are no atheists in foxholes." Originally, the expression was used in wartime, referring to the faith of the soldiers hunkered down in the trenches. According to the syllogism, people universally reach out to God when their lives hang in the balance.

The previous year had been a time of major religious upheaval in my life. Although I had been raised in a Mormon household, I had discarded the faith of my upbringing the summer before leaving for college.

When I was a child, I spake as a child,
I understood as a child, I thought as a child:
but when I became a man,
I put away childish things.

Family and friends had warned me that I was making a mistake by leaving the fold. I was a lost sheep, a prodigal son. In my comfort and my pride, I had abandoned the truth. But someday God would humble me. He would show me his power. And faced with my mortality, peering through the thin veil separating this world from the next world, I would tremble in fear and cry out to God for comfort and mercy.

Every knee shall bow and every tongue confess that Jesus
is the Christ.

I smiled.

In that moment, hunkered down in my own foxhole with the Spectre of Death just moments away, I stopped for a moment to consider my faith. And I was happy to realize that they were wrong about me. I didn't feel compelled to reach out to a creator or believe in an afterlife. I didn't tremble at the void. In fact, I felt an even clearer sense of identity and pride, with my senses attuned to the moment. I felt like the universe made sense.

This was just an accident. It wasn't part of any cosmic plan. It wasn't God's will. It wasn't a punishment for bad behavior or a reward for a life well lived. It was just an accident. Shit happens. Just like the uncountable multitudes of people before us, our lives were about to end.

I felt like a citizen of the earth, both human and animal, connected with nature in a way I had never felt before, bonded to all other living creatures by our common mortality.

These are the thoughts that raced through my mind during those interminable moments before our car hit the ground.

When we landed — about 30 feet below where we left the road and about 60 or 80 feet forward — we landed squarely on all four tires and still facing forward, our momentum carrying us another 50 or 60 feet until the underbrush finally slowed us to a stop.

We exhaled.

And in exhaling, we realized that we could breathe. Which meant that we were alive. And when we realized we were alive, we laughed. And we shouted. And we hugged one another.

Nobody was hurt.

Full of adrenaline, we walked down the mountain road together. An hour or so later, we met up with a major highway and hitched a ride back into town in the back of somebody's pickup truck.

I still don't believe in God.

At least, not according to any definition of the word "god" that I've ever seen. Someone with a rational mind. With opinions and intentions and memories and powers.

A soul.

Some people think of God as an old soul or a wise old soul. Some think God is a disembodied soul, and some think he's embodied in the fabric of the universe itself. Some think of him as a him. But regardless of the incarnation, the basic concept of God that I'm familiar with is that God is a soul.

But then again, what is a soul anyhow?

Is it a ghost? A mind without a body?

For me, a person is an event. A soul is like a waterfall. A waterfall is something that definitely exists. You can see it and you can hear it. But if the cliff crumbles and the water flows down the ruins, that's just called a river, and the waterfall vanishes into the air, as though it never even existed. It would be a mistake to ask "where did the waterfall go?" It didn't go anywhere. It just ceased to be.

Our souls are like that. A person is like a waterfall, an airborne river of personalities, emotions, memories, and gestures. When someone we love dies, we hesitate to clean out their homes or rearrange their stuff, because a person's soul is evident in the things they touched and organized and arranged.

So I do believe in souls. I just don't believe in ghosts.

18

"Don't let go of that rope!" Emily had seen me loosening my grip, as my mind drifted.

Back when the ship had first begun to sink, and the tables and chairs toppled over from the incline, the slope kept getting worse and worse, making it difficult to stand up straight without holding onto something. But now, the ship had rolled almost completely over onto it's side, and the place where we were sitting felt almost like a picnic spot on the cloudy side of a gently rolling hill.

The image of that picnic persisted a moment in my mind before I remembered that we were sitting on the *side* of an *overturned ship*, in a spot that had been — until just a few hours ago — underwater for more than *six years*.

"Keep holding on tight," said Emily. "You're not just a boyfriend anymore. You're somebody's husband."

Up above us, we heard the buzz of helicopter blades whirling and chopping through the sky from off in the distance. Within a few minutes, a spotlight shone down on us from above, and we felt a cyclone of cold air whipping down upon us from its rotor. It skittered back and forth and round and round, looking down on us like a seagull trying to find a safe perch on a crocodile's head.

Maybe it was a news-copter from CNN or the BBC. Maybe they were broadcasting live footage all over the world right now! Maybe my mom could see me on TV, through the zoom lens of a CNN news camera on the other side of the world.

We waved our arms back and forth over our heads, simultaneously pleading for rescue and waving to our families back home.

Out in the water, a miniature fleet of tiny boats — Coast

Guard boats and lifeboats, and local fishing boats from a near-by marina — had gathered in the water in front of us. Just like the helicopter zipping around above us, the boats sailed back and forth along the length of the ship uncertain how they could do possibly do anything to help.

Meanwhile, a few people around us found ropes of their own and climbed down the hull of the ship, just like we had done. And a few of *those* people got fed up with waiting for somebody to rescue us, instead jumping into the water and swimming toward the Coast Guard ships.

"No, no!" we shouted to them as they leaped from the hull, plunging into the inky-blue blackness of the midnight sea. "Come back, come back!"

Only then did a sailor from one of the rescue ships speak into a megaphone, telling us to *please not jump into the water.*

Thanks. Thanks for that helpful tip.

Emily tapped me on the shoulder.

"Guess what?" she said. "I have to pee. Really bad."

"Oh boy," I replied. "That sucks. I'm sorry."

"Would you be ashamed of me if I wet my pants?" Emily asked, her voice shaking a little bit with worry.

"No, of course not." I squeezed her hand. "I'm proud of you. You do whatever you've gotta do."

Emily nodded her head. "I'm gonna try to hold it. But no promises."

"Benji and Emily!" called John, waving his arms in our direction. "Come closer and take a picture."

Emily and I scooted a little further down the hull, towards where John and Apple were sitting. He had been carrying a small black pouch, but now the top was open, and we saw that he had his digital camera.

We took a few pictures… Pictures of the line of people behind us, and pictures of the helicopter and of the boats in the water. Pictures of all six of us sitting on the hull of the ship, and holding onto the rope.

"Someday, somebody is going to tell us we don't have any proof that we got left behind," I said. "We might be in court someday, and they'll say 'How do we know the six of you didn't escape on the lifeboats with everybody else?' We need to prove that we got left behind."

"Maybe we should make a video?" suggested Apple.

So we passed the camera around and pointed it at our faces, and we narrated our experience. For documentation purposes.

"My name is Emily Lau."

"And I'm Benji Smith."

"We are cruisers from Boston, on board the Costa Concordia." said Emily. "Tonight, right after dinner, I would say at around 9:30 or 9:45, we felt a movement in the boat. Like it was tipping. And I was a little scared, so I asked Benji, I asked him, 'what is going on?' and then wine glasses started falling the TV started moving and things started shattering. People were running around in the hallway."

I took the camera from her and added, "People were screaming. The lights flickered on and off. People ran from deck to deck with life preservers. There was no instruction on the PA system yet. We went to deck four because we knew that's where the safety boats were. But when we got to deck four, no one told us what to do. No one told us what the situation was or what had happened."

We kept talking into the video camera for the next five minutes or so, explaining all the events that had unfolded so far, making sure to describe everything we could remember. When we finished, we put the camera back into John's little black pouch.

One of the coast guard boats finally came up close to the ship, pulling a black rubber raft in its wake. I couldn't quite see what was going on down at the waterline, but there were a few other people ahead of us, people who had gone down a separate rope from us, I think. And they were talking to the Coast Guard people.

Finally, it looked like someone was going to rescue us.

"Take off your shoes!" shouted a voice from down below us.

"Our shoes?" asked Emily. "Why? It's cold out here."

"I don't know." I said. "Maybe they're worried about people with spike heels poking a hole in the rubber raft."

"Take off your shoes!" repeated the voice. "Everyone, you must take off your shoes!"

I turned around and looked up the slope of the ship.

A short, smiling little Filipino crew member had come down behind me on the rope and was now sitting, without holding onto the rope at all, a little uphill from us and to my left.

"Stopped sinking, huh?" He smiled at me and Emily.

Wait... *what?*

For a moment, my brain couldn't accept it.

But then suddenly, I realized he was right. For a long time, we had felt the ship moving and shifting beneath us, but now some tiny sensor deep down inside my inner ear told me that, yes, the ship had actually stabilized. Emily tilted her head too, testing out her own sense of balance.

"He's right." Emily marveled. "We stopped sinking."

Emily called down to John and Apple, talking to them in Cantonese. After a few words, each of them also closed their eyes and tried to feel the different equilibrium.

I turned back toward the little Filipino guy.

"Take off your shoes," I told him.

"My... my shoes?" he asked. "Why?"

"I don't know. But the people on the boat down there told us all to take off our shoes." I looked up at the people lined up behind us. "Pass it on."

He turned around and passed the message along to the person behind him, who turned to the person behind her. All the way up the line, people began taking their shoes off.

"I'm keeping my own shoes on," I said, turning back to Emily. "Maybe I'll take them off when we jump into the raft, but until then, there's no sense getting cold feet."

"Yeah," she replied, dreamily.

I looked at the people getting ready to jump into the rubber raft down below. A man and a woman. First the man jumped, down a ten-foot drop and into the little rubber raft. Then the woman got ready to jump. But before she did so, she handed her shoes to Apple.

"Here, hold these," she said, thrusting the shoes — a pair of expensive-looking black high heels — into Apple's hands.

"Who do I look like?" scoffed Apple, as the woman jumped down into the raft. "You get saved in boat, and I take care of your shoes?"

And then the little coast guard boat, with the little black rubber raft, pulled away from the cruise ship and back out into the darkness. They had taken a grand total of two passengers.

Apple tossed the woman's shoes down into the sea, folding her hands across her chest and shouting down to the life raft. "Next time, you carry your own shoes, okay?"

There were now at least forty or fifty people along our rope, forming a dotted line between the water-line and the third-deck railing (where another fifty or a hundred people sat against the railing).

News passed up and down the rope like a telephone line.

Our life jackets had a small flashlight-sized bulb on the front, inside a three-inch plastic casing with a moisture sensor on top. If we fell into the sea, these sensors would detect the water and the light would turn on. Someone behind us in line had discovered that you could spit onto this sensor and the light would blink into existence.

One by one, up and down the rope, the life jackets lit up like a string of lights on a Christmas tree. I tried to do it myself, but it didn't seem to work for me. I spat and spat, but the light never came on.

I imagined what would happen if I ended up in the water somehow. This little light was how my rescuers were supposed to find me. They would look out into the blackness of the sea, and they'd see my little light bobbing and blinking in the water. They'd use that little point of light to find me and throw me a life preserver and steer their raft towards me. Without that little light, would they leave me behind?

After a few minutes watching me spitting and licking to no avail, Emily shrugged her shoulders. "Maybe you just have really dry spit."

I tried licking the sensor a few more times, and then gave up. "Der blinkenlights isst kaputt!"

"I guess that means you're the one who dies," Emily smiled. "The cats are really going to miss you."

"Just the cats? You'll be fine?" I asked.

"I'll learn to cope somehow."

It wasn't that big a deal. We would probably be fine. I probably wouldn't end up swimming. And even if I did, I'd probably be able to swim to a nearby boat on my own. And even if I couldn't swim on my own for some reason, somebody would probably still be able to see me and help me out, even without my blinking light. Probably.

But maybe not.

We kept waiting.

19

By now, there were over a dozen tiny boats in the water in front of us. It was after two o'clock in the morning, but the only people who had been rescued so far were the two people who jumped into the rubber raft from the Coast Guard boat. Hundreds more still waited.

"I hope Ronald is okay," whispered Apple, as we all pulled our jackets close around our shoulders.

Up above us, near the top of the rope, somebody — some kind of crew member, based on the uniform he was wearing — stood up and started walking down the side of the ship. Without even holding onto the rope.

Now, granted, the slope wasn't all *that* steep anymore. The ship was almost completely sideways in the water, but the hull had a natural curvature to it, and we were definitely still sitting on a downward incline. I could imagine what might happen if somebody tripped and fell; they might slip and roll all the way down to the water. And they might knock somebody else over too. He had a sloppy, clumsy demeanor — like the kind of person who would probably walk around with untied shoes all the time — and he looked like he was going to trip over his own feet. He was the only person not holding onto the rope, and I didn't appreciate him being so cavalier with safety (an attitude which, incidentally, is how we all ended up on a sinking ship to begin with).

"Sit down!" I shouted, shooting him a dirty look, but he kept walking without acknowledging me.

Finally a ship approached. It didn't look like a Coast Guard ship or a fishing boat or any other kind of boat I was familiar with. Maybe it was a local tour boat taking people for trips around the nearby islands. It was about forty feet long and yellow with a covered roof. There was a small door on one side, and the crew of this little boat was coming close, trying to approach the cruise ship.

As it got close, we realized why all the other little boats had been staying further back, shining their lights onto us but not approaching.

All the commotion from all those tightly-packed ships was creating rough choppy waters. Many of the boats zipped back and forth, fretting about what to do and whether to get closer. In the process of doing so, each boat churned the already turbulent sea just a little bit more.

This ship now approaching was doing no better. When it finally got within a few feet, the two ships crashed together with violent force, creating a thunderous clap of metal-on-metal. Again and again, the ships knocked into one another, the smaller one bouncing four or five feet up and down in the water with the passage of each new wave.

The first mate of the little boat stuck his head out the side door and reached for our rope. Obviously, he thought he could stabilize his own little boat by securing it with a nearby rope.

With a swoop, he waved his arm out and snapped up the dangling end of our rope.

And then, of course, when his little boat bounced and bounded and lurched with the waves, the slack between us pulled taught. The rope we had been holding loosely in our left hands suddenly swung to the right. We ducked our heads and passed the rope to the other hand, each of us terrified of losing the rope entirely and losing that source and symbol of security.

"No! No!"

"Let go of the rope! LET GO!!!"

He continued tugging wildly against our rope, ripping it from the hands of some of the people in our line and leaving them holding nothing. The side of the ship wasn't vertical, so nobody fell, but the slope was steep and letting go of the rope was madness.

"LET GO! LET GO, YOU LUNATIC!!!"

And then one of the other mates on the ship realized what was happening, and he tripped over himself running to the other side of the ship to knock the rope from his co-worker's hands.

Confused now about how they would safely approach the

cruise liner, this boat too retreated, only to come back a few minutes later with a new plan. The men on the boat had now gotten hold of a few different ropes, affixed to other parts of the massive ship, and not held by any of us desperate castaways. With these two ropes, the men pulled the little boat close and tight until it could no longer crash back and forth against the ship.

But they couldn't do anything about the up and down motion of the boat. The waves were still bobbing the little boat up and down in the water. And every time it moved, there was a scraping crashing sound of metal grinding against metal.

Somehow, we had to get into this boat.

As the boatmen tried to stabilize their craft, we crouched and tried imagining ourselves leaping from our current position, perched five or six feet above the waterline, and onto this wild thrashing boat four feet below. It wasn't a huge jump, but the movement and the crashing made it terrifying.

Just like before, Erik went first, jumping onto the fiberglass roof of the little boat. He landed with a loud crunch. It was a big jump, and he's a solidly built man, and the roof of this little boat was not meant for these kinds of landings.

Erik got up and brushed himself off and called out words of encouragement to Chui Lin. She was crying and shaking, but she built up her courage and took the leap too.

CRUNCH!!

Someone reached out to grab my hand. It was *that guy*. The non-rope-holder. He clasped his hand around my wrist, but before he could knock me off balance, I snatched my arm away from him.

"Don't touch me" I hissed.

I know he was just trying to be helpful, but he struck me as unpredictable and maybe a little volatile, and I wasn't willing to put up with his risky behavior. Even if he was trying to help.

Apple and Emily looked down into the door on the side of the little boat. The boatmen were encouraging us to try jumping directly down into that door, and Emily and Apple seemed to think it was a better option than jumping onto the thin surface of the roof.

To me, that little doorway looked like a broken leg or an amputated foot waiting to happen: Two of the boatmen reached their arms up out of a three-foot-wide door, their heads at

107

our waist-level. If they stretched their arms up as high as they could reach, they could take a person by the underarms and guide their jumps down into the door between them.

But the little boat was still rocking up and down, smashing into the hull of the cruise ship with violent force. If someone tripped, or if the boatmen lost their grip, someone's leg could slip down into the crack between the two boats.

That would be the end of their leg.

I looked at this situation and decided not to accept their help down into the doorway. I have a habit of tripping on stairs. For some reason, I'm always falling on steps.

Instead, I followed Erik's lead and jumped onto the roof.

CRUNCH!!

I landed on my hands and feet at the same time. Not like a cat, but more like a dog, confused and disoriented, and only on my feet for a split second until I stumbled over onto my side.

Wrists not broken? Check. Both legs and ankles intact? Check.

I stood up and turned around to look for Emily. She had already jumped on the boat somehow, though I hadn't seen her land, and now she was headed down the doorway into lower deck.

But there were still more than a hundred people behind us, holding onto the rope and scooting their way down the hull of the ship, all headed toward this lifeboat. At the head of that line was the non-rope-holder, reaching his hands out again to grab somebody.

"Hey!" I shouted. "Get that guy away from everybody! He's going to knock somebody into the water!"

"Thank you for your help," said a crewmember of this little boat, putting his arm around my shoulder and leading me down into the lower deck, "but your job here is done now. Go down and sit."

I was getting in their way.

There were five of us down in the lower deck now. The whole area down there was filled with wooden benches, and we sat down immediately, grateful to finally be off the cruise ship, but disoriented by the wild waving motion.

As the boatmen got better and better at their rescue routine, they could lower people down into the doorway in assembly-line fashion. There was a rhythm, punctuated by the up and down movements of the little boat.

Swing-up, wave their arms at the person still standing on the edge of the cruise ship.

Swing-down, reach up and get ready.

Swing-up, grab the castaway by the underarms. The castaway jumps.

Swing-down, guide the castaway down the arc of their jump and into the doorway, where they would land with a thump (and sometimes a slide on the wet floor).

I watched these guys help rescue us, and I was grateful. I didn't know if they were fishermen or if they drove this little tour boat for a living, but I was thankful they were here. And as I heard the ongoing crunching noises of people landing on the roof of their boat — and as I saw the fiberglass begin to splinter and crack of the stress — I was grateful that they were willing to destroy their little boat to help save us.

I watched as people stumbled, one by one, down into the lower deck of this little boat.

"Hey, check this out," said Emily, pulling a cardboard box from beneath her seat. She read from the side of the box: "Drinking water."

Inside the box, there were 24 plastic pouches — each about the size of a grapefruit — filled with water. On the side of the bag, in four different languages, there were instructions for avoiding dehydration at sea in an evacuation emergency. There were more boxes like this, underneath all the seats in the lifeboat.

For a moment, I thought "I don't want to use up the emergency water on these guys' little boat. They should save their water for an emergency!"

And that's when I realized that this little ship we were on was actually one of the lifeboats deployed from the cruise ship itself. I don't know why I hadn't figured that out before. Evidently, it had already dropped off its first load of passengers somewhere and had now come back for us. It didn't belong to these guys. They weren't tour boat drivers. They had been crew members on our own ship.

Emily gave me one of the plastic drinking-water pouches, and I took a drink.

It was sweet.

I mean… actually it tasted terrible. The water itself had an old, dusty, metallic taste. And then on top of that, it had the flavor of ten-year-old plastic bags stored under the seat of an unused lifeboat.

But still, we held those bags up to our lips and sucked them dry. When they were empty, we tore open the next bags with our teeth and drank and drank and drank.

It was sweet indeed.

Apple sat on a wooden bench across from us, between an old Vietnamese woman and a middle-aged German man, holding hands with both of them as her face turned pale and greenish, with seasickness and dehydration and shock. The drinking water didn't seem to be helping her.

Emily spoke with the guy for few seconds — until her German vocabulary had been exhausted, leaving nothing to discuss — and then she turned back to me.

"He lost his friends," she said. "They got separated on the ship somehow. You know, that's almost what happened to us. What if we hadn't run into John and Apple? How horrible…"

The little lifeboat thrashed up and down, and Apple squeezed hard on the German man's hand. When she couldn't keep it in anymore, all the muscles in her body clenched, and she vomited, right onto his chest.

He whispered softly as he held her, saying sweet soothing words none of us could understand, hugging her close and stroking her hair as she convulsed.

We didn't even know his name.

When the little boat had taken on 120 or so castaways, and there was no room left for anyone else, we pulled away and headed for land. As we put more distance between ourselves and the cruise ship, I saw scores of tiny twinkling lights all in a row, blinking from the hull of the ship where we had just been.

Those were the water-activated light bulbs from the life jackets of a hundred or more people just like us who hadn't yet escaped. Everyone in the lifeboat looked back at those little twinkling lights, and I think we all felt a bit ashamed that we had been rescued, and there were still so many people back on the cruise ship still hoping and waiting to be saved.

"I hope Ronald is okay," said Apple, wiping her mouth and finally regaining her color. "I am so *worry* about him."

As our little boat carried us back to *terra firma*, those little blinking lights disappeared from view.

PART THREE

20

Our lifeboat docked at a once-lazy marina in a tiny Italian village, though now the docks had become crowded with yellow escape boats and orange rubber life rafts. The lifeboats had looked so small hanging from their nooks on the side of the cruise liner, where they had been tucked away just in case of disaster. But now in this quaint little marina, they overwhelmed everything. It was like having thirty school buses parked at your own house, filling the driveway and leaving muddy tire tracks through the flower beds and tearing into the front lawn.

We got out of the lifeboat and walked — our arms wrapped around each other's shoulders and waists; our heads hung low — to where the thin wood-plank dock met the dry land.

Solid earth again. Finally.

The whole marina was packed with people. Hundreds sat on the sidewalks, hundreds more paced anxiously back and forth, clinging to each other for warmth as much as for security. Some with tears still trickling down their cheeks or shoulders shaking. A few people had been wrapped in blankets. Some pulled blue plastic tarps around their families, huddled together on the streets. I could see their panic and anxiety rising, like trembling waves of heat from a desert highway.

A paramedic next to me cast her eyes over the ten or fifteen other emergency medical personnel under her supervision, the ambulance's red and white lights spinning above them. There were stretchers all around us, and a trembling passenger with an oxygen mask lying on each. One of the EMTs stood watch over a stockpile of fuzzy woolen blankets.

"Can we get a blanket? For our group?" I gestured to the six of us.

She looked me over and said "If someone in your group

has hypothermia, you bring them to me, and I will give them blankets."

"None of us has hypothermia," I said, "but we're very cold."

She turned away from me. "I'm sorry, but these are *emergency* blankets."

We turned away from her and walked across the marina parking lot. Two charter buses sat idling on the blacktop, both filled with people.

"Where do you think they're taking those people?" Emily asked.

I furrowed my brow. "I don't think they're going anywhere. I think they're just sitting there with the heat on, getting warm."

Haunted faces looked out at us through the windows of the bus, and I wondered if that's what we looked like ourselves.

From our vantage point, you could look out over the boats moored in the marina and see the massive husk of the capsized Costa Concordia.

We couldn't take our eyes off it.

On the pavement next to the sidewalk, there was a huge pile of discarded life jackets. Probably five hundred of them, piled into an enormous heap. It was weird, though, because nearly everyone we could see was still wearing their life jackets. Even people who had escaped on the first round of lifeboats more than four hours earlier still had their life jackets around their necks and buckled at the waist, as though still harboring a sliver of concern that this island might also sink into the sea.

Emily and I looked around. Who was in charge here? Was there somebody from Costa with a clipboard somewhere, assessing the situation or starting a headcount of survivors? Where should we go? Did somebody have our passports?

A thin woman stood teetering on the sidewalk, a look of shock and derangement in her eyes. As we got closer to her, we could hear her calling out.

"Housekeeping? …Housekeeping?" over and over again in a desperate mournful refrain.

I looked into her eyes.

"Housekeeping?" she asked again.

"Have you seen Ronald?" Apple asked the girl. "We looking for Ronald the waiter. *From the restaurant.*"

The woman looked confused for a second. But then she turned away from us and called out again, "*Housekeeping?*"

114

We walked away.

* * *

"If I don't pee *right now*, I'm going to wet my pants." Emily declared.

"Where should we go?" I asked. "I don't see any place that looks like it might have public bathrooms, especially not at 3 a.m."

"Let's go up this hill," Emily said, pointing up the small main road heading from the marina uphill. "That's where everyone seems to be going."

Indeed, anyone who wasn't sitting on the sidewalks against the buildings or pacing back and forth across the marina or enjoying the warmth of the idling buses was walking up this hill.

We followed them, blending into the steady trickle of people climbing the sidewalk up away from the waterfront. John and Apple followed us, Erik and Chui Lin trailing close behind.

We walked along the sidewalk, up a hill and past a huddle of palm trees, on a street lined with stucco buildings, each of them three stories tall with a red tile roof, painted in muted shades of orange and yellow and dusty pink. Wrought iron balconies jutted from most of the upper levels, and I could easily imagine some other couple on their own honeymoon, perched on one of these balconies under the starlit night with wine glasses in hand, toasting their good fortune.

This was exactly the kind of seaside Mediterranean village we had imagined when we first planned this trip.

"How about over there?" Emily asked, gesturing toward a fenced-in patch of grass and gravel behind one of the apartment buildings on the hill where three cars and a van were parked. "If I squat behind a car, will you guard me while I pee, to make sure nobody watches?"

"Sure."

I stood watch, with John and Erik, while the three women found their own corners of the parking lot. Emily crouched behind a powder-blue van. I stood in front of her and folded my arms, looking outward toward the sidewalk, which curved steeply up the hill and wrapped around our makeshift outhouse area.

115

If I craned my neck, I could see almost see the top of the hill, where the road curved again. There was a light on, and everyone climbing the hill seemed to be headed toward that light.

"Oh my god. I feel so much better." Emily came up from behind me, zipping and tucking and snapping her clothes back into place. She had a new spring in her step. "Do you need to go? Want me to stand watch?"

"No thanks, I'll be fine." I was still looking uphill. "I think I can see where everyone is going. See that light?"

"Yeah. Let's check it out."

Another two minutes' walk led us up the sidewalk, around the bend, up a dozen or so steps and to the source of the light: the doorway of a modest little neighborhood chapel.

Inside, images of saints rendered in stained glass loomed above us. But without the illuminating glow of daylight, their robes appeared to be sewn from sackcloth, their ashen faces hidden in the blackness of night, like phantoms. They slept, sequestered in darkness, unaware of the pitiful situation unfolding on the shores of their tiny island home.

Beneath them, throngs of people covered every available inch of space, filling the pews and sitting on the floors. At least three or four hundred people had gathered here, probably the most that had ever been inside this church since its construction.

Groups of five or ten or twenty castaways snuggled together, their heads on each other's shoulders, their children curled up in their laps. Like a family of wild dogs huddled together for security, resting and licking their wounds after a perilous fight with a pack of hyenas.

A few people actually slept, but most still had their eyes open, staring blankly out into space, doubtlessly replaying the events of the night in the theatres of their minds. The few with their eyes closed didn't look peacefully lost in dreams, but rather like they had clenched their eyes to shut out those same visions.

All across the room, almost everyone still wore their life jackets, resting their heads on the padding wrapped around their necks, like those travel pillows that people use on airplanes.

Two men walked past, draped only in white bed sheets.

Their hair was wet, and somehow, they had lost their clothes. Each of them wore a pair of makeshift shoes, built by slicing a life jacket into pieces and putting their feet into slits in the orange nylon fabric.

Their eyes were distant and cloudy. They didn't speak.

We looked around for a place to sit, but every pew was already filled with people. Their bodies filled the aisles and packed the nave. Every place to sit already had someone sitting in it, and every place to stand was already occupied by those pacing back and forth to relieve their nervous energy.

There was no room for us here.

21

A little further up the hill we saw another light, and more people. We followed the sidewalk another hundred feet and up another flight of stairs to an outdoor patio lined with plastic deck chairs and packed with more stone-faced shivering survivors. Walking past all of these led us to the front door of the *Hotel Bahamas di Fanciulli.*

Inside, there were two rooms. First, a simple entrance foyer with tile floor and a tall front desk counter, its wood paneling faded and pale. Eight or ten people sat here too, in the same plastic deck chairs as outside. And a dozen or so people sat on the floor, leaning their backs against the wall. In the corner, a staircase lead up to the hotel rooms on the upper floors, and underneath the stairs a small bathroom.

Past the foyer area and through a round arching doorway was a lounge area with country-style couches and chairs arranged conversationally around a coffee table. Bleary-eyed castaways filled the couches and chairs, every face turned toward the old TV set in the corner, tuned to an Italian national news network.

Beyond the TV area, there was a bar with five bar stools, and behind the bar, a middle-aged man with curly brown hair attending to his patrons, filling their glasses and smiling into the eyes of these tired terrified guests. Behind him, the shelves were nearly bare.

This was Paolo Fanciulli, obviously the owner of *The Hotel Bahamas di Fanciulli.* After emptying bottle after bottle of wine and spirits, he opened cartons of milk and poured water into paper cups. He opened boxes of crackers and brewed coffee. People tried to give him money but he closed his eyes and shook his head, saying softly

"No no. Please. This is the least I can do."

The six of us found a seat near the entryway, a patch of empty floor space where four of us could sit, and two empty chairs we could each take turns claiming as our own.

"In Hong Kong police," said Apple as she took off her life jacket and used it as a cushion to sit on the floor, "one day I go out on a very strange assignment. A very old man die in his house. He was very rich, and he wants to give money to his family. So he puts all his money into secret hiding places all over his house, hoping his family come there after he dies to take care of his body. And while they are there, they will find all the money, and they will be so happy. But when he dies, his family does not come. The police try to find his family and tell them, but we don't find anyone to call. Maybe all his family are gone. Or maybe nobody cares enough to come to see him."

"Wow." I said. "Poor guy. What ever happened to his money?"

"Very sad. His family never show up." Apple shrugged. "Police keep the money."

I sat down on my own life jacket. It made a decent enough cushion. Not exactly comfortable, but much better than sitting on the hard floor.

A few minutes after we situated ourselves, someone from the crew came through the front door and looked around. She approached a few other crew members in the room and talked with them quietly for a moment. Then she turned and walked back out the front door. The others did the same. Within a minute, all the crew members at the Hotel Bahamas had walked out the front door.

We sat for a long time, staring blankly at the walls.

Watching the other passengers try to sleep.

Listening to the soft sound of people crying.

It was almost four o'clock in the morning.

"Let's go back outside," I said to Emily. "I want to see if anything is happening down at the marina."

"Good idea," she answered. "And I want to see where all the crew members went. What do you think they're doing?"

"Probably trying to get their stories straight."

"Or maybe they're taking a headcount," Emily suggested.

"Why isn't anyone trying to take a headcount of the passengers?" I asked. "Who's in charge here?"

119

"I don't think there's anybody in charge."

We zipped up our jackets and told the rest of the family we'd be back soon.

"Also… I kinda want to see the ship again." I put my hands in my pockets and glanced out the window. "You know, just to look at it."

"Yeah. Me too."

We walked back out of the hotel and down the hill toward the marina. Lots of other people just like us were up and walking around, some going down the hill and some climbing up; walking back and forth; pacing restlessly.

Down at the marina, nothing had changed. The same people still sat in the idling buses. Others still sat on the sidewalks or against the buildings. Others stood still along the waterfront, staring out at the ship.

We hovered there with them for a moment and gazed outward.

Why?

Why did this happen?

Why did it happen to us?

What was going to happen to us now?

We turned around and walked back up the hill. There were no answers for us here.

22

When we got back into the lobby of the Hotel Bahamas, the crew members had returned. Five or six dancers from the ship's entertainment department sat on the floor near our group, with their backs against the front-desk. With them sat a tall wiry man with a shaved head — the singer from their act — wrapped in nothing but bed sheets and wearing the same big square orange shoes made from torn-apart life jackets that we had seen back at the church.

In the corner, a group of cabin stewards and housekeeping staff had gathered. They were sitting on the floor, against the wall and behind the front desk. When Emily and I walked into the room, one of them approached us. He still had a name-tag pinned to his chest.

It was Jonathan, our mysterious cabin steward!

"I am so so sorry," he said. His face was twisted with guilt and shame. "I told you that everything was okay. I said everything was under control."

Emily took his hand and reassured him. "It's okay. It's okay."

"I didn't know that the ship was sinking. I was just telling you the same thing that they were telling me. That everything was under control. I am so sorry."

We smiled at him and reassured him that it wasn't his fault. We gave him a hug and asked him if he was okay. He hadn't been hurt but he was tired and cold, and he was a little bit nervous about his job.

"It's going to be tough for the next month or two." said Jonathan, squinting his eyes and looking at the ground.

"Where will you go?" Emily asked. "Back to the Philippines?"

"I'll stay here!" He seemed surprised at this question. "But I

121

won't be able to work until they fix the ship. And it'll probably take at least a month, maybe two, before they can get the ship up and running again."

"This ship?" Emily was confounded. "This ship will never sail again."

Jonathan's eyes darted to the window and his expression dimmed a little. "If they don't fix this ship, I don't know what I'll do." He paused for a moment, and then his expression changed again, a big bright earnest smile spreading across his face. "They'll fix the ship. I'm sure of it."

Jonathan settled back into a corner with his friends, seven or eight other Filipino cabin stewards. They talked quietly for a while and then rested their heads on each other's shoulders and gradually all fell asleep. All across the room, people stretched their arms and yawned and rested their heads on their loved ones' laps.

I've always considered yawning one of our most basic fundamental animal instincts. A way of signaling to the other members of our pack that it's time to cuddle up together and sleep, nestled into each others bodies for safety and warmth.

Jonathan and his friends looked like a litter of puppies sleeping in a cardboard box.

Beyond them sat a female crew member in her mid-twenties, wearing a crisp white shirt and a navy-blue blazer with a bronze nametag. She was talking on the phone, in English but with a heavy Italian accent.

"Yes, yes. Of course. My name is Isabella Paccagnella. I work in the guest-services department for Costa Crociere. Yes… yes…"

Emily and I cocked our ears toward her to eavesdrop. She was talking to a news reporter somewhere.

"Yes, that's true… Everything is under control, and people are safe."

Emily and I exchanged a quick glance.

"The evacuation was smooth and orderly. When the captain gave the 'abandon ship' order, the passengers gathered at their muster stations and boarded the lifeboats, and we brought everyone safely to shore."

Emily could not tolerate this any longer.

She tapped the woman on the shoulder. "Excuse me."

"Yes?" the woman was surprised and a little annoyed.

"Are you talking to a reporter?"

She hesitated for a second.

"Yes."

"Tell the reporter that there is a passenger who would like to also make a statement."

She gave us a look of pure contempt and then spoke back into the telephone.

"After I finish, do you want to talk to a passenger?" She paused for a moment, listening to the reporter saying something. "Wait… now? You want to talk to her now?"

Her lips pursed and her eyes narrowed into a scowl, she handed the phone to Emily.

"Hello. Who is this?" Emily asked. "Al Jazeera?"

She looked at me quizzically.

"Al Jazeera is huge." I whispered. "They're the biggest news network in the Arab world."

Her eyes widened ever-so-slightly, but then she turned back to the phone, focused and driven.

"I just want to say that the other woman was lying to you." Emily said. Subtlety has never been her strong suit. "I heard her telling her story and I couldn't help but speak out. Everything is not okay. Everything is not under control."

I sat next to her and put my arm around her shoulders while she spoke.

"My husband and I were trapped on the cruise ship until 3 o'clock in the morning, holding onto a rope and climbing down the side of the ship. Our lifeboat was broken, the crew didn't know how to operate the equipment, and the captain was nowhere to be found. The officers of the ship didn't help us evacuate. They left us behind to die."

"So when I heard that woman from Costa telling you that everything is under control and that everyone is safe, I couldn't just sit here and listen without speaking up."

For the next few minutes, Emily sat quietly, just listening to the voice on the other side and occasionally saying "okay". Then she hung up and turned to me.

"She wants me to do a live interview in twenty minutes. She said she'll call back this same number, so we need to stay by the phone."

"Okay. How do you feel? Are you nervous?" I asked.

"No… I don't think so…" she said, and then after thinking for a moment, she asked "How many people do you think watch Al Jazeera?"

"I don't know. A lot."

(We later learned that Al Jazeera is available to 130 million homes in over 100 countries. So yeah, that's a lot.)

In spite of the sullen weary mood in the lobby, there were still lots of people coming and going, and with the occasional background noise of people chattering, it wasn't a great place to talk on the phone. Especially not for a live interview on international television. So we climbed the stairs to the upper floors where all the guest rooms are, looking for a quiet corner where Emily could sit and wait for the phone to ring.

In every hallway and around every corner, people huddled together in groups of two or three or four, collapsed from exhaustion with their heads on each other's shoulders and laps and shivering with cold and shock. Most of these were crew members, who had spent sixteen hours on the job before the evacuation had even begun.

When the phone finally rang, Emily answered. She spent a few minutes talking to a producer and then sat quietly waiting for the interview to begin.

"Yes, thank you." she said, finally speaking live on the air. For the next five minutes, she told the interviewer everything she could remember about the evacuation, especially focusing on the chaos and confusion.

"When we got to the muster station, people were just utterly hysterical. Not because the situation itself was so scary, but because nobody seemed to be in control. It was just utter madness."

She paced back and forth through the hallway as she spoke, trying not to speak loudly enough to wake the people sleeping around us, but not so quiet that she couldn't be heard over the phone.

"People were tripping and falling over," she continued "because the ship was actually sinking quite fast. And then we heard the 'abandon ship' announcement, and we all had to embark onto our lifeboats, and people were rushing to escape, and there was no order of any sort. No one ever told us what to do. Costa has been saying that they had everything under control, but it's not true."

When the interview finished, we went back downstairs

124

again and found the innkeeper.

"Can we use your phone again?" I asked. "Just one more call... So that I can call my parents?"

He didn't speak much English, so we had to communicate primarily in pantomime, but as soon as he understood what we needed, he took us into the private office area behind the bar and off to the side. The room was cluttered with knick-knacks, and the wood-paneled walls were hung with dozens of pictures of the innkeeper posing with his guests in front of the hotel or in the lobby or on a fishing boat in the harbor or in the restaurant — dozens of these photos — always with a bright smile and an arm around someone's shoulders. These were pictures of a man who loved his job because he loved people. A true old-world innkeeper at heart.

I dialed my parents phone number. My mom picked up the phone.

"Hello?" she asked, not recognizing the international phone number on her caller ID.

"Hi mom. It's Benji."

"Benji, hello!! How are you? How is your honeymoon? Are you guys having fun?"

She didn't know.

"We're okay. We're fine. I don't have much time to talk right now, but there's been a horrible accident. Our ship sunk and everyone had to evacuate. We're safe on shore now, but I just wanted to call and let you know that we're okay before you end up seeing us on the news."

"Oh... Okay. Are you having fun?"

She didn't understand.

I could hardly blame her. It takes awhile for the word "sunk" to sink in.

"I'll call you again as soon as I have a chance, but I've gotta go right now."

"Okay, thanks for calling! We're glad you're safe. Have fun on the rest of your honeymoon!"

"Okay, tell Dad I love him."

"Okay, I will."

"Talk to you soon."

"Buh bye."

I hung up the phone. Soon my parents would turn on the TV and see the first bits of news finally trickling into the slow-to-react American news networks. But for now, at least they knew we were safe, and when their understanding finally clicked, they'd at least know we were alive.

We thanked the innkeeper again and went back to sit in our spot on the floor, with the rest of the family.

23

Erik and Chui Lin rose from the chairs they had been sitting in, offering them to Emily and me. John and Apple sat on the floor.

Chui Lin sat on the floor next to me, trying to make herself comfortable on top of the discarded life jacket. I put my arm around her and laid her head down on my thigh. On the other side, Emily held my hand.

We sat silently like that for a long time.

Across the room, a tall slender woman with a perfect face and a perfect body wearing a little black party dress sat in an armchair and scowled. The look on her face told us she might seriously believe that the shipwreck had been cooked up specifically to ruin her night.

She had somehow managed to take two chairs for herself, her feet propped up on the second chair while most of the people in the room sat on the floor with their heads and feet in each other's laps.

Without saying a word, Emily stood up and walked toward the woman in the little black dress. They made eye contact for a second, and then Emily pulled the chair out from under the woman's feet and gave it to a crew member who had been sitting nearby on the cold floor.

The woman gasped as her feet fell to the ground and mumbled obscenities in Italian as the crew member gratefully accepted the seat.

And then suddenly, the energy in the room changed.

The people who had been quietly talking to each other fell silent. Someone said "shhhhhh". The people who had been sleeping rubbed their eyes. Everyone turned toward the TV set in the corner.

"We now return to the island of Giglio, where the survivors of the Costa Concordia shipwreck are gathering in a tiny hotel lobby and watching the story of their own shipwreck on a television news report."

Or at least, that's what I imagined they were saying.

The broadcast was in Italian, so I couldn't understand a word of it.

The whole report was only about five minutes long, and most of the video footage was from before the accident. Since this was a breaking news story, they hadn't had enough time to get a camera crew out to the island yet. Instead, they showed stock footage of the Costa Concordia docked in some sunlit Mediterranean port, surrounded by smiling tourists, the yellow lifeboats looking like a string of bright bananas strung along the ship's hefty waistline.

A grave, serious voice cut through the festive panorama, narrating some somber detail about the shipwreck. Watching the news broadcast, it was hard for me to imagine what she might be saying. We had so many questions about what had just happened, and why, but we couldn't fathom that the TV lady would have unearthed any of those answers yet. Or what the answers might possibly be.

And the broadcast finished. The anchor woman said "buona notte" and the closing music began to play, like a national anthem.

I looked around for someone who might be able to translate. The only people who had been able to speak fluently to us were the crew members, and they were on my shit list right now.

A woman with blond hair and blue eyes sat on the far corner of the couch next to the TV. As she lowered her eyes from the TV, I made eye contact with her and saw (or imagined) a spark of recognition and camaraderie. She paused to meet my eye, and I asked "Do you speak English? Can you translate?"

She smiled. "Yes. A little. I'll try."

"Thank you."

"On the news, they say… At 9:45, the ship hit a coral reef and then water start coming in. Everybody have to evacuate. Very much people got scared."

Nothing new about any of that.

"Is there anything else?"

128

"No. Nothing else."

It was about 4:30 in the morning. There probably wouldn't be any real news until well after sunrise.

It was hard to make sense of the passage of time anymore. It had been less than seven hours since the big wave and the spilled box of capers in our cabin, but it felt more like three days.

"Let's go back down to the marina," Emily said.

We zipped up our jackets again and hiked back down the sidewalk to the marina. The scene hadn't changed much. It looked like the same people standing in the same spots staring out into the sea at the image of the sunken ship, floating like a hologram out there in the darkness.

But then again maybe these weren't the same people we had seen out here earlier. Maybe just like us, they had gone back up the hill to the church or to the hotel and sat in some corner waiting for something to happen.

After a few hours, maybe they had come back down here just like us, drawn by some primitive instinct to gaze out at the glowing unfathomable wreck.

We couldn't help but return to look and leave again, drawn to this mournful hulk like wolves howling at the moon. We turned back around and climbed back up the hill.

As we entered the lobby of the Hotel Bahamas again, the innkeeper poured us each a styrofoam cup of hot cocoa, luke-warm and very watery. Still though, it was comforting to have something a little bit warm and a little bit sweet going down my throat.

I sat back on the floor and sipped at my cup, and Emily sat beside me and held my hand.

An hour passed.

Mostly, we didn't talk.

To an outside observer, it might have looked like all of us were just sitting in that room staring at each other, too exhausted to sleep.

But really, most of us had turned our vision inwards. With no more energy to walk down to the marina, we imagined the ship in our minds. Over and over again, we remembered the lifeboats, the rope, the water. We remembered saying goodbye.

Eventually, I slipped out of consciousness. And in my mind, those interminable loops of memory softly transformed into the vivid dreams of shallow sleep. I dozed for about twenty minutes, my mind back on the ship and then deep in the ocean, sinking.

Sinking into the sea.

The soft silent cold dark deep blue sea.

24

When I finally washed up onto the shores of the waking world again, the sun had risen and golden beams of light shone in through the big picture window. From there, we could see the cruise ship, yes, still toppled over on its side.

Just where we left it last night.

Seeing the abandoned ship in the daylight made it much more real than it had been in the shadows during the wee hours of the morning, under the nightmare fog of nighttime. I think when tragedies happen in the darkness, some primitive part of our brains expects the morning sunlight to set things back in order and bleach away the horrors.

"People are going down to the marina." Emily said. "There are ferry boats."

"How long did I sleep?" I asked, rubbing my eyes.

"Half hour." said Emily. "Maybe forty-five minutes."

We stretched our arms and dusted off our clothes and left the Hotel Bahamas, with nothing in our pockets but our hands. In just a few hours, this place had become a very much like a home to us. We found the innkeeper, shook his hand, and hung our weary arms around his shoulders. We had been welcomed with open arms, and we wanted him to know the depth of our gratitude.

"Thank you so much… for being so kind." Emily said. "And so generous."

"It's okay. It's okay… This is my job." He held out his hands, gesturing up toward this hotel he loved so much, and then shrugged his shoulders. "I'm just… just doing my job."

He smiled and returned each embrace, and I could see a deep reservoir of pride welling up inside him. He knew that he had done good in the world; he knew that his kindness had been appreciated. Paradoxically, it was through this pride that he showed us his humility.

We left with the warmth of his welcome in our hearts, walking down the hill to the marina. This path was starting to feel familiar: well-trodden, after just one night.

At the marina, a massive throng of castaways now gathered, at least a thousand people strewn across the seaside streets and sidewalks. A blue and white ferry boat had been tied to the main dock, and a dense crowd had packed themselves at its rear plank, pushing each other out of the way to get onto this boat.

Unlike Americans, who never touch each other except in sudden bursts of violence, Europeans are comfortable standing shoulder to shoulder and applying long slow constant pressure to the people surrounding them. The strongest of them always squoze their way to the front of any line, and the weakest (or least willing to push) eventually found themselves squeezed out the back.

The ironic truth though, was that nobody was in any kind of mood to get back on another boat again. One old man standing near us on the periphery of the marina stood with his wife, scratching his head.

"Can't we just take a bus?" he asked.

"This is an *island*," she replied.

We felt the same way.

Getting on another boat was the last thing we wanted. And it was impossible to get into these lines without either pushing people out of our way or being pushed aside ourselves.

"We should wait... for next boat," said John, as he surveyed the situation. "No rush."

This is why I like John so much. He doesn't panic. He doesn't get all worked up. No need to worry. He's always calm and patient and thoughtful.

At a bakery across from the marina, we bought a few pieces of bread and cups of coffee. Some of the other nearby shops had doubled or tripled their usual prices to take advantage of this rare tourist extravaganza. But here, the woman at the counter wished us good luck getting home. John reached into his black pouch to pay her a couple euros for our breakfast.

Emily and I had left our wallets and cash and credit cards behind — when we left our room, we hadn't known that we would never come back — but John and Apple and Erik and Chui Lin had all been back to their room, and they had gathered up all their cash. We had about a thousand euros to split among the six of us. And to get us all back home again.

I pulled my hood around my head. The wind on my cheeks was giving me chills.

We waited on the sidelines of the marina while ferry after ferry moored at the docks, and we watched while the most persistent people pushed their way to the front. Each time, we looked out over the crowds and decided not to take this ferry but the next one, or the next *next* one.

Better to go last than to get trampled.

Each time a new ferry docked, nobody gave us instructions. Nobody addressed the crowd. The ferry would tie up its ropes and lower its gangplank, and then people just boarded the new ship, streaming onto the ferries as though they knew where we were going next. As though it was part of the plan all along.

But nobody ever told *us* where we were going next. We didn't know who was from Costa or who was from the coast guard. We didn't know whether anyone from Costa headquarters was aboard the ferryboats, and nobody came forward to give us an update. The crew members from our own ship were no different than us. The evacuation had been their final official duty, and now they were just castaways too. They didn't know where we were going either.

"Excuse me?" Emily waved her arms toward one of the crew members of the ferry, finally catching his attention. "Where are we going?"

"Yes. Everything is under control," he told us.

"But where are we *going*? What's *happening*? Nobody has told us anything."

"We are taking you off of this island."

"Yes, I can see that," said Emily. "But we must be going *somewhere*, right? Can you tell me *where?*"

The man rolled his eyes. "What? You want to stay here? Get on the boat."

So, with no idea what would happen next, we got on one of the last boats to leave Giglio Island.

25

By the time we got in line, the mob had shrunk considerably, but it was still impossible to board the ship without passing through the pushing squeezing throng of people.

Right in front of me, a tiny old British lady stood by herself.

"I was here with two of my friends," she said, her lower lip trembling, "but I haven't seen them since last night after dinner."

I tried to imagine my state of mind I would be in if I hadn't seen Emily since before the crash, but the concept was beyond the abilities of my imagination. I just couldn't fathom it.

As the ferry boat tied its ropes to the dock and the crowd packed itself into an ever-denser loaf of human flesh, I looked down at this fragile little woman and worried about her. I reached my arms out in front of me, over her shoulder, and put my hands on the shoulders of the man standing in front of her. He didn't even notice. He was, himself, pressing his own hands against the shoulders of the guy in front of him, squeezing in more tightly so that he could ensure himself a place on the ferry.

When other people pushed against my back, I stiffened my arms against the guy in front of the old lady, creating a little courtyard where she could continue to exist without getting trampled.

Slowly, we all moved forward. One by one, each of us stepped on the gangplank, ignoring the voice of reason shouting in our heads shouting *stay off of that ship!*

I wiped a few droplets of sweat from my forehead, trying to fend off the dizzy feverish feeling overcoming me. I shivered and folded my arms tightly against my body, hugging my own torso to generate a little warmth.

"Are you okay?" asked Emily. She touched the back of her hand to my cheek.

"Yeah, I think I'm fine." I said. "Maybe a little bit woozy, I guess."

"You feel warm. Do you have a fever?"

"I don't know." I replied, pressing the back of my hand against my forehead, trying in vain to detect my own fever. "It's probably just the same thing I was feeling last night at dinner."

And just then it hit me how much time had passed. Or rather, how much had occurred in such a short span of time. Last night, we had been eating dinner on the cruise ship. It was a normal day on a normal vacation in a normal life. But now it seemed like such a distant memory. It felt like we had been escaping from this shipwreck for *years*, and everything before the shipwreck had already receded into a far-distant past.

"Are you going to be sick?" asked Emily.

"No, I'll be okay. I just feel dizzy. And cold."

We were aboard the ferry now — the walls painted bright blue with a thick coat of paint, now peeling away in leaf-sized flakes — in the very back, where the cars would ordinarily have been parked if this was an ordinary ferry ride. But there were no cars. Instead, the crew had set up two small square tables, and behind each of the tables sat two people on metal chairs, their shoulders hunched over a clipboard.

"And you?" the man in the chair looked up at me.

"Sorry... what?"

"What is your *name?*" he looked mildly annoyed.

"Oh, right... Smith. Benjamin Smith."

With the dull nub of a yellow pencil, he scratched down my name at the end of a long list of hand-written names on a sheet of plain white paper, atop a stack of other pages just like it.

It wondered why they didn't have a checklist somewhere with our names already on it, ready to be circled or crossed off or check-marked. There was no central record-keeping system. Just a couple of guys with a couple of clipboards.

He turned to Emily now.

"Name?"

She closed her eyes for a fraction of a second and took a deep breath, knowing that this was going to get complicated.

"The last name is *Lau*. L - A - U. My first name is *Kuk Yuen Emily*. Let me spell it for you." and she went through the tedious process of reciting and then spelling the English names and Chinese names of everyone in our party. It took a few minutes, and several corrections, before we were all correctly accounted for on the survivor lists.

Then we climbed the stairs to the passenger deck and sat down on the cold aluminum benches surrounding the cold aluminum tables. We put our elbows on the table and our head in our hands. A few minutes later, the motors hummed and the boat chugged out of Giglio harbor, passing close by the sunken cruise ship again on our left before heading back in toward the mainland.

Emily sat next to me. Erik and Chui Lin sat across from us. John and Apple sat at the end of the table, across from each other.

"Good thing we buy travel insurance, right?" said Apple, as we sat and looked out at the hulking vessel toppled over onto its side, like the corpse of the great-grand-daddy of all wales, rotting in the sun.

"Travel insurance?" Emily asked, her face completely crestfallen. "You guys bought travel insurance?"

Erik and Chui Lin told us that, yes, they had also bought travel insurance. Their son is an insurance agent, so they bought it from him.

"Maybe you get free travel insurance from your credit card?" Apple asked Emily.

"Maybe." Emily replied. "But anyways, at least you guys have travel insurance for all your lost bags and everything."

"I don't want it," said Apple, sticking her chin out. "I only want Ronald get home safe. No insurance. No money. Only Ronald."

We all nodded our heads in agreement. We didn't yet know how many people might have died the night before, but we hoped they hadn't been people we had known. We hoped it hadn't been people who had treated us kindly. We had seen Jonathan and Karledys Lopez, but we still hadn't seen Ronald, and we hoped he was okay.

Emily put her hand on my face. Her fingers were cold.

"Hanging in there?" she asked.

"Yeah. I'll be fine." I replied. "I just have to make sure I remember all this. Gotta take good notes so I can write a book about all this someday."

Apple seemed very excited about the idea. "You will write a book? About the shipwreck?"

"Yeah, well I was actually working on a novel when we left on this trip," I explained, "but I think now I'm going to set the novel aside for a while and write this story instead. Don't you think this would make an amazing book? I can hardly even believe it's real myself. And someday they'll make the book into a movie."

Everyone laughed.

"No, I'm serious." I said. "Someday, they'll make a movie about the shipwreck. Maybe it will be based on something I write, or maybe it will be somebody else's story. But this will definitely be a movie someday. I promise."

"That's true." Emily said.

"And if they do make a movie about the shipwreck," I continued, "I don't see why we wouldn't be characters in that movie. Our story is completely crazy."

"That's true too." Emily said.

"And if they make a movie about the shipwreck," I went on, "then there will probably be a scene where some of the survivors are riding the ferry from Giglio back to the mainland."

"Yes, yes!" shouted Apple. "This boat! A scene from the movie, right here!"

John laughed too. "Maybe they get Tom Cruise to play me."

"And in that scene," I said, "the characters will be talking about how someday they'll write a book about the shipwreck and how that book will get turned into a movie."

Emily closed her eyes and in her very best hippie-stoner voice, she said "You just totally blew my mind. Like… *totally*."

I pretended to cry. "I'm just so happy I could be involved in a project like this with you guys."

Apart from our half-hour nap at sunrise, we had been awake for about 27 hours at that point, so we were starting to get very loopy and silly. The weird thing about a disaster like this is that you start making jokes about it pretty much immediately. The whole thing is so big and ridiculous and mind-boggling, you can hardly believe that it really happened to you.

And for some reason, that's really funny. Like really really absurdly funny.

We laughed and laughed until our faces were sore.

It took about an hour to reach the mainland.

As the ferry crew tied up the ropes, the passengers climbed down the stairs and packed themselves against the gang plank, eager to be done with boats forever. Of course, we stayed at the back of the line and waited for all the eager push-and-shove people to exit first. Meanwhile, my head throbbed with fever.

26

A gaggle of TV news crews pointed their cameras at us as we walked down the gangplank and onto solid ground again.

(In fact, somebody there shot a piece of footage that got broadcast live on Fox News back home, and a few of our friends first discovered that we had been in the shipwreck by recognizing us in the background of that live TV news report on the other side of the world. Crazy, huh?)

This marina was very different.

When we got off the ferry, there was an entire... operation, I guess... set up on the blacktop next to the port. Someone stood at the bottom of the gangplank with a stack of blankets — maybe from the Red Cross or some local government agency — and as I passed by, she draped a tan fleece blanket over my shoulders and around my arms. I pulled it around my body like a cocoon.

Maybe there would be *somebody* around here somewhere from Costa.

Huge crowds packed the sidewalks. Hundreds of people. All of us crowded together and moving like a glacier down into a big green canvas military tent.

This must be the headquarters for the evacuation! The command tent!

Presumably, someone would finally tell us what was going on or why our honeymoon cruise ship had just sunk into the sea. Maybe somebody would stop for a moment and ask us if we're okay. Maybe somebody would say "You must feel terrible. Can we give you a hug?"

Maybe we would have to sleep in a tent, in a refugee camp somewhere out here in Tuscany.

Maybe, if our passports had gotten left behind in the ship

and washed out to sea and we couldn't make our way back home again, we would become street-people in Tuscany, moving from village to village and earning a living doing odd-jobs around the vineyards.

Someday maybe we'd buy a house in the countryside and sit on the patio at dusk in the summertime, painting watercolors and eating grapes right off the vine.

Or maybe we'd live on the streets, consigned to eek out the rest of our days in rags. There was no telling. When you walk off a sinking ship, nothing surprises you anymore. Anything is possible.

Behind the command tent stood a pair of ambulances and a few people lying on stretchers, breathing oxygen through a plastic mask.

A woman approached us, carrying a big black plastic bag. We saw her speaking to other people in Italian, but she didn't even bother trying to speak to us, five Chinese people and an American. Instead, she just reached into her bag and pulled out a brand new pair of black socks. She repeated the trick, producing a fresh clean pair of socks for each of us.

"Yes yes!" I cried. "Oh my god, thank you!"

Of the small joys in life… few are so wonderful as putting on a fresh pair of socks twelve hours after a shipwreck.

Then someone else brought us water bottles. And yogurt. And chocolate. And butter cookies.

The water was sweet. The cookies were soft and salty and buttery.

We stuffed all of these things into the plastic bag we had gotten at the bakery, hoarding an extra pair of socks and a few extra water bottles. We went back to the girl with the juice boxes and stockpiled a few extra. When we had each eaten a granola bar, we went back for seconds, so that we could each have a granola bar to carry with us. For later.

This was our first piece of luggage. A plastic bag with a spare pair of socks and a few things to eat. We felt sneaky, like we weren't supposed to be taking this stuff. Like it hadn't been brought there specifically for our benefit. But still, we felt like we would get in trouble if someone caught us stuffing an extra cracker or two into our pockets.

"I've never felt like this before." said Emily.

"I know. Me neither." I replied. "But, it's like… we don't

know when we'll have another opportunity to get a juice box. Maybe we won't see food again for the rest of the day."

We shuffled past a group of journalists interviewing survivors in Italian and scribbling furiously into their little notebooks, around a corner and into the big green tent. More of a canopy, really. Inside, there were three long tables, lined up lengthwise along the left-hand side. A man in a blue uniform stood next to the entrance.

"Are there any injuries in your group?" he asked us as we approached.

Emily put her hand on the back of my neck.

Of course, I still had the hood pulled over my head, and I still had a blanket wrapped around my shoulders.

"My husband has a fever and chills. And a headache."

The man looked at us.

"Please go into the tent. Go to the last table."

Yes. Finally.

We walked to the last table, and a woman with short curly hair looked up at us.

"Your names, please."

"But… my husband has a fever." Emily started. "He's shivering."

The woman looked at me for a moment, and then back at Emily.

"Yes yes. But your names. I must take your names."

And so we went through the long process of telling her all six of our names, both English and Chinese. We spelled them out and fixed the mistakes.

She wrote those names on a blank sheet of white paper, just like the blank sheet of white paper where they had written our names on the ferry. When we finished, she gestured out the other side of the tent.

"This way please."

Emily looked out the way she was pointing. "Is there someone who can check up on my husband's fever?" she asked. "Nobody is helping us."

"Yes yes. Please." the woman insisted. "Out this way. Please."

What else could we do?

We walked back out into the sunlight and found ourselves being shuffled along in another mob of people, pushing and packing tightly together again, making our way toward a line of buses parked along the curb. Every few steps somebody would accidentally poke an elbow into someone else's side or step on somebody's heels.

I felt like a zombie, walking and walking and walking, with no human energy left in my bones. Driven forward only by an inexorable march toward an unknown goal.

Braaaiiins!!!!!!

Another man in uniform approached me. "Your blanket, sir. Please."

"Can I keep it?" I asked. "I'm still feeling cold."

He smiled a faint smile and shrugged his shoulders. "Yes. But there are many many other people. The next boat will bring more people still. Also, they are cold. They will want blankets too."

He was right. Four thousand people, all of us shivering. All of us cold.

I gave him back the blanket.

Before long, we reached the curb and looked up into the open door of a bus.

A uniformed worker held up his hands and gestured for us to stop.

"It is full. No more, please."

He signaled to the driver, and the bus drove away. Moments later, another identical bus pulled forward to take its place, and the door opened up.

"Hello, please… Where are we going?" Emily asked the bus driver.

"Keep moving. Yes. Come come, onto the bus and sit down" he replied.

"But where?" Emily was losing her patience. "Where are you taking us?"

"We are taking you *home*, of course." We stood still and blinked our eyes for a second, not quite sure what he meant. Home? Now?

"Sit. Sit, please! Many many people are behind you!"

He was annoyed with us, like he thought we were causing some great inconvenience. Like this whole shipwreck had been our idea of a fancy vacation, and now this poor bus driver was having to suffer because of our silly shipwreck obsession.

We sat down, defeated.

A few minutes later, all the seats were full, and we left the little marina with the big green tent.

Emily spent a few minutes talking to the rest of the family in Chinese. I closed my eyes and leaned my head back. At least it was warm on the bus.

Ten or fifteen minutes passed, and then we stopped in front of a grey concrete-block building. It was some kind of school building. Possibly the most depressing kindergarten in all of Italy. Maybe someone from Costa would be here.

We squeezed our way through the crowd and into the middle of the building. But we still couldn't find any official Costa representative. Or anyone from the police, or from the government. Just confused castaways in every direction, filling the hallways almost no room even to breathe.

Suddenly, Apple gasped and pointed her finger up the hallway, back toward the doorway we had just come through. She jumped up and down. "Ronald!" she shouted "Ronald! Ronald! Ronald!!!"

There he was.

His right arm was tied up in a makeshift sling, and it looked like he might have broken it. But at least we knew he was alive.

"Well hello, my favorite dinner group!" said Ronald as he approached us. "I'm glad to see that you're okay."

"Ronald, Ronald!" said Apple. "We keep thinking about you. We always hope you okay."

"I made it," he said. "I made it."

"What happened to your arm?"

"What this?" shrugged Ronald. "It's nothing. I'll be fine."

Watching Apple and Ronald's happy reunion, I couldn't help but think about the rest of Ronald's family. He had told us at dinner a few nights ago about his wife and daughters — one of whom had just started college last year, and he paid her tuition by waiting tables at the cruise ship for sixteen hours a day for the past ten years. But what would happen to that daughter now? We all knew he wouldn't find another job like this in the Philippines.

"Everyone, please!" shouted a barrel-chested man at the far end of the hallway. "Your attention, please!"

The noise from the crowd made it almost impossible to hear his voice. Why didn't anyone around here have a bullhorn or a loudspeaker or something?

"Quiet please! Everyone! Shush!!"

143

The shushing lasted a few minutes, to very limited effect.

"Please line up, according to your city of embarkation."

Really? Four thousand people are going to sort themselves into groups and just *line up?*

"Please, everyone!! If you embark the cruise ship in Rome, please come *this* way! If you come from Palmero or Cagliari, go *that* way. Barcelona and Palma de Mallorca, please go over *there*."

We turned in the direction of the Barcelona crowd, since that was where we had originally boarded the cruise ship.

Why did they care about our original embarkation city anyhow? Were they going to take us back to Barcelona? *Now?* It didn't make any sense.

People were really starting to really push. Hard.

To keep my balance, I had to put my hands on the shoulders of the person in front of me. And then when people pushed me from behind, I couldn't help but push the person in front of me. We moved like a giant self-destructive amoeba of an organism, compression waves rippling through the crowd like an earthquake.

Someone could get trampled to death like this.

I could see the whole thing unfolding in my mind. A weak old woman would twist her ankle and fall. Someone would scream. The screaming would invoke a panic. In the panic, we would all try jumping out of the way, to avoid stepping on the old woman. But those sudden movements would knock other people to the ground and cause a chain reaction. In my mind, I could hear the sounds of people screaming and shoes scuffing against the tile floor and bones cracking.

I held my breath and tried not to move.

But the pressure against my back pushed me forward. I held Emily's hand, and we moved downstream together, riding along on this river of people. Eventually, we found ourselves at the end of the hallway, looking out a double doorway leading back out of the school.

"What city?" a man at the end of the hallway shouted at us.

"Barcelona," Emily replied.

"No no no!! Barcelona is on the *left* side! Mallorca is on the *right*! Pay attention!!"

He made a sweeping gesture with his arms.

"Barcelona, here!" he swept his arms to the left.

144

"Mallorca, there!" he swept his arms to the right.

But the only people who could hear him were the people within a radius of ten feet. All down the rest of the hallway, for forty feet behind us, nobody could hear his instructions.

And even if people could hear his voice, there was no room to maneuver in this crowd. We couldn't move to the left side of the hallway, no matter how hard we tried.

Finally, the shouting man gave up his idea about the two different lines, and he signaled us all to move forward. As we funneled out the door, he asked each person "Barcelona or Mallorca?" and then twisted them by the shoulders, pointing their bodies in the right direction.

We still weren't sure where he was leading us until we finally emerged from the hallway and back out into the sunlight again, walking down a sidewalk to a curb where a line of buses sat idling, a different bus for each city: Rome, Cagliari, Palermo, Palma de Mallorca, and Barcelona.

27

What is the *plan* here?
Where are we *going?*
Is anyone ever going to tell us what *happened?*
Although our world remained shrouded in mystery, and though we asked each other the same questions over and over again, we didn't bother actually asking the bus driver anything. We couldn't bear to hear the same vague bullshit any longer...

Everything is fine!
Everything is under control!
Yes please, we are taking you home!

We dragged our feet to the back of the bus and sat on the second-to-last row. A frazzled-looking family sat behind us, a pair of elementary school aged kids — a boy and a girl — sitting between their mother and grandmother.
One of kids kicked the back of our chair over and over again, unleashing plumes of dust into the stagnant recycled air.

Thump. Thump. Thump.

"Mommy, did that ship really sink?"
"Yes, sweetheart. It did."

Thump. Thump. Thump.

"Why?"
"What do you mean, why?"
"Why did it sink?"
"I don't know. Somebody messed something up, sweetie.

146

Somebody wasn't doing their job, and they crashed the ship."

"But why, mommy? Why weren't they doing their job?"

Thump. Thump. Thump.

"I don't know, honey. I don't know."

The chair-kicking was driving me a little bit crazy, but I felt bad for the kid. She had just gotten off a sinking ship and would probably spend the next twenty years of her life in therapy. I didn't turn around. I didn't give the family dirty looks. I closed my eyes and tried to sleep.

But the kid just kept kicking and kicking.

Thump. Thump. Thump. Thump. Thump. Thump.

Emily leaned her head on my shoulder.

"This kicking is really annoying," she whined softly into my ear.

"I know. I know. First the shipwreck, and now *this?*" I put my hand on her leg and squeezed. "Haven't we suffered enough?"

We tried to ignore them. We tried to sit and rest. We tried to relax and sleep.

But those kids kept asking their sad questions and kept kicking and kicking and kicking and kicking, the incessant thumping of sneakers in our backs creating a manic drumbeat, like a metronome with cardiac arrhythmia.

Thump thump thump thump thump thump thump.

"Mommy, where are we going?"

"I don't know."

"Are we going home now? I want to go home."

"I don't know, honey… I don't know where we're going."

THUMP THUMP THUMP THUMP
THUMP THUMP THUMP THUMP

"I'm hungry, mommy. When are we having lunch?"

147

THUMP THUMP THUMP THUMP THUMP THUMP
THUMP THUMP THUMP THUMP THUMP THUMP
THUMP THUMP THUMP THUMP THUMP THUMP

We tried diverting our attention by looking at the Tuscan countryside flying past us outside. But the afternoon sun shone down upon us with punishing intensity, the brutally bright beams of sunlight slicing through the window glass like razor blades and refracting through the stale air, casting a scorching glare upon the thousands of dust particles floating in front of our faces. And with every breath, with every spoken word and every sigh, we sent this swarm of fireflies into motion, encircling our heads with white-hot blades of light slashing at our eyelashes and stabbing at our stinging squinting brows.

That's when everything began to reel.

THUMPTHUMPTHUMPTHUMPTHUMPTHUMPT
HUMPTHUMPTHUMPTHUMPTHUMPTHUMPTH
UMPTHUMPTHUMPTHUMPTHUMPTHUMPTHU
MPTHUMPTHUMPTHUMPTHUMPTHUMP...

I squeezed my eyes closed, shutting out the thumping conflagration surrounding us and trying to find some comfort in darkness. But there in the darkened theater of my mind, I couldn't help but watch the images projected on the screen behind my eyes. *Running. Screaming. Flooding. Climbing. Crying. Fear and panic and confusion.*

THUMPTHUMPTHUMPTHUMPTHUMPTHUMPT
HUMPTHUMPTHUMPTHUMPTHUMPTHUMPTH
UMPTHUMPTHUMPTHUMPTHUMPTHUMPTHU
MPTHUMPTHUMPTHUMPTHUMPTHUMP...

"Are you okay?" asked Emily. "You look like your fever is getting worse."

She touched my cheek with the back of her hand.

"Hey, does anybody have any Advil?" she asked, standing up in the aisle and addressing the people around us.

A few faces turned toward us, their hollow eyes downcast and their cheeks sallow with sleepless exhaustion.

"Now let me just see here..." a fifty-something woman with

a thick Irish accent was sitting in the row in front of us, on the other side of the aisle. She had a box-shaped face, surrounded by springy blond curls that bounced back and forth as she rummaged through her purse. "I've got two of these green ones… They're not exactly Advils, but they should do the trick for yeh."

She unfolded a small square of white paper, revealing a rainbow assortment of capsules and tablets and pills. She saw me staring at her collection.

"I traded for them," she smiled. "Back at yonder schoolhouse, while we was waitin' and waitin' for something to happen, a few of us girls rummaged 'round in our bags and shared all our medicines and toiletries and whatnot."

"Thank you." I said, taking the two green pills from her as she wrapped the rest back in paper. "What are these?"

"Can't say that I quite know," she shrugged and gave me a weak smile. "But they're meant for back pain or sore muscles or some such thing… Might help with a headache and a fever."

"Do you know if they have codeine?" I asked. "Codeine makes me dizzy. Gives me vertigo."

"I'm afraid I can't say…" she replied.

Sitting next to her, with arms folded across his chest and a scowl on his lips, her husband nodded his head. "If I see you startin' to keel over, I'll catch yeh before yeh can hit the ground."

"Thanks," I said, slipping one of the pills into my mouth and swallowing it dry.

Emily put the other pill into our plastic bag of supplies, adding it to our inventory of crackers and juice boxes and other emergency necessities.

"A right feckin' mess, innit?" the Irishman said to us, his wife now tucking her purse back underneath her seat.

"Yeah," I replied, rubbing my temples and waiting for the mystery-drug to kick in. "A huge mess. We'll probably be stuck in a lawsuit for the next ten years."

"Ha! Don't make me laugh!" He puffed out his chest. "Costa is a shabby little cruise line with debts even bigger than its ridiculous ships. They'll be out of business before they pay a bloody dime to a single soul."

I turned back toward the window and stared out into the gleaming sunlit landscape. With the pounding in my head,

I couldn't think about what might happen over the coming months or years. The financial future of Costa was too much to wrap my head around. I just wanted to know what was happening to us *now*.

Where were they taking us?

Everyone on this bus had boarded the cruise ship in Barcelona, so maybe they were going to drive this bus all the way back there. How far would that be? Eight hours? Twelve? Would they really drive us all the way back to Barcelona? What would they do with us when we got there?

Maybe they would take us to Genova, about an hour south of Rome, to the Costa headquarters. Maybe, finally, somebody could tell us what's going on.

Or maybe they were taking us to Rome. The ship had set sail from Civitavecchia three hours before hitting the rocks, and Civitavecchia is about an hour away from Rome. But then we had ridden the ferry for an hour and a bus for another twenty minutes before ending up at the school, and then another forty-five minutes on this bus.

So where did that put us now? Which direction were we travelling?

I looked out the window and looked for clues in the landscape or on the street signs. For long stretches of time, there was nothing on the horizon but long winding roads surrounded by farms and vineyards. The street signs were few and far between, and none of them had names I could recognize.

We could have been anywhere.

But eventually, as the rolling countryside melted away into the periphery of urban sprawl, I saw a sign for Rome.

"Look," I said to Emily, pointing out the window, "They're taking us back to Rome."

But then, just a moment later, we saw another sign.

This time, there were no words. Just a blue background behind the silhouette of an airplane.

"They're taking us to the airport?" gasped Emily. "Do they think they can just put us on a plane and send us home? Without anybody ever even talking to us?"

"I don't know." I answered. "I really don't know. Maybe."

"But we don't even have passports," she said. "We don't have tickets."

"Maybe we don't need tickets." I said. "It's an international catastrophe. Maybe we don't even need passports. Maybe someone from the U. S. government is already here, waiting to take us home?"

Emily frowned. "I don't know. What if they just drop us off at their airport? What if we have to fend for ourselves? What will we do then?"

"Yeah. What if we're stuck?" I asked. "What if we can't stay in Italy, but we can't go home either? What if we're trapped at the airport, with no money and no passports? What if we can't go home?"

Or maybe the moon would drop into the sea.

We would hardly be surprised. Anything could happen now.

But the idea of getting off this bus and right onto a plane seemed horrible and crazy and wrong. Wasn't anyone going to *talk* to us? Wasn't someone from Costa going to stand in front of us and say "here's what happened to the cruise ship, and here's what we're going to do to get you home"?

Or would they just send us home with no explanation and no apology?

The airport was getting closer now. We could see planes taking off and landing. We could see the color-coded street signs guiding cars and taxis toward various different airport regions and zones and parking lots.

We exited from the highway.

They were really going to do it. They were really taking us to the airport.

I couldn't believe it.

And then, suddenly, the bus pulled into a parking lot and stopped, the front door heaving open with a sigh in front of the *Airport Marriott Hotel Roma*.

28

A hotel?

We were definitely not expecting this.

We figured they would eventually bring us all to a big arena or a gymnasium filled with tables and volunteers and row upon row of army cots or bunk-beds. We thought there would be dedicated emergency management personnel ready to deploy food rations and a public address where the CEO of Costa would get up in front of us with a microphone and apologize to us for the accident, promising to make everything right and telling us about the company's detailed emergency plan.

It hadn't occurred to us that the company's plan included hotels rooms for all of the survivors. It was surprisingly generous, for a company that hadn't yet bothered communicating with any of us.

We shuffled off the bus and into the hotel lobby.

Within moments, sixty people crowded into the lobby area, mobbing the front-desk. Emily and I once again found ourselves at the back of the crowd, letting everyone else push their way ahead of us. At least this time, we knew the hotel wasn't sinking.

"Hello, yes?" a hotel employee greeted us as we finally made our way to the front desk. "You also are from the cruise ship?"

"Yes," I answered.

"I must have the full names of each person in your party." He had a pencil in hand, poised above a blank sheet of white paper. I wondered what had happened to the names we had already given to the people on the ferry boat? Or the names we had given to the people in the army rescue tent? What about the computer system that scanned our Costa cards when we left the ship in Palma de Mallorca or Palmero or Sicily or

Rome? What about our passports?

Lost. Even after all that, they still didn't have our names. They still didn't have a master-list anywhere of all the passengers and crew.

So Emily once again went through the tedious process of reciting and spelling everyone's English and Chinese names.

"Thank you. I have three rooms for you. Here are the keys. The elevators are at the other side of the lobby. Dinner will be served at seven o'clock in the restaurant, down the hall and to your left."

We took the keys and turned toward the elevator.

But then I thought again about that logistical meeting I had been imagining earlier, where the CEO of Costa would explain everything. Obviously, I knew now that there would be no such meeting. But still… there must have been *somebody* who could talk to us and answer some of our questions.

I turned back to the guy at the front desk "Excuse me, can you tell me who here is in charge?"

"You want to talk to the hotel manager?" He seemed a little hurt, and slightly defensive, as though I was accusing him of bad service.

"No, no, no. I mean from Costa. From the cruise company."

Now he just seemed confused.

"Nobody from Costa. Not here."

I tried to clarify. "Yes, there must have been somebody from Costa on the bus? Or maybe someone called you on the telephone to we were coming?"

He looked me straight in the eyes. "No. Nobody from Costa on the bus. Nobody ever call us to say you are coming."

This was astonishing news.

I turned to Emily. "So they just dumped us here."

"Yeah, you're right." she replied. "They just dumped us here. Like trash."

We took the elevator upstairs and found our room. It was so tempting for us to just collapse into a pile of skin and bones and then just sleep for a million hours — we were so completely and utterly exhausted — but how could we rest when there was *so much work to do*? If Costa wasn't going to do anything to get us home, we would just have to do it ourselves.

And time was wasting.

We each took a quick shower, and then put our same smelly

clothes back on again, ready to go back out and take some action.

"First things first," said Emily. "We need to make some phone calls. People we can really trust to drop everything and focus on research for the next day or two."

Other than my own, I only know two phone two numbers by heart: my parents' house (where I grew up, and where my happily-married-for-forty-years parents still live) and my best friend from college, Daryn Tufts.

Before I go on, I want to say a few words about Daryn. We started brainstorming story ideas back in 1996 when we were roommates at BYU. Both of us wanted to be screenwriters. But after we finished college, I somehow became an artificial intelligence programmer and quit writing for ten years. But Daryn actually stuck with his writing. He's written dozens of TV commercials, a YA novel, and more screenplays than I can count. Now he's a movie producer and director too. He's not exactly Steven Spielberg (yet!), but he's climbing the ladder pretty quickly. He's directed Alyssa Milano, Beau Bridges, Carol Kane, and William Shatner.

Seriously, William Shatner.

Anyhow, I knew Daryn would be an ideal point-man back at home. He's great with logistics and he knows tons of people. He could communicate with all our friends and family back home, and he'd be the perfect person to find an obscure friend-of-a-friend in Italy who might be able to help us out.

"I'll call him," said Emily. "You go downstairs and see if you can find a computer with an internet connection. Post a message on Facebook. Something really urgent. We want everybody we know to jump into action."

So I gave Daryn's phone number to Emily — they've spoken once or twice, but don't know each other very well — and she gave him a call.

"Hi, Daryn, it's Emily," she said. "Our cruise ship just sunk, and we need some help. I need you to do the following five things in the next hour… Yeah… Clear your schedule."

While they talked, I went downstairs to the hotel's "business center" where they had a fax machine and a dusty old computer. It took a few minutes for me to get used to the Italian version of Windows 98. Some of the letters were in different places on the keyboard, and all the apps had different names (even the "start" menu was called "avvio"). I had a hell of a time typing in my password. But after a minute or two, I figured out how to login to Facebook, and I wrote the following message:

PLEASE HELP! THIS IS AN URGENT EMERGENCY! IT IS NOT A JOKE. Last night, an enormous cruise ship (3000 passengers and 1000 crew) sunk in the Mediterranean Sea. The name of the Ship is the "Costa Concordia" and I was on that ship honeymooning with my new wife Emily Lau. THIS IS THE BIGGEST CRUISE SHIP DISASTER SINCE THE TITANIC, and it isn't being reported yet by CNN or any of the major news outlets. The cruise operator is essentially holding all the surviving passengers hostage, without any information and without returning our passports. Thankfully for us, none of our friends were hurt or killed, but we know there were at least six casualties, and based on what we saw on the ship, we think there were a lot more than that. My guess is that there were at least 100 people killed in this disaster. Please share this message with everyone you know. Help us out. We are stranded in Rome without clothing, passports, money, phones, etc. Please contact your favorite newspaper or website and convince them to make this a huge story.

I read through it a few times.

This would definitely get people's attention.

I logged off the computer and went back upstairs to see how Emily was doing.

"I called Daryn and gave him the job of finding us some friends on the ground in Italy." Emily scratched some notes onto a sheet of paper from the desk next to the TV set. "We don't know how long we'll be stuck here, and we don't know how long this hotel will give us free room and board."

"That's perfect. " I said. "He's one of those weird people with connections. A few years ago, he took a trip to Japan without even booking a hotel room. He doesn't know anybody in Japan, but he found a friend of a friend who had seen one of his documentaries, so there you go."

"So then I called my dad back in Hong Kong," Emily continued, "and asked him to get us the phone numbers for the U.S. Embassy and the Chinese Embassy in Rome. Plus the phone number for CNN's international news desk."

"Very smart," I said. "You're really good at this."

"If there's one thing I know how to do, it's getting shit done." She smiled and shrugged. "That's what I do."

"So, should we call CNN?" I asked.

"Already done." Emily looked up from her notes. "It's just an answering machine, but I left a message. I said 'My husband and I are survivors of the Costa Concordia shipwreck, and we have breaking news to report. Please call us back at the Airport Marriott Hotel Roma, in room 330.'"

"Wow, you've been quite productive." I said, scratching my head and marveling at her accomplishments. "I just posted this one Facebook message. And I think it probably makes me sound like a crazy person."

"So now we need to call the Embassy." Emily said. She gave me the number, and I dialed.

"United States Embassy" said a voice with a strong Italian accent on the other side of the line.

"Hello. My name is Benji Smith. I'm a United States citizen and a survivor of the Costa Concordia shipwreck. My wife and I lost everything we had. All of our clothes, cash, credit cards, identification. We have no passports."

"Today is a Saturday. We're usually closed on the weekends," said the voice.

I stopped for a second, confused.

"Is this the emergency line?" I asked.

"Yes, this is emergency phone." The voice sounded annoyed. Frustrated. Exasperated. "We are open today, though. Because of this shipwreck. We are all working today. But usually, we are not working on a Saturday."

Was he trying to pull a guilt trip on me, for getting shipwrecked, *over the weekend?*

"Okay. Well… thank you." I said.

"You must come here by five o'clock."

"We're in a hotel next to the airport. How far away is the Embassy?" I looked at the clock on the bedside table. It was almost three.

"You can hire a taxi. It will take one hour for driving."

A taxi? Seriously? A taxi would cost a fortune.

"But we have no money. We lost everything in the shipwreck. Can you send someone to pick us up?"

"No, I am sorry. It is not possible. We cannot send a car. Perhaps you will borrow some money from a friend?"

"No, we can't borrow any money from a friend." I was starting to get angry. "Everyone we know in this country just got off a sinking ship. With *nothing* in our pockets. There were more than a hundred American citizens on this cruise ship, some of them are still wearing the same wet clothes they were wearing when they *swam* to shore. Every single one of these people needs your help. Can you send a bus or a van to come pick us up?"

"That is very sad, and we are very sorry." He spoke slowly, condescension dripping from every syllable, as though speaking to a very stupid child. "But we are doing everything we can do. We are working very hard to help you. And let us not forget that this is a *weekend*, and we are not usually *working* on a weekend."

"So you won't send anyone to help?"

"You must come to the embassy before five o'clock, and we will make for you a new passport."

I hung up the phone and shook my head at Emily.

"Pathetic."

29

We met back up with the rest of the family at 3:15, in the lobby near the restaurant.

Emily had also called the Chinese Embassy, and the situation was the same with them as with the American Embassy. They wouldn't send a car or a bus. They wouldn't offer any food or clothing or logistical help. They wouldn't provide transportation home. They didn't offer to help contact our families. They couldn't loan us a couple hundred dollars.

In short, they were practically worthless.

They would give us our new passports (actually, they weren't going to *give* us anything; we would have to *pay* for our temporary replacement passports — they reminded us to bring exact change for the passport photo machine in the lobby — so it was actually more like they were *selling* us new passports), and then they would send us on our way without any other kind of help.

We asked the woman at the hotel concierge desk to call us a cab. Something with enough room for six adults.

"Oh no, I'm very sorry," she said. "There are no taxis today. There is a protest with the drivers. They are having a strike."

Of course.

"Can you call the taxi dispatcher for us anyhow?" pleaded Emily. "There might still be a few taxicabs that aren't striking today. It wouldn't hurt to try."

She rolled her eyes and scoffed, but we had nothing better to do than hanging around the concierge desk asking her to please please *please* try again. It didn't take long for her to relent. After a minute or two speaking in Italian, she put down the phone again and turned toward us.

"You are very lucky. I have arranged for a taxi to come for

you. It will be here in ten minutes."

"Thank you. Thank you!" Emily and I were ecstatic.

The concierge almost smiled, but then reconsidered. "The taxi protest was yesterday only. Today, taxis are driving again. Tomorrow, who knows?"

Ten minutes later, a little white sedan pulled up to the curb, and the six of us squeezed in. The driver winced and fretted, watching as Emily climbed up onto my lap in the front seat, and Apple sat on John's lap in the back. He didn't seem to speak any English, so he expressed his dismay entirely by twisting his lips into complicated contortions.

"Please take us," said Emily slowly and loudly, pantomiming with her arms as she spoke and gesturing at the two addresses scratched on a scrap of paper, "to the United States Embassy. And then to the Chinese embassy."

The driver scratched his head and stared at the addresses. "No, no, no. È molto lontano." We waved his hands dismissively, like he wanted us to get out of the cab. "Too far. Too far."

"Please, please! We just got off the Costa Concordia," said Emily, pronouncing her words carefully pantomiming a colossal sinking ship in the air with her arms, "and we lost our passports, so we *must* go to the embassies tonight."

"Yes yes, please. Too far," he said again. "Too too far."

"You know the Costa Concordia?" Emily asked, starting to get very creative and detail-oriented with her pantomime act. "Big cruise ship? Sinking into the sea? Many people died, yes?"

"Yes, yes…" he waved his hands at us again, his annoyance mounting. Then, suddenly, his eyes widened and he pointed at Emily. "You? You were on this ship? This ship, which… which… *sinks* into the sea?"

"Yes! That's what I've been trying to tell you!" said Emily.

The cab driver pushed the gas pedal to the floor, and we whipped through traffic on our way back into Rome.

"Yes, I take you both embassy." His English had improved quite considerably over the past minute and a half. "You will pay… one hundred fifty."

John looked into his wallet. A hundred fifty euros figured out to be more than two hundred dollars. At this rate, we'd be completely out of money in two days. Three tops.

But the cab driver put his heart into it. For the first time, we felt like somebody other than one of us castaways actually felt a sense of urgency about this whole ridiculous catastrophe. Of course, we paid him handsomely for that urgency, but it still felt sincere.

As we approached the heart of Italy, Emily said, "I think we're going to need to split up."

"What? Why?" I said. "I don't understand."

"We don't have enough time to go to the U.S. Embassy to get your passport," Emily explained, "and then go to all the way to the Chinese Embassy to get all of our passports. They'll be closed."

"I hadn't thought about that," I said.

"Plus," Emily continued. "I need to get my green card replaced. But I can't do that until after I've already gotten my Chinese passport."

"So you think we should split up?" I asked, suddenly feeling like I was back to the deck of the ship when somebody called out for *women and children first*. "But we don't have phones, and we don't speak Italian, and we're an hour away from our hotel. What if we split up and then we can't find each other?"

Emily thought for a moment.

"Okay, we'll go to the U.S. Embassy first and drop you off. John and Apple will give you fifty euros for cab fare. You'll go inside and get your passport while the rest of us head over to the Chinese embassy for our passports. When you finish, stay outside the embassy gate and wait for us. I need to come back to the U.S. Embassy anyhow to get my green card."

"Okay," I replied.

"But if we don't arrive by six o'clock," Emily continued, rummaged through her plastic bag for a pen and scribbling an address on a scrap of paper, "then take a taxi to this address and wait outside the Chinese Embassy for us."

"Sounds good," I said. A few moments later, we pulled up to the gate of the U.S. Embassy. I gave Emily a kiss and stepped out onto the curb, and then the cab whipped back out into traffic and disappeared around a corner. Emily was gone.

The guard at the entry gate of the American Embassy smiled awkwardly as he asked for my identification.

"Sorry," I said. "No papers. Everything got sunk in the shipwreck."

"Yes, yes. Of course." he slapped his forehead. "How stupid of me! Please, please, come in."

He was an eager young Italian man, freshly enlisted from the look of it.

"I have been watching on the news all day," he continued. "And then all day I was reading about the captain, and about the lifeboats, and I read that six people have died. Very *very* bad, this accident. I am so so sorry."

"Thanks," I said. He seemed like a nice kid, and he gave me a bright, warm smile as he motioned me past the security desk and through a metal detector. When he finished his inspection, he opened a metal door and I walked out into an open air courtyard between the outer wall and the embassy complex.

I followed his instructions to the visitor's entrance, then through the hallway and up a flight of stairs to the passport office. It felt unnatural and surreal to be here, navigating these winding corridors and staircases without Emily by my side.

"Hello," I said, to a woman behind a thick pane of glass. "I'm a survivor of the Costa Concordia shipwreck."

She looked up and nodded her head.

"I lost my passport when the ship sunk. All of my documents and identification and money were there in the closet in our cabin. My wife and I… all our luggage is just… everything is just *gone*."

"Please fill out this passport application." The woman slid a page underneath the glass. "Don't forget to turn it over when you're done, and sign it on the back."

"Is there anything else you can do for us?" I asked. "We don't have any other clothes to wear. And we don't know how we're getting home."

"There's nothing we can do." she said, "It is not our policy to provide financial assistance to distressed travellers."

"Okay," I muttered. "Thanks anyhow."

She gave me a sour look. "There's a photo booth downstairs. It's six euros for two pictures, and the machine only accepts exact change."

I found a pen and carried my paperwork to a table nearby, scratching out all the important details about my identity: name, place and date of birth, address and social security number.

About halfway down the page, there was a big empty box with this question written at the top:

161

How, where and on what date did the loss or theft take place? What efforts were made to recover the passport?

I uncapped my pen and wrote:

On January 13, 2012 at 9:45 pm, the Costa Concordia cruise ship sank into the Mediterranean Sea off the coast of Giglio. My passport is somewhere on that boat, probably under water. No efforts were made to recover the passport.

When I finished, I went downstairs (with my exact change) and posed for a pair of passport photos. When I finished, I walked back upstairs to the desk and slid my paper under the counter.

"Thank you." said the woman. "We'll call your name when we're ready for you."

I sat down in a plastic chair halfway across the waiting room and watched the TV set mounted to the wall. It was tuned to CNN International, so I sat and watched the news. It seemed so strange that other newsworthy events might be unfolding elsewhere in the world right now.

But every half hour or so, they played an updated news blurb about the Concordia shipwreck. Three bodies had been found, with more than fifty people still missing.

"The captain of the ill-fated vessel, Francesco Schettino, was arrested and taken into custody early Saturday afternoon," said the CNN anchor, "on charges of abandoning ship and manslaughter."

My heart pounded.

No wonder we hadn't heard anything from the captain during our evacuation. No wonder we hadn't seen him during the three hours we had spent holding onto the rope and waiting for rescue. The captain had found his own way to safety, leaving us behind to die.

"Mr. Smith," a voice called from behind the glass. "Mr. Benjamin Smith."

"Yes," I said. "Thank you. Is my passport ready?"

"No, Mr. Smith. We will call your name when we're ready for you. Right now, there's just a phone call for you."

"A phone call?" I asked. "For me?"

"Yes, there is a phone call. For you." She pointed over to other corner of the room. "You can pick it up on the white phone, over there on the table."

I picked up the phone and fiddled with the various unmarked buttons until I heard a clicking sound.

"Hello?" I asked.

"Hey, it's me!" said Emily. "How are things going over there?"

"Oh hey, sweetheart. It's good to hear from you." I said. "Things are okay, I guess. This place is exactly like a driver's license office. It's the epitome of bureaucracy. Anyhow, I gave them my paperwork a few minutes ago, so now I'm just waiting. How about you? Making progress?"

"It's a mess," said Emily. "The Hong Kong government issues its own passports, which are different than Chinese passports. But Hong Kong doesn't have its own embassies, so we have to deal with the Chinese Embassy here, and then they'll talk to the Hong Kong government. The Chinese Embassy can print the paperwork on behalf of the Hong Kong government, but the passport needs to be approved by the Hong Kong officials."

"Wow." I said. "Sounds complicated."

"Yeah," replied Emily, her voice starting to break. "And nobody even *cares* about us. They all act so annoyed that we would come in here asking for help. Like we crashed the ship on purpose or something. Everybody's being so *mean* to us. I don't understand."

"I don't get it either." I said. "But it's exactly the same thing here."

"Benji, they're saying I might have to go back to Hong Kong to get my passport reissued."

"Really?" I asked. "That's… that's crazy."

"I've been on the phone with somebody at the American Embassy too," Emily continued. "Her name is Susanna — from the State Department — and she says I need to get my passport replaced before I can get a new green card. And if I don't get my green card replaced, then I can't go back to Boston with you. Maybe I'll have to go back to Hong Kong."

"Do you think it'll come down to that?" I asked.

"Maybe," she replied. "I don't know… But if that happens, and if I *do* have to go back to Hong Kong instead, will you

163

come with me? I don't know what I'll do if we can't go home together."

"Yes. Absolutely." I said it without a moment of hesitation. "I'll go back to Hong Kong with you and stay there for a few months, if that's what we've gotta do. I'm not going to leave you behind. Not after everything we've been through. No matter what, we're sticking together."

"Okay, thanks." she said, breathing a deep sigh of relief.

Then, from behind the inch-thick glass behind me, a man's voice called out my name. "Benjamin Smith!"

"Oops. I've gotta go." I said. "They're calling my name. Call me back if anything changes."

"Okay," she said. "I miss you."

"I miss you too."

I hung up the phone and turned back toward the desk.

"Mr. Smith, please complete section two of the application document." The man behind the counter slid my paperwork back through the slot. "We need to know if you're applying for a full passport replacement or an emergency passport."

"What's the difference?" I asked.

The man sighed and rolled his eyes. "A full passport replacement costs $135. In local currency that's about 180 euros. An emergency passport is free — except for the cost of the photos — but you can only use it once, to return back to the United States. After that, it becomes null and void."

I stood still and thought for a second, not sure what to do.

"Mr. Smith," the man persisted, "are you applying for a full replacement passport, or for an emergency passport? We cannot proceed with your application until you complete section two."

"I don't know…" I said. "My wife might not be able to get her green card… We might have to fly to Hong Kong… I don't know…"

"Then you'll need a full replacement," the man interjected.

"But… I don't have $135…" I reached into my pocket and unfolded the crumpled bills. I only had 44 euros, and I still needed most of that to pay for a taxi to the Chinese Embassy. Even if I could get more cash from John, we didn't have enough money between the six of us to pay full price for passports.

"Maybe if I could talk to Susanna…" I said, "from the State Department… She's working on my wife's green card."

164

"Yes, I'm aware of the situation," said the man.

"Okay okay, good." I said, the wheels in my head starting to turn. "So, maybe if I could talk to Susanna and ask her about the progress on Emily's green card, then…"

"No." He cut me off mid-sentence. "I already gave your wife Susanna's phone number. I'm not giving it to you too."

"Well… Isn't there anything else you can do to help?" I asked.

"It is not our policy." He shrugged his shoulders. "And anyhow, we are already doing everything within our power to help. You know this is a weekend, right? A *holiday* weekend."

"Okay then," I responded, biting my lower lip. "I guess I'll apply for the free emergency passport."

If we end up going to Hong Kong, I'll have to find the money somewhere, but for now I'd just cross my fingers and hope we could make it home. I checked the appropriate box in section two and slid the application back through the slot in the bulletproof glass.

As the man behind the counter disappeared into another room, I sat back down in a chair and put my head in my hands.

And only an hour and a half later, I finally walked out the door with an emergency temporary passport.

30

Dusk had fallen, and the evening wind was cold outside the American Embassy. I tucked my new emergency passport into my pocket and raised my hand to hail a taxi.

The sky dripped with amber beams of light from the setting sun, casting a dreamy glow across the streets of Rome. Swaddled in that honey-colored haze, I felt dizzy and heavy-headed, exhaustion weighing me down like a lead helmet. I fantasized about lying down on the sidewalk and taking a nap. Maybe for just ten minutes.

Yeah, the sidewalk would be bitter cold, and the crowds of people passing by would probably step on me, but the taste of sleep would be so sweet… so intoxicating… so warm and buttery and comforting like a symphony of caramel-colored blankets.

Or something like that.

I felt like my brain had been rewired, and all the sensory connectors had been hooked up to the wrong places. Was that the sound of blurry vision rattling in my lungs? Or the smell of car horns stinging my eyes? I couldn't tell. Everything had become so confusing.

Finally a taxi pulled to the curb and I stumbled into the back seat.

"The Chinese Embassy, please." I said to the cab driver. I reached into my pocket for the address Emily had given me. "Number 56, Villa Bruchella."

The cab driver snatched the paper from my hands and cast a doubtful eye on it.

"*Via Bruxelles*," he said, correcting my pronunciation with a roll of his eyes.

"Yeah, whatever," I mumbled.

The cab whipped around the streets of Rome for the next ten minutes before depositing me in front of the gates of the Chinese Embassy. Emily stood on the corner with John and Apple and Erik and Chui Lin.

I paid the taxi driver, who started driving away almost before I could even close the door, and joined the rest of the family on the curb.

"Everybody got their passports but me," said Emily.

"Why? What happened?" I asked.

"All of us have Hong Kong ID card," said John, his hands in his pockets. "So we get passport nice and easy."

"Nice and easy?" scoffed Apple. "They make us wait two hour! And then they make us pay extra 'urgent fee' to get passport today. And these not even real passports. After we get home, they make us throw it away and get new passport all over again. It make me so angry!"

"The whole time, they couldn't stop talking about how we made them come to work on a weekend," said Emily, her hands clenching into fists. "Anyhow, I don't have my Hong Kong ID card. I don't have a drivers license or a birth certificate or anything with my name on it. They kept saying 'how do we know it's really you?' I swear to god, I could punch somebody in the face right now."

"Seriously?" I asked. "They accused you of being an impostor?"

"They said they couldn't do anything for me without an ID card, unless they had authorization from the Hong Kong government. But I already *talked* to someone from the Hong Kong government. They already *sent* my information to the embassy, and they were really nice and they were trying to be helpful and everything."

"But the embassy just want to get rid of us," said John. "Tonight, they having a big party. Very fancy."

"What?" I asked. "A party?"

Emily's eyes narrowed. "They told us we had to get out. The ambassador is having a black-tie party, and we were in the way."

"You've got to be kidding." I gasped.

"Nope. Not kidding," said Emily, fuming with rage. "They looked at us in our dirty baggy refugee clothes, and they told us we had to leave because the guests were starting to arrive. They told us to get out and come back tomorrow. Which means we have to take another taxi and spend another hundred euros. And they don't even *care*. That's what makes me so mad."

Just then, a young Chinese woman stepped out of the embassy gate and approached us, speaking loudly and waving her arms, pointing at the embassy building and then at the gate and then down the street.

Emily and Apple only listened for a second before whipping their heads around and responding with their own loud speech and wild gesticulations. I didn't understand what was going on, but I could tell this was a particularly nasty argument. Finally, Emily turned her back and stormed off in the other direction, grabbing my hand and pulling me along with her.

"She told us to go stand on the other side of the street," growled Emily. "She said this is where all the cars are trying to drop off the party guests, and she doesn't want them to look at us. And you know what? Fine. Fine. If they don't want to look at us, fuck them anyhow. I don't want to be where I'm not wanted."

Down the length of the street, a line of black Mercedes had formed; at the head of that line, dignitaries dressed in black tuxedos emerged from each car and then disappeared through the embassy gates to enjoy the luxurious gala within. Thanks to the embassy staff, none of the ambassador's honorable guests had to injure their delicate sensibilities by laying eyes on a dirty smelly band of castaways.

We crossed the street to hail a taxi from the shadows, far from the embassy's floodlights and red carpet.

31

It was impossible to find another cab driver willing to pack six adults into an ordinary taxi, so we took separate cabs back to the hotel. Before hailing a cab for ourselves, Emily got a cab for John and Apple and Erik and Chui Lin.

"Airport Marriott, please," Emily said to the driver, as the four passengers climbed aboard.

"Which one?" asked the cab driver.

Emily hesitated. "I think there's only one… It's called 'Airport Marriott Hotel Roma.'"

"Hmmmm…" shrugged the driver. "I don't know… There are many many hotels at airport."

Emily held up the plastic bag she had been using as a purse, the name and logo of the hotel emblazoned in red ink on the white plastic. "This one! This is the hotel! Please drive them to this hotel."

The driver shook his head. "I don't know… I don't know how to… go to there."

"Figure it out!" Emily shouted, slamming the back door shut and pointing out toward the highway. "Use a GPS or call your dispatcher. I don't care how you do it. Just go!"

Annoyed but defeated, the cab driver spit a ball of phlegm out his window and then put the car into gear, spraying gravel from the rear wheels as he shot out into traffic.

* * *

Forty-five minutes later, we dragged ourselves through the front door of the hotel, stopping for a moment at the front desk to see whether we had missed anything important during our five-hour embassy excursion.

169

"Hello," I said. "We've been away for a few hours, trying to get our passports. Did anyone from Costa ever show up here tonight?"

"Yes," she replied. "Two or three hours ago, someone from Costa come here."

"Really? What did they say?" I asked eagerly. "Did they leave us any instructions?"

She shrugged. "I don't know."

"Will they be back again?"

"I don't know."

"Did you get contact information?"

"No."

"Does anyone at this hotel have a phone number for anyone at Costa?"

The look on her face was withering. She was reaching her limit of annoyance and disgust. "No, sir. No, we do not."

It was maddening. How could these people be so inconsiderate?

"Why not? Why wouldn't you ask for contact information?"

Her voice was icy cold. "Because this is not my job to do this."

She gave me a sheet of white office paper and said "You can use this to fly home. If you have no passport, you can use this instead. Show it to them at the airport, and they will let you onto the plane."

I looked down at the paper with astonishment. It looked exactly like this:

NAME _____
DATE OF BIRTH _____
COUNTRY _____
OTHER DECLARATIONS _____

What a joke. I could have printed this page myself in less than five minutes.

Emily and I walked away from the desk. What a waste of time.

We looked around for John and Apple and Erik and Chui Lin. Their cab still hadn't gotten back from the Embassy. Why would it take so long? We went outside and waited for their taxi to arrive.

Five minutes passed, but their taxi still didn't show.

And then suddenly, Emily tilted her head and focused her attention on some distant sound.

"I think I can hear them," she said. "I think they're back in the lobby."

We rushed back into the hotel lobby, only to find it empty.

Were we hallucinating? Maybe it's because of the lack of sleep or the stress, and now we're hearing voices? Or maybe we're just so exhausted that we're imagining that we're hallucinating? Is that even possible?

"That's weird," I said. "I thought I heard them too. Maybe they went back up to their rooms."

So we went upstairs and looked for them there too.

Each time, we thought we heard their voices, talking quietly in their rooms. But then we knocked on the doors and nobody answered.

Finally, we went back to our own room, figuring maybe they had been out looking for us, the same way we were looking for them.

But there was nobody at our room either. So we just sat down and waited.

The thing we were most worried about was whether their cab driver had taken them back to the wrong hotel. To one of the other airport hotels, or to a different Marriott.

Emily started making phone calls.

One after another, every hotel operator said that no, they hadn't seen a group of four Chinese people. One by one, Emily thanked them and told them to call our hotel if they saw our family members.

While she called, I walked back and forth between the lobby and the three different hotel rooms, just in case they showed up without us noticing.

Emily was starting to get frantic. And we were both starting to get hysterical. We had been awake for more than 36 hours. And we had hardly eaten anything. Throughout the day, we had gotten our hands on a few cups of coffee, a few hunks of bread, and a few granola bars. But none of us had eaten a meal. We were starting to feel a little dizzy.

"Maybe we should call the cab company and get their dispatcher to call all the cabs in the area," Emily said.

"I think that's a good idea," I said. "But before we do anything, we need to eat dinner."

"Yeah… I am pretty hungry…" said Emily, closing her eyes and yawning. "But we have to find them. What if they're lost?"

"We'll keep looking for them later. But right now, you need to eat. No negotiation."

She looked at the phone and sat silently for a second. "Okay," she finally said.

"Let's eat."

So we dragged our feet down the hall and down the elevator and into the restaurant.

When we walked through the door and into the dining room, John stood up from his chair and said "Benji and Emily! Finally!" John and Erik and Chui Lin looked up at us and smiled.

They had been here all along. They had already finished their dinner, but they were waiting for us to show up.

Emily collapsed into a chair and breathed a deep sigh of relief.

I looked at her in admiration. She cared so much for everyone, and so often exhausted herself taking care of people. It was just like in Barcelona when she had run herself ragged (and driven me crazy) tending to everyone else's needs.

Even now.

Really she should have been getting something to eat. Just looking at her, I could see the last of her energy reserves bottoming out. But she was focused on her family anyhow, asking them how long they had been back (about an hour) and why hadn't we seen them anywhere (they had gone directly into the restaurant upon arrival).

Watching Emily, I knew that she'd stay focused on her family, neglecting her own hunger and exhaustion.

So I got up myself to make her a dinner plate.

The restaurant had set up a buffet table full of food in a special section of the dining room just for shipwreck survivors. Salad greens and fruit. Pasta with pesto sauce. Some kind of saucy herb chicken. Roasted potatoes.

I loaded up a big plate and brought it to Emily.

All around us, the other shipwreck survivors sat at their tables and ate their dinners too. Forty or fifty of us, all together. A few people still wore a stunned expression on their faces, silently pushing peas back and forth on their plates. But most of us ate ravenously, shoveling down forkfuls of delicious savory food. Buttery, garlicky, juicy, delicious food. It was like an entire lifetime had elapsed over the past twenty-four hours, and this was the first meal of a new era. Epic and monumental.

While we ate, we talked.

This was the first time we started hearing everyone's stories, and it's the first time we began telling our own story.

"We were just sitting there in the magic show, when the lights went out..." said a short, middle aged woman.

Someone else chimed in "When we heard the first announcement, we knew it was bad." He was a young Filipino, with an athletic body but no trace of an accent, probably in his early to mid twenties. "An electrical failure? Seriously? That's bullshit."

Emily quickly engaged in this conversation. After an afternoon spent tangled in bureaucracy, trying in vain to get help from embassy employees who didn't understand our situation and didn't seem to care anyhow, it was an enormous relief to be back in a room with fifty other people who knew exactly what we were going through.

But then I noticed Emily wasn't eating her food. She had taken a bite or two. But in general, she was so tired and so distracted talking to everyone else, she scarcely paid any attention to her food.

So I picked up a fork and gave her a bite, then another and another. I brought a glass of ice water to her lips and wiped the corners of her mouth with a napkin.

We talked about the crash and the evacuation. The lifeboats that worked and the lifeboats that failed. About eighty percent of the people seemed to have gotten off the cruise ship on that first wave of lifeboats, reaching Giglio Island by 11 o'clock that night.

The other twenty percent of us, who got left behind and abandoned, scrambled back and forth on the cruise ship, looking for the safest way to dry land. Some stayed on the high side of the sinking ship, climbing over the rails and clinging to the rope. Others went to the low side, down where the water was flooding the decks, washing through into the windows and doors. They went there because someone had told them to go. They went down to the water and looked for lifeboats close enough to take them. Some of them jumped onto the roofs of

173

other lifeboats, already overcrowded with refugees. But some of them jumped into the water and swam to the nearest lifeboat. Or to the shore, a hundred yards away.

As we finished eating dinner (some of us wolfing down second and third helpings; a side-effect of having forgotten to eat all day long), we sat at the tables and kept talking and talking.

Patrick and Elizabeth introduced themselves to us.

He was the young Filipino-American we had heard earlier at dinner, and she was his newly-wed wife; they were on their honeymoon too. They had saved money for a year to pay for this trip, even paying a little extra to fly first class.

When the ship ran aground, they did the same thing as everyone else, grabbing their life jackets and going to the muster station on the fourth deck. And just like us, their lifeboat got tangled or stuck trying to descend, and just like us, they found themselves back on the ship fending for themselves.

But unlike us, they actually got onto a second lifeboat. A second lifeboat that *also* got tangled and stuck trying to descend.

"You know, most of the crew on this ship are Filipino." He said. "I was *born* in the Philippines, and I speak Tagalog, so I can understand every word they're saying. Even before the shipwreck, at dinner, I can hear them talking about the passengers and saying which women have a nice ass, or whatever. And they're saying all that stuff while they're serving us food. That's just completely unprofessional, you know?"

He lowered his voice a little and came in close, as though he was telling us a secret.

"But out on the lifeboat, when they're supposed to be lowering us down to the water, I can hear them shouting at each other. Saying stuff like *I don't know what I'm doing. I don't know how this works. Something's broken.* They're arguing with each other and shouting. All of them are confused. Like none of them ever got trained or had a drill or anything. It's fucking ridiculous."

When the second lifeboat didn't deploy either, they got really scared and panicked. They had to do something. They had to escape. To somehow get the fuck off this death trap.

So when somebody suggested they go over to the starboard side of the ship, they listened and crossed over to the other side.

The sinking side.

"When we got down there, there was water everywhere," he told us. "And all the boats were gone. But there was a rubber raft down at the end, so went down there and jumped in."

Patrick's story was intense. His voice quavered as he spoke, and his eyes focused somewhere else. Watching him tell the story, we could see him seeing the mental images replaying in his mind. And because he could see that imagery so vividly, we saw it too.

"But there were so many people in that little rubber raft. It wasn't built to hold so many people. Which caused the water to start coming in over the top. And the water kept coming in, until the whole raft was just *flooded* with water. So I said *fuck this*, we just got off a sinking ship, and now we're on a sinking *raft*? I don't think so."

Patrick wiped a line of sweat off his forehead. His young wife Elizabeth, quiet and sweet and timid, instinctively put her hand on Patrick's shoulder.

"So I said to Elizabeth, *Do you trust me?*"

Elizabeth spoke up for second to tell her part of the story, "And I was like… *Yeah, I trust you.*" Patrick nodded his head quietly for a second. His eyes still focused inward.

"So I said, *We're going to have to swim. We're going to have to jump into the water and swim to land.* And I don't even know how to swim. But I've got a life jacket, and I can kick my feet like a motherfucker. So we're gonna be all right, you know?"

We all nodded our heads, rapt in attention.

"I told Elizabeth, *Hold onto my hand and don't let go. Don't you dare let go of my hand.*"

Tears are starting to come into his eyes. First just glistening at the corners but then erupting down his cheeks.

"So we jumped in and started swimming. And we held onto each other's hands. And we're swimming and *swimming*. And I've never held onto anything so tight in my whole fucking life. I'm serious."

"But then this lifeboat comes by, and it's coming toward the ship. It's gonna crash into the ship, and we're gonna be crushed. Like literally *crushed* between these two boats. And the only thing for us to do is just go underwater. We've gotta go underwater and swim under the lifeboat and come out the other side. But then we're underwater and it's so dark, we can't see anything. It's just completely, totally, utterly pitch black. And freezing cold."

"And then all of a sudden, I lost her hand. *I lost her*. I reached everywhere, trying to find her and thinking *oh no oh no, I fucking lost her hand*. My brand new wife. My bride. And I fucking let go of her hand."

He reached for her fingertips and held them tightly. I knew how he felt. The taste of rat poison rose in my throat again as I remembered losing Emily to the "women and children" group.

"When I came up for air on the other side of the boat, there she was. I've never been so happy to see anyone. I held her hand again, and we swam back to shore."

She smiled a small, meek, exhausted smile. "Our shoes are still a little wet."

At the table next to us, a group of six people laughed loudly as they raised their glasses and somebody said, "Drink up, friends! Eventually Costa will have to pick up the tab for every bottle of wine we drink."

The rest of them giggled with glee and said "cheers!"

Listening to their conversation, it quickly became clear that they had gotten off the cruise ship during the initial evacuation, on one of the first lifeboats to leave.

I looked back over at Patrick and Elizabeth and I couldn't help but contrast them with this other group of early escapees. Where did Emily and I fall along that spectrum?

I wondered how Emily and I might have been affected if we had escaped on the first lifeboat? What if we had never had to climb that rope? How would that have changed our lives?

And then again, what course would our lives take — how would our future be different — if we had been forced to swim to shore, through that cold dark terrible water?

I shuddered at the thought.

Emily touched my hand, and I turned to face her. From the look in her eyes, I could tell she was thinking the same thoughts as me. What if we had had to swim too? Her shoulders shook as the tears welled up from deep inside her and poured, in glassy cascades down her cheeks.

From the next table over, the jolly toastmaster looked in our direction. "Hey now, there's no need to cry!"

He stood up and walked in our direction, carrying a glass of merlot and setting it on the table in front of Emily. "Drink this, and try to chill out. Hey, free wine can't be bad, am I right?"

Emily turned and looked at him, her eyes squinted and locked upon his gaze with a laser focus.

"No thanks," she said.

32

After dinner, we dragged ourselves out the restaurant and headed back toward our room on the third floor.

Notwithstanding a few minutes of drowsy nap time, I had basically been awake for 40 hours at this point. And I'm pretty sure Emily hadn't closed her eyes for longer than a blink or two since the ordeal began.

"The only thing I want in this world is to sleep." I leaned my head against the wall as I pressed the elevator call button.

"Well, hello again," said a woman's voice from behind us. We turned to face the Irish couple we had met on bus, earlier that afternoon.

"Hello," I said. "Good to see you again."

"We missed the two of youse, back a few hours, when the Costa lady was here," she continued. "Yeh didn't sleep through it, did yeh?"

"No," I said. "But I do wish we had gotten some sleep. We're exhausted."

"We went to the U.S. and Chinese Embassies," said Emily, "trying to get our passports back."

"You had to go all the way out there yourself?" asked the Irishwoman. "They didn't send someone here?"

"No, and it makes us crazy," said Emily. "We called them and asked if they could send a bus or a van or something. But they said no. They told us to take a cab."

"Well isn't that lovely of them!" exclaimed the Irishman. "Tonight, the Irish ambassador himself came here to check on us, and we're the only two people on the whole ruddy ship from Ireland."

"Really?" I asked. "Your ambassador came here?"

"That's the truth. I swear it." he answered. "And right about

178

the same time, there was other ambassadors. I can't remember them all, but I know I seen somebody from England and Spain."

"And Wales," said his wife. "I do believe I saw the ambassador from Wales."

"Wait a minute… Let me get this straight in my head," he continued. "Every wee country in Europe — with no more than two or three people aboard the ship — sends a diplomatic convoy to check up on their people. But the two richest and mightiest nations in the world can't get off their duff to help out a hundred or more of their own?"

My thoughts exactly.

* * *

I looked at my phone. There was an email message from my younger brother, Michael, asking if he could do anything to help:

I can wire you whatever money you need if you let me know where you could pick it up. I've also contacted Carnival Cruise Line (parent company of Costa) and gave them your contact info. I haven't been able to get through to Costa Cruise Lines yet, but I'll keep trying in the morning. Let me know what you need and we can help. If it would help for my to fly there and be with you to help you guys get home, I would buy plane tickets without hesitating.

I hope you get some rest and I hope to talk to you soon.

Much love,

~Michael

I thought about the wire transfer. In a desperate situation like this, it's always nice to have more cash. But we didn't know how much longer we would be in Rome, and what if we ended up leaving the country without actually figuring out how to get our hands on the money?

And then suddenly, I realized the best way for him to help.

179

Actually, there's one huge thing you could do for me. A really important job. Would you mind checking in with Julie? Give her a call and take her temperature. See whether she's told the kids about the cruise ship sinking and whether the kids are scared. Did they see the news video? Did they hear me tell my story? If that's the case, then I'll definitely make some time to call the kids and let them know that I'm okay. Otherwise, I'll wait to call them until I'm home safe. Thanks for doing that for me, and I hope to talk to you soon.

benji

33

I collapsed on the bed and curled into a fetal position.

"Let's go to sleep," I said.

But Emily was thinking ahead.

"We need to wash our clothes."

She was right. We only had one change of clothes: the ones we had worn on our day in Rome and throughout the entire evacuation ordeal. They were filthy and smelly, and caked with the palpable dust of panic and despair.

"Take everything off and put them in the sink," Emily said. She did the same.

We stood naked for the next five minutes. Emily peeled the paper off the tiny bar of hotel soap and then ran it under the stream of water in the bathroom sink. She rubbed the soap against the palm of her hand to build up a foam and then used her hands to scrape the spots of grime out of our clothes. When she ran out of soap, she opened the small bottle of shampoo nearby on the counter and squeezed it too into our makeshift laundry tub.

Just then, the phone rang.

The phone meant news: probably from Daryn, with some sort of important information about people who might help us in Rome. Or maybe it was our parents, calling to send their love and check in on us.

Emily picked up the phone.

"It's CNN."

The news network was calling back to arrange an interview. They had gotten Emily's message on the tip-line earlier in the day, and they were very interested in booking an on-air interview with her to hear more of the details.

"I think you should talk to my husband Benji."

I stood next to her. I was naked. I wasn't sure about this. Emily had been the one who talked to Al Jazeera, and she had been so calm and so clear. She had remembered to say all the important details. Would I be any good at talking to the press?

"Really?" I whispered to her. She cupped her hand over the phone and looked me in the eyes.

"Yes. You're so articulate. You're such a good storyteller. It should be you."

"Okay. I'll try my best."

"And besides," she said, "I think I'm too angry to do this. If I start talking, I'll just end up shouting or crying, and then nobody will hear me anyhow. I think I'd just be a mess."

Emily finished making the arrangements. Someone from CNN would call us back at ten o'clock. I would spend a few minutes talking with a producer, who would prepare me for the live interview.

I hung up the phone and waited. It was 9:45.

Emily wrapped a blanket around my shoulders.

"Are you nervous?" she asked.

"Yeah. A little."

She put her arms around me.

"You'll be amazing."

When the phone rang, I took two deep breaths before picking up the receiver.

"Hello?"

"Hi, is this Benji?"

"Yes."

"Hi, my name is April. I'm a producer with CNN International. Thank you so much for agreeing to this interview."

"No problem. I'm just glad I can help tell this story. Emily and I think it's really important."

"That's great. We're glad you called us. From what we've seen so far, it sounds like you guys have been through a lot, and we're grateful that you're safe."

"Thanks. Yeah, we're really happy to be alive."

"So are we. Okay, now let me just give you a heads-up so that you know what to expect during the segment."

"Okay."

"In a few minutes, I'm going to patch you into the live audio stream. You'll be able to hear everything that's broadcast on the network. You can just sit and relax and listen to the show for about five minutes. And then the news anchor will introduce you and ask you an opening question. At that point, your microphone will be live."

"Sounds good."

"The anchor's name is Ralitsa Vassileva. She'll ask you about your experiences aboard the ship and talk to you about your escape."

"Okay."

"Do you have any questions?"

"How much time will I have?"

"Probably about two or three minutes. In these kinds of interviews, we like to get to the point quickly and go straight into the details."

"Okay. I'll do my best."

"I'm sure you'll do fine. Just sit back and relax for a few minutes, but listen for the start of your segment."

"Okay."

My heart was starting to pound. I closed my eyes and took a deep breath. After a moment or two, I could hear the audio stream coming through the phone, but I couldn't focus on what they were talking about. I was just thinking about the things I wanted to include in my story. There was so much to talk about already. So many details. How would I be able to tell our story in two to three minutes?

Emily came back out of the bathroom, where she was still scrubbing our clothes.

"What's up?" she asked.

"I'm waiting a few minutes. Our story is up next."

She kissed me on top of my head.

"Are you nervous?"

"Yeah."

She sat next to me on the bed and put her ear up against my head so that we could both listen.

And then I heard my name.

"We want to turn now to Benji Smith and his new wife Emily, who were enjoying their honeymoon cruise aboard the Costa Concordia when the disaster occurred. Benji is joining us now by phone from the couple's hotel room in Rome with details of their harrowing experience. Benji, thank you very much for joining us."

I swallowed hard and opened my mouth.

"Yeah, yeah. I'm happy to."

The anchor's voice was calm and soothing and kind. She had a soft eastern European accent. "Describe to us what happened."

"Once the lifeboats started to be deployed, there were a certain number of them that actually went out, and those people pretty quickly went to safety. But there were three of those lifeboats that malfunctioned. Or maybe the crew didn't know how to work them. Or maybe some combination of the two. And those lifeboats, as they're being lowered down to the deck are twisting and turning, and people are getting thrown around."

As I started to tell the story, I could feel a sense of fury building up inside me. I wanted to tell this story to everyone and let the world know how we had been treated. "And then they pulled the lifeboats boats back up and just put the people back onto the ship, and then they never came back for us."

The news anchor paused for a half second. "Really? And so how did you... did you just self-evacuate?"

"Yeah. We scrambled around the ship, looking for the best way to go. Some of us ran to the lower deck. Some of us ran to the upper deck. When we were afraid that the stairways were flooded with water, we made ladders out of ropes, and we used those ladders to climb down from the outer fourth deck to the third deck, where we could kind of... shimmy our way down the side of the ship."

The anchor started to ask a question "Did the ship..." but I cut her off before she could finish her question. My mind was already racing faster than my mouth could keep up, and I knew what I wanted to say without having to be asked any leading questions.

"We climbed down the ship with rope ladders. And we waited, clinging to those rope ladders, for three and a half hours."

I continued. "My family was picked up at three o'clock in the morning by one of the lifeboats that had brought people to shore and came back. The people manning these boats were just cooks and shopkeepers. They weren't the sailors. It wasn't the captain or the officers. We never heard from any of those guys. Never heard their voices. Never saw any of them. They never helped us to evacuate. We were totally abandoned."

"When we got to shore, we were never told where to go. We were never told to gather anywhere. People curled up in churches and in shops."

"And then in the morning, boats came and we were just told to get on the boats, but we were given no reason why. We weren't told where we were going or what the next plan was. We were never told who was in charge or what was going to happen to us. We didn't know who was alive. We didn't know where we were going."

The whirlwind of these events was buzzing around me like a swarm of bees.

I looked at the bedside clock. I had already been on the air for five minutes, and the story was just getting started.

"We arrived at a school where we were packed in really dangerous, riot-like conditions and forced through hallways to sort ourselves into embarkation cities, and then they put us onto another set of buses that took us back to Rome. When we arrived, we found out there was no one from Costa on our buses at all. We tried to ask questions: 'Who is the person from Costa?' But there was no one there.

"We asked the hotel manager 'Where is the person from Costa?' And the hotel manager had never heard of any person from Costa. They weren't told about this drop-off in advance. We were just randomly dumped at the hotel."

I pulled the blanket tightly around my shoulders. "We still, to this point… I've been awake for 40 hours. It's been 24 hours since the catastrophe, and I still have never spoken with a person from Costa." My voice was trembling. My body was trembling. I felt naked. "We still haven't gotten any clothes or food or money. We're just stranded. We have nothing."

"That's… that was my next question…"

Now her voice was trembling too. "You probably don't even have your passport on you. No money? Nothing…? And where are you going to spend the night? How are you going to feed yourself and your wife?"

"The hotel that we're staying at has been very generous. We asked who their contact person is at Costa, and they said they don't have one. They don't have a person they talk to at Costa, so this is all just the generosity of the hotel. But thankfully, they've given us food and they've given us a room to stay in. But if we're going to be able to get home, then we need to get our passports sorted out. We need to get our flights. We lost a lot of our stuff… All the things we brought with us on our

185

honeymoon are just gone."

"Benji, I want you to take us back to the evacuation, to when it actually happened. You said that you thought that something was wrong long before it happened, and that you were stranded for three and a half hours?" Her voice was incredulous. It was like she couldn't believe what she was hearing. "Just hanging off of a rope ladder? Until you were rescued? Tell us a little bit more. Take us through that experience again, which is simply shocking."

I looked at the clock. The interview had been going on for more than five minutes now, which was a little weird. Time had taken on an unearthly quality, and I had a hard time deciding whether it felt more like I'd been doing this interview for over an hour, or just a few seconds.

"It started when my wife and I were in our cabin on the second level, and the whole ship seemed to tilt — over the span of ten or fifteen seconds — up to maybe thirty degrees. And cups, wine glasses, wine bottles were falling off of the chairs."

Did I really just say that wine bottles had fallen off the chairs? I blinked my eyes and shook my head. I was so tired that it took a very dedicated effort just to construct a sentence that made sense from start to finish.

"Then the TV slid down and almost fell onto our heads. If we hadn't jumped up to grab it in time… Furniture was falling over. Then the lights flickered out and came back on. Then we grabbed our life jackets and ran to the fourth deck… Because that's where the muster stations were."

The news anchor asked "Now how did you know to go there? Was there any instruction given by the ship to evacuate? To do something? Or any explanation as to what had happened?'"

"We read that information in a packet that was in our bunk. We attended a safety presentation on our first day, which turned out not to actually have any safety information in it. It was only a sales pitch for excursions, so we read in the safety information that the evacuation boats were on the fourth deck in our book."

In the background, I started to hear other sounds. As the news anchor started her next round of questions, I could hear the muffled sounds of people shouting in the distance.

"Benji, as you are describing your harrowing experience, I

186

just wanted to tell our viewers that a little bit earlier, we were watching amateur video of people just like you who were trying to evacuate. We've also received some video in which people are screaming. It's chaos. People are just... the look like they're lost. They're just looking around. They're lined up... And then, this disturbing video... in the dark..."

I listened to the sounds.

"I think those... those are from... the early parts of the ordeal, where everyone was rushing up to get to the lifeboats, and people were pushing and shoving. There was no order. There were no lines. There was no system in place, and there was no one in charge. Every crew member who walked past would shout different instructions. But the instructions contradicted each other. At one point we were ordered to go back to our cabins and await further instructions, but when we got to the main stairwell, we were ordered to stay at the muster stations and go back to the lifeboats. And there were children shouting and panicking. Since the boat had turned up on its side, people were sliding and falling on the slippery decks, and landing in broken glass from wine glasses in the restaurants."

The pictures were so vivid in my head. Retelling the story was like watching a movie.

"Benji, as you're talking, I just wanted to reintroduce you. For those of our viewers are just joining us, I'm talking to Benji Smith, who is a survivor from the cruise ship disaster there off the western coast of Italy..."

I looked at the clock. Nine minutes had passed.

It seemed weird to me that after less than ten minutes, she would have to do a whole new introduction. How long does the average CNN viewer tune in for? Five minutes? Less?

On the other hand, we had already long since blown through our two to three minute allocation for this segment, and I wondered how long we would keep talking. The interview was going really well, and I was feeling good about how the story was finally being covered.

"Benji," continued the anchor, "it seems to me that it would have been disastrous if you and your wife had followed some of the instructions that told you to go back to your room at that point."

"Oh, absolutely. Absolutely. It would have been catastrophic. For me, though, the worst part of the whole ordeal was on one of the lifeboats. When we were boarding, one of the crew members told us 'women and children first'. And all of these families who were clinging to each other had to separate. The women got on first, and it just…" I felt a lump in my throat. "It just tore everyone to pieces. That was the worst part for me, because, why go through all of this if we just have to be separated? It was just truly awful."

There was a long pause — or at least it felt like a long pause — while Ralitsa Vassileva the CNN anchor reconsidered the idea of women-and-children-first. I felt like I could hear the gears of cognition turning through the phone line. Finally, she said, "And… and you said that the lifeboat that you got onto was broken? Wasn't working?"

"I don't know if it was defective, or if the crew members just didn't know how to work it. The lifeboats have to be pushed away from the ship ten or fifteen feet and then lowered down… I don't know… sixty or seventy feet. And it was like the Marx brothers watching these guys try to figure out how to work the boat. They couldn't coordinate. They were shouting at each other. One of them would suddenly drop one end of the boat, and everyone would scream. And then they'd reel that side of the boat back up and try to get it even. I heard that there were other boats that twisted and turned so that the passengers were falling down into the ceiling parts of that boat. I felt like the disaster itself, hitting the reef, the capsizing of the boat was manageable. But I felt like the crew was going to kill us."

"And add to that the darkness?"

"Yes, yes. The lights went out. When we got to the outer deck of the ship, our eyes adjusted to the moonlight, and we could build our rope ladders and navigate over the railings by moonlight and starlight. But inside the ship, it was just impossible."

"So basically, you and your wife never made it onto the lifeboat? You were just hanging there… on those ropes you were describing?"

"You know, there was one more thing that truly amazed us. There were a dozen or more small boats floating next to the ship, just watching us. They had their spotlights on us, but none of them approached us for more than an hour and a half or two hours. Just sitting there watching us while we held onto this rope on the side of the ship. After a while, a small coast guard boat approached with a rubber raft in tow, and a few passengers jumped onto that rubber raft. But after three or four of those passengers, they left again, and we didn't know what was coming next. Finally, one of the lifeboats, after dropping its passengers, came back for us. And we jumped, one-by-one, onto the top of that boat."

And then I remembered the number of people involved. So far, I had been telling the story as though it was just our own family going through this process, hanging onto the rope.

"But there were three of these lifeboats that didn't deploy correctly. Each of those boats has a capacity of… I think it was a hundred and fifteen people?"

I turned to Emily. "Is that right?"

She nodded her head. "Yeah."

I continued talking into the phone. "So I have to think that's 350 people who didn't get off the boat and had to scramble around with no instructions, or with contradictory instructions, and those 350 people… Some of us ended up clinging to the ropes. Some people jumped into the water and tried to swim."

Quietly in the background, Emily said, "Some people died."

I swallowed hard, and kept talking "Other people, I have to assume, went back inside and" I tried to find a way of saying it that wasn't so grim and hopeless. I tried to say it without using the word 'dead'.

"And some people are the subjects of manhunts right now."

It wasn't any better. There are no good word choices when people are suffering and dying.

"It's just… It just is the most awful disaster."

The interview was winding down.

"Benji, we are very sorry to hear about this harrowing experience on your honeymoon. We wish you and your new wife the best of luck. And… We hope you make it back safe and…"

"Thank you."

"…and get over this horrible experience. We're glad that at least you're safe. And thank you so much for reliving those harrowing moments and sharing them with us. We wish you all the best, and we thank you."

"We're really grateful that we made it out safely. But our hearts are with those people…"

The news anchor finished my sentence "…who are still

189

missing… Yes, definitely. Our hopes go out that they're found safe and sound. Benji, thank you very much."

I hung up the phone…

…

You're welcome.

I'm glad I could help report this important story.

34

Please indulge me while I pause the narrative for a moment to tell you a quick side-story.

Right now, as I'm writing this book, I just went back to the CNN website and listened to that interview about a thousand times in a row, so that I could transcribe everything for this book. I put on headphones, listened closely, and tried to write down every word. And because I was listening so closely, I could also hear some of the background sounds from the hotel room in Rome where I was talking on the phone when we recorded the interview.

One of those background sounds is Emily's voice, quietly answering me when I asked how many people would fit in each of the lifeboats:

"I think it was a hundred and fifteen people?" I said, turning to Emily for confirmation. "Is that right?"

Emily said "yeah."

And that's it. That was the only thing she said… Just one word.

But when I heard it, my heart skipped a beat.

Hearing her voice at that moment was like opening up a portal through space and time, awakening my memory and bringing the details of that hotel room back into sharp focus. When I heard her voice, the whole conversation transformed from being something that happened a long time ago on the teevee with millions of viewers into an intimate moment between Emily and me, both of us sitting naked on the edge of the bed, wrapped in blankets in a hotel room in Rome.

Hearing her voice reminds me that this was real.

35

It was about 10:30 when I finished the CNN interview. I was simultaneously energized from the interview and teetering on the brink of exhaustion, as I hung up the phone and pulled the blanket tight around my body.

Emily smiled. "I love you."

"I love you too."

"You did a good job."

"Thanks."

We sat for a few minutes and didn't say anything at all.

"I finished washing the clothes." She finally said. "But my hands aren't strong enough to squeeze all the water out of your jeans. And the jackets."

"It's okay. I'll help."

Back in the bathroom, we finished wringing the clothes. Then we patted them with bath towels to soak up as much of the left-over moisture as possible, and we hung everything to dry.

If the clothes weren't dry by the morning, we'd have to wear them anyhow. We had another busy day ahead of us, trying to figure out how to get home.

The thought of "tomorrow" was a little dizzying, though. In my mind, I knew we would spend the next day working on the logistics of getting home, running around the city and getting our paperwork straightened out. But in my gut, the idea of "tomorrow" felt as far in the future as "yesterday" felt in the distant past.

The passage of time had taken on a mystical quality. Just yesterday, we had been here in Rome, sightseeing and laughing and posing for pictures with big smiles on our faces. Tomorrow, we'd be back in Rome again, trying to find something to wear, something to eat, and some way home.

It felt like a thousand years had passed.

"It was the fountains." Emily said. "When you throw a coin into the fountain, it means you will someday return to Rome."

"I just… didn't think we'd be back so soon."

"Exactly." She smiled a weak, tired smile. "This is all the fountain's fault."

With the clothes all washed and hanging to dry, we took a hot shower together and let the warm water soothe our fried, frazzled nerves.

We got into bed and huddled together. She put her head on my chest and cried a little. In spite of our exhaustion, we spent another hour or so talking in the darkness before finally drifting off to sleep a little after midnight.

When we finally slept, we slept well.

PART FOUR

36

We woke early the next morning.

Someone at dinner the night before had told us that a Costa representative would be in the lobby at 7 o'clock, and we didn't want to miss them again, so we had set our alarm for 6:30.

I don't think I've ever enjoyed six hours of sleep as much as I enjoyed them that night. When the alarm went off, I opened my eyes feeling more refreshed than I could ever remember feeling. I felt like some kind of pulsing glowing thing had been implanted in my breast; an inexplicable source of boundless manic energy.

We got out of bed and pulled our clothes back on. They were still damp, but not so much that we'd be cold or uncomfortable. By the time we finished breakfast, they'd probably dry out anyhow.

We were out the door and in the elevator by 6:45, heading down to the lobby.

"I want to be there the moment somebody from Costa arrives." said Emily. "I don't want to miss them again."

We had so much we needed to accomplish today: we needed to go back to the Chinese Embassy to get Emily's passport, and then we'd head over to the U.S. Embassy to get her green card. Or if we couldn't get her a green card, we'd upgrade my emergency passport. Then we had to do some shopping for basic necessities and whatnot. We needed toothbrushes and toothpaste, and probably another change of clothes. We needed to file a police report for John and Apple's travel insurance, and we had to start figuring out how we'd get home. We needed to talk to somebody from Costa and somebody from the airline, and we needed to find an attorney back in Boston and probably an attorney in Rome too, and then we had to go and check back in with Daryn to see if he had found us a friend in Rome and then probably talk to more journalists and eat lunch and call our families and cancel our hotel in Paris and send some emails and post an update on Facebook and it was a beautiful bright sunshiny day and we felt like a million bucks — like if we could survive a shipwreck, then we could do *anything* — and we had so much *energy* and so much *focus* it was almost scary.

The lobby was empty when we got there, but we found a couple of chairs in the corner where we could sit and wait.

A little after seven, someone from a local charitable organization arrived, bringing boxes of clothing for the survivors. Not the Red Cross, but something like that. The clothes were all delivered in brown cardboard boxes, wholesale bulk, probably straight from the manufacturer.

These were our refugee clothes: fleece shirts, socks, and some very small boxer shorts (for elves?). There were no specifically feminine clothes, and oddly enough, no pants. Emily gathered up a few things for the rest of our family. Mostly fleece jackets. There were lots of fleece jackets.

The boxer shorts were way too small for me. I'm not terribly fat by American standards, but I'm no European. I picked up a few pairs of socks and a fleece jacket.

We changed into our new fleece-jacket-based wardrobe and gathered back into the restaurant for breakfast. All the survivors who we had just seen the night before were back in the dining room, mostly wearing the same clothes and sitting in the same chairs.

Emily made up a few breakfast plates with pastries and fruit from the restaurant, but we hardly touched them. We were too focused! Too driven! And we didn't want to risk missing the Costa people when they arrived, so we paced back and forth in the lobby, only returning to our pastries once or twice for a few nibbles.

By this point, the lobby was buzzing with activity. We and our fellow refugees were getting anxious and impatient.

The Costa representatives finally arrived at around 7:30; there were actually two of them. A tall, slender woman with perfect facial features and long straight blond hair, wearing a navy blue uniform with the Costa insignia on the breast pocket. By her side, a tall handsome man with chiseled features and bright blue eyes. They could have been in a sunscreen commercial together.

They didn't try to gather the castaways together for an announcement or coordinate any logistics. They didn't have a checklist of people to talk to, and they didn't proactively seek any of us out. Instead, they just stood in a corner of the lobby trying to look invisible, probably hoping nobody would talk to them.

Our schedule for the day was too complicated to achieve by foot. And we couldn't possibly afford taking a taxi back and forth between the embassies again. So Emily focused all of her manic energy on a singular goal: getting us a car.

"Listen," Emily said to the woman. "I've got nowhere else to go and nothing else to do, all day long. So I can just stand here right next to you and ask you over and over again: Can you get us a car? Can you get us a car? Can you get us a car?"

"Yes, yes," she said. "Please sit down and wait. I am already doing everything that I can do."

So we sat and waited. An hour passed. Every fifteen or twenty minutes, Emily would ask her again. And every time, she waved us away, rolling her eyes and telling us she was doing everything she could do. Finally, Emily approached the guy and asked him why everything was taking so long. At first, he rolled his eyes too.

But then Emily softened, "Please, don't treat me like a disgruntled customer," she said, looking him in the eyes. "Just treat me like a person."

He sighed and looked at his feet.

"We want to help you, but we have no power," he said, offering a feeble smile. "Costa give us no money, no authority. And no instructions. If we need anything, we must call main office in Genova. But that phone is not working now, because so many people is calling it. So we call them again and again, but they still don't answer. We are not very helpful, I know. But we are doing everything we can. If you keep waiting, we will get you a car."

So we kept waiting. And eventually, they succeeded.

After two hours, a car and driver finally arrived at the hotel to pick us up and take us on our errands.

37

When we stepped out onto the curb in front of the Chinese Embassy, it was hard to shake off the rage from last night's humiliation. This was where we stood last night, when the embassy had been so ashamed of our appearance that they asked us to stand on the other side of the street.

We knocked on the door, and a guard let us inside.

Behind the desk, a young pretty Chinese girl with horn-rimmed glasses and a cashmere sweater sat behind a computer screen.

"She's the intern," Emily whispered to me as we walked through the hallway and into the reception area.

"Do you like her?" I asked, whispering in return.

"Yeah, she's nice." Emily replied. "She's the only person around here who didn't look at me like I was a piece of dirt."

I sat in a chair in the corner while Emily stepped up to the desk and checked in with the intern. "*Qǐng wèn wǒ de hù zhào bàn hǎo le méi yǒu?*"

"*Chà bu duō la!*" replied the intern, smiling up at Emily. "*Zài guò jǐ fēn zhōng jiù bàn tuǒ hǎo.*"

Emily returned her smile and leaned in close, "*Ā! Wǒ zhēn de hěn gǎn xiè nín. Nín shì zuó tiān zhè lǐ wéi yī dāi wǒ hǎo de rén.*"

I watched the two of them talking, though of course, I had no idea what they were saying to each other. The whole trip had been a mess of linguistic confusion, even before we got on the cruise ship. From the very beginning of this voyage, the only person I could communicate with fluently was Emily, and she spent a huge chunk of her time translating for John and Apple and Erik and Chui Lin. In most of those cases, I sat nearby and read a book while they spoke to each other in

Cantonese.

The intern nodded her head at Emily and said, "*Nǐ men zhēn dǎo méi. Chuán jìng rán chén mò le! Wǒ zhēn de xī wàng kě yǐ bāng nǐ huí jiā qù.*"

"*Xiè xie!*" Emily put a hand on her hip and pointed her index finger into the air. "*Zuó tiān nà ge nu rén zài mà wǒ, shuō wǒ yāo qiú tā zài gōng gòng jià qī shàng bān. Tā shuō wǒ yīng gāi gǎn jī tā. Wǒ men gāng gang sǐ lǐ táo shēng! Zhēn shì gǒu pì!*"

"*Duì a, zhēn de shì duì bù qǐ,*" said the girl, now looking down at the floor.

Emily went on, the speed and pitch of her voice both gradually rising, "*Wǒ zhēn de bù gǎn xiǎng xìn tā men jìng rán huì yǐ kāi jiǔ huì wéi míng qū gǎn wǒ men. Wǒ men gāng gang chén chuán, shēn shàng jì méi yǒu qián, yě méi yǒu yī wù. Wài miàn de tiān qì yě lěng dé bù xiàng yàng!*"

The intern didn't say anything.

"*Nǐ kě yǐ bāng wǒ yī gè máng mǎ?*" asked Emily. "*Qǐng wèn nǐ men de dà shǐ jiào shén me míng zi? Wǒ xiǎng xiě yī fēng xìn.*"

Finally, the intern looked up and made eye contact, "*Duì bù qǐ, zhè ge wǒ bù fāng biàn dā nǐ.*"

A look of rage rose up through Emily's veins and washed over her face.

"*Nǐ bù néng gào su wǒ dà shǐ de míng zi?*" she asked, incredulously. "*Zhè kě shì dà shǐ guǎn!*"

The intern shrugged her shoulders sheepishly and said "*Wǒ míng bai, dàn shì zhè shì wǒ men de guī ju. Wǒ men bù kě néng jiù zhè yàng gào su nǐ.*"

"*Bà le, nǐ yòu jiào shén me míng zi?*" Emily asked. "*Wǒ dā ying bù huì gěi nǐ zhǎo má fan.*"

She replied, "*Wǒ zhǐ shì yī gè shí xí shēng. Zhè shì wǒ de míng zi,*" writing something down on a sheet of paper and giving it to Emily.

"*Zuó tiān nà gǎn wǒ zǒu de nu shēng?*" Emily asked, tapping her fingers on the counter. "*Tā yòu jiào shén me míng zi?*"

"*Duì bù qǐ, zhè ge wǒ yě bù fāng biàn dā nǐ.*"

Emily's voice turned cold and icy, and as she spoke, her words intensified, building to a crescendo. "*Nǐ zhēn de zài gēn wǒ shuō, zuò wéi shì jiè shàng zuì dà zuì yǒu quán lì de dà guó de gōng mín, wǒ men gāng gang yù shàng le kě pà de zāi nàn, nǐ men bù dàn bù yuàn yì bāng máng, gēng yāo luò jǐng xià shí: shōu wǒ qián, rǔ mà wǒ, gēng yāo shāng hài wǒ de jiā rén? Nǐ*" *men jìng rán bù yuàn yì gào su wǒ nǐ men dà shǐ de míng zi wǒ men kě shì yǒu nà shuì de ya!"*

The intern stood up during Emily's speech, walking out the door and into a small room behind the reception area. Emily raised her voice and kept talking — she was almost shouting now — so that the intern could still hear her from the back room.

"Nǐ zhī dao wǒ kě yǐ shàng wǎng zhǎo de?" Emily called out. *"Rán hòu tā men dū huì rě lái yī shēn má fan?"*

The intern came back into the room and placed Emily's temporary travel pass on the desk. *"Duì bù qǐ,"* she said quietly. But Emily and I were already on our way out the door.

"What was that all about?" I asked Emily as we walked back toward the car. And for the next five minutes, she told me the whole story, translating everything into English.

* * *

One of the behind-the-scenes notes for this book is that almost everything you've read on these pages happened in real life in some other language and got translated and re-translated so that everybody could understand what was going on. Luckily for you, dear reader, I don't usually subject you to the confusion. But in this chapter, I thought it would really help convey the constant sense of confusion we were dealing with by traveling with Americans and Chinese people in Italy.

I wanted to write this chapter in Mandarin, as it actually occurred, so that you can see the scene from my perspective and experience just how confusing it can feel when you don't understand what anyone is saying.

But the conversation is worth hearing from Emily's vantage point too, so that you can understand why she was so frustrated. So I'm going to rewind this scene back to the beginning and let you watch the English-dubbed version…

* * *

I sat in a chair in the corner while Emily stepped up to the desk and checked in with the intern. "Is my passport ready?"

"Almost," replied the intern, smiling up and Emily. "It will just be a few minutes."

Emily returned her smile and leaned in close, "Hey, I just wanted to say thank you. You were the only person who was nice to me yesterday."

The intern nodded her head at Emily and said, "I'm sorry your ship sank. I just hope I can help you get back home."

"Thank you!" Emily put a hand on her hip and pointed her index finger into the air. "Last night, that lady complained to me that I was making her come in on a holiday. She said I should be grateful. We almost died out there! Unbelievable!"

"Yes, I'm sorry," said the girl, now looking down at the floor.

Emily went on, the speed and pitch of her voice both gradually rising, "I really can't believe that they told me that we got in the way of the ambassador's fancy banquet. We were in a shipwreck! No clothes! No money! And it was freezing outside!"

The intern didn't say anything.

"Hey, do you know what you can actually do for me?" asked Emily. "Would you please give me the name of the ambassador? I think I'm going to write a letter."

Finally, the intern looked up and made eye contact, "Sorry, I can't give you that."

A look of rage rose up through Emily's veins and washed over her face.

"You can't give me the name of the ambassador?" she asked, incredulously. "This is the embassy!"

The intern shrugged her shoulders sheepishly and said "Yes, I know, but that's our policy. We can't give out the name of the ambassador just like that."

"Okay, what's your name then?" Emily asked. "I won't get you into trouble."

She replied, "I'm just an intern, but here's my name," writing something down on a sheet of paper and giving it to Emily.

"What's the name of the girl last night?" Emily asked, tapping her fingers on the counter. "The one who told us to go away?"

"Sorry. I can't give it to you."

Emily's voice turned cold and icy, and as she spoke, her words intensified, building to a crescendo. "So you're telling me that — as a citizen of one of the biggest and most powerful countries in the world who just suffered a horrible disaster — not only can you *not* help me, but you also want to charge me money, yell at me, and insult my family? And to top it off, you won't even tell me the *names* of the people in your staff? I pay tax money for this!"

The intern stood up during Emily's speech, walking out the door and into a small room behind the reception area. Emily raised her voice and kept talking — she was almost shouting now — so that the intern could still hear her from the back room.

"You know I can just find those names on the internet, right?" Emily called out. "And then they'll be in trouble anyhow, won't they?"

The intern came back into the room and placed Emily's temporary passport on the desk. "I'm sorry," she said quietly. But Emily and I were already on our way out the door.

38

At the U.S. Embassy, we finally met Susanna, the woman from the State Department who had been working on Emily's green card situation. She had chestnut colored hair and big brown eyes.

"Hey guys," she said when we arrived, greeting us through the bullet-proof glass, "I'm so sorry for everything you've been through."

"Thanks," said Emily. "How does it look? Do you think I'll be able to get a green card today?"

"It looks pretty good, actually." Susanna replied with a warm smile, "especially now that we've got your Hong Kong passport. We won't be able to give you an actual green card today, but I can issue you a travel document that will let you enter the United States again."

Emily's face fell. "You can't even give me a real green card?"

"Once you're back home, you can apply for a replacement green card," said Susanna, trying to sound upbeat. "First, you'll have to get a full passport replacement from Hong Kong; this temporary passport doesn't qualify. Then there's a $450 replacement fee, and you'll have to wait six to twelve months for processing. In the meantime, you won't be able to travel internationally. I know it's not ideal... but that's the best I can do for you today. Now, go ahead and take a seat, and I'll call your name when I'm ready."

We sat and waited. An hour passed. Then another hour.

The TV was still tuned to CNN, and about every 40 minutes, they broadcast a segment with breaking news about the shipwreck. They played lots of clips from my interview the night before, and it was kind of surreal to listen to my voice over and over again.

But more details kept trickling out as well, and I learned something new and crazy about the shipwreck: the captain had been performing a risky maneuver when he crashed the ship into the rocks. The head-waiter for all of the restaurants aboard the ship had been born on the tiny island of Giglio, and his family still lived there. So the captain had been performing a "salute" to the head-waiter's family by bringing the behemoth ship as close as possible to land and whizzing past the port with all the lights on. He was, quite literally, showboating. He had done this particular "salute" maneuver many times in the past, though this time he had come too far into shallow water and hit an outcropping of rocks.

Transfixed, I wiped a few droplets of sweat from my brow. *This was how it happened?*

A van full of Americans had just been dropped off at the embassy, and now there were twenty or thirty people buzzing around in the little room, filling out paperwork and snapping pictures in the photomat machine. Last night, I had been here alone, but today the place was hopping with activity. And when one wave of people finished up with their business and left, another wave arrived. Throughout the afternoon, we saw more than fifty people come through that office.

I had an idea.

I found a sheet of blank office paper and tore it into thin strips, about two inches long and a half-inch wide. On each of those strips of paper, I wrote my email address.

Then I walked around the room and talked to every single person, one by one.

"Hey, how are you guys doing?" I would ask. "Is everybody okay? How long were you guys trapped on the boat before you were rescued? Did anybody in your group end up swimming?"

I'd listen to them tell their escape stories and I'd tell them about me and Emily and the rest of our family. Whenever the CNN news loop turned back to the Concordia story, everyone in the room would fall silent, and we would all turn toward the TV in rapt attention.

Sometimes they'd play clips from my interview the night before, and then when it ended, people in the room would come up to me and say "That was a great interview." Then, forty-five minutes later, the whole thing would repeat and everybody would hush up and watch the same story all over again.

When the story finished, we'd pick up on conversations right where they left off.

"Hey, why don't I give you guys my email address?" I would say. "And then we can keep in touch after we all go home."

They would tell me that sounded like a great idea, and they'd love to keep in touch.

"In fact, I'd like to create a bunch of Facebook groups for Costa Concordia survivors," I explained. "One group for English speakers and one group for Italian speakers — groups for all the different languages spoken on the ship. And multilingual people can join multiple groups, and we'll use these groups to collect all of our stories and materials in one centralized location, so that we'll have a complete record. We can assemble a complete repository of documents and photos and videos and affidavits. Written stories and audio recordings. You know, we'll probably all end up in court someday, and it'd probably be good if we can get our evidence organized up front."

People would say, "of course, that's a great idea! We would love to be a part of that group!"

And then I would give them my email address and ask them to contact me sometime soon after they had gotten home, and I'd take on the responsibility of organizing the group.

I tried not to approach people while they were in the middle of their paperwork; I knew how tedious this process could be, and I didn't want to slow them down. But I'd wait until after they turned in all their paperwork and were just waiting around for their passports to be printed. It took between 30 and 60 minutes for each passport to materialize, so that's when I could have people's mostly undivided attention (except for the occasional CNN interruption).

When I finished giving away all my little improvised business cards, the room was almost empty.

"Emily Lau!" A voice called from behind the bulletproof glass. It was Susanna. "Please come to the window. Your permanent residency paperwork is complete."

Emily and I rushed back to the window and pressed our faces up against the glass like cuttlefish.

"Yes, we're here!" Emily answered breathlessly. We had been waiting for more than two hours.

"Please sign here and here," said Susanna, while Emily

scratched her signature on all the designated documents, "and then you're free to go. Here's your travel document."

"Thank you so much!" Emily said.

"Your so welcome!" Susanna replied. "And good luck, you guys. I hope you get home safely."

"Thanks, Susanna." I said. "I just want to tell you how grateful we are to you and to the other people working at the Embassy today. You guys have really gone out of your way for us. You've been really helpful, and we really appreciate how you guys have worked on a holiday weekend to help send us back home. It means a lot to us, and I want to thank you personally for your kindness."

Her eyes watered a little.

"But I also want to say how disappointed we are with the Embassy's response. When we got off that sinking ship, we had nothing. We needed food, shelter, dry clothes, transportation, and a little bit of cash to get us by for a few days. The embassy never offered to help with any those basic necessities, and when we specifically asked for help, the embassy told us to fend for ourselves. We feel forgotten and abandoned."

I kept my voice slow and measured, tapping my finger on the countertop as I spoke.

"Other countries sent their ambassador to the hotel to check up on their people and help them get home. Our ambassador didn't even bother showing up at the embassy to ask us if we needed anything. Some of these people are in shock and need help. The ambassador didn't offer any help making travel arrangements, and we still don't know when or even *how* we'll get home. As a citizen of the United States, I thought my country would have reached out to lend a helping hand."

Susanna nodded her head.

"I know you personally did everything you could for us, and I want to reiterate how grateful we are to you. But I hope you'll pass along the message to your superiors that we feel very disappointed with the embassy."

She nodded solemnly. "Okay. I will."

39

When we finally left the U.S. Embassy, we found our driver waiting outside next to the car, smoking a cigarette.

"Can you take us shopping?" asked Emily.

"Scusi?" he replied.

"Can we go to a *store*?" she said, carefully articulating her words. "To buy clothes? Not too much money."

"Ah... sì sì sì sì sì..." he flicked his cigarette butt into a puddle and then held the rear car door open for us, like celebrities.

We drove around for a while, the driver tut-tutting quietly to himself about this little shop or that one, shaking his head and tapping his fingers on the steering wheel. Finally, he parked the car in front of a shabby little shop and exclaimed "perfetto!", hopping out to open the door for Emily and me.

As he stood there holding the door, I imagined a roll of red carpet popping out from a hidden compartment underneath our door frame and unrolling itself from the sidewalk in front of us to shop entrance, just like in the cartoons.

When we stepped through the shop door, a tiny bell tinkled, announcing our arrival. The linoleum tile floor was grubby from years of foot traffic, and the fluorescent lights above us flickered and hummed.

We thumbed through the racks, not quite sure what we were looking for but looking at every price tag and keeping a mental tally of all the best deals. Sweatpants for ten euros. Tee shirts for five. Although everything was brand-new, the stitching was shabby and the materials were all third-rate. These clothes would fall apart after being washed three times.

I found a pair of black sweatpants for only five euros, and Emily found a few things for herself before picking out a couple pairs of underwear for Apple and Chui Lin. There was nothing fancy about these clothes; we'd still look like refugees, but at least we'd have two full changes of clothes now, so we could wash one set of clothes without having to be naked while they dried. Altogether, we had gathered probably thirty euros worth of stuff by the time we made our way to the cash register.

We put all of our items down on the counter and looked up at the tall teenage boy standing on the other side. He brushed a shaggy lock of brown hair away from his eyes as he listened to Emily speak.

"Hello," she said, "we just got off the Costa Concordia."

I brandished my Costa card, showing him the picture of the monolithic cruise ship and pointing my finger at the words "Costa Concordia."

He nodded his head while Emily continued, "We lost all our clothes when the cruise ship sunk last night. Is there *any* way you can offer us a discount on these clothes? It would mean so much to us."

He smiled and turned his head toward a small Chinese woman standing behind him. She cocked her head to one side and listened while Emily explained our situation again, this time speaking Mandarin.

The Chinese woman listened for a moment but then shrugged her shoulders and said something in return. I couldn't tell exactly what she said, but whatever the words, the intention was icy cold.

Wordlessly, Emily reached into the plastic bag she was using as a purse and fished out a few bills. The teenage boy looked ashamed as he took her money.

As soon as we walked out the door, I asked "What was that all about?"

"I told her we had just lost everything in a shipwreck, and I asked if she could give us a discount so that we could save our money for food."

"And what did she say?"

"She said, 'Not my problem.'"

40

Back at the hotel that afternoon, after we gave John and Apple and Erik and Chui Lin their share of the underwear and sweatpants, we called Daryn to check up on his progress.

"Hey there stranger!" he exclaimed as he answered the phone.

"Hey, little buddy!" Daryn is six-foot-five, so I like to address him using whatever diminutive endearments I can think of. "Thank you so much for helping us out. We really truly appreciate it."

"Let me tell you Benji, it's just nice to hear your voice. I've been so worried about you guys, ever since Emily called me yesterday."

"She's pretty fantastic, huh?" I said.

"Yeah, she's great," he replied. "I can't wait to meet her in person."

"When we get back home again, you should take a trip back east and hang out for a few days in Boston. We have a spare room."

"Definitely. For sure." he said. "But first, let's find you a friend in Rome."

"Sounds good," I replied. "What have you got for me?"

"Okay, one potential option is the Mormon mission home. You can call the mission president and I am one hundred percent confident that they'll take excellent care of you."

Daryn gave me the address and phone number of the *Italy Rome LDS Mission Home*, and I scratched it down on a scrap of paper from the hotel desk.

Mormons are well known — all over the world — for being kind and generous and helpful. If we couldn't find someone else, calling the Mormon missionary headquarters would actually be an excellent option, but I still hoped we might find someone a bit more savvy about the legal and political landscape in Italy.

"Awesome," I replied, finishing up with my notes. "Who else have you got?"

"I've got one other option," Daryn continued, "and this one is very interesting. Somebody named... Nancy something-or-another. Nancy and her husband Jim are Americans living in Rome. She and her husband Jim have diplomatic status in Italy, which might be helpful."

"Okay then!" I exclaimed. "That sounds perfect. How do we get in touch with them?"

"I've got phone numbers and email addresses for Jim and Nancy. They're already waiting for your call" Daryn dictated all the relevant details and I added them to the bottom of our list.

"Thanks, man." I said. "Nice work. This is hugely amazing."

"I accept checks and money orders," Daryn said.

I laughed. "I'll have my accountant send you a sack of gold doubloons."

"Seriously though," said Daryn, "if there's anything else I can do to help, just pick up the phone and call. Twenty-four-seven."

"I will. Thanks."

After I got off the phone, Emily called Nancy to set up a dinner date for tonight. At six o'clock, Jim and Nancy would come pick us up at our hotel and take us out to eat somewhere. They'd introduce themselves and listen to our story and then they'd try to help us out with whatever they could. Maybe they'd help us find an attorney, or maybe they'd help us figure out how to get home.

"Ask them if they can bring us a laptop," I suggested.

41

After Emily got off the phone with Nancy, she turned to me and said "Hey, we have an extra hour before Jim and Nancy get here. Want to come with me, and we can try to file a police report?"

Apple and John had travel insurance on this trip, and they had already called to make a claim, asking for some emergency cash or reimbursement for their lost belongings. The insurance company said they wouldn't be able to file the claim unless there was a police report. We were a little bit stunned. Didn't they watch the news? The shipwreck was pretty well documented at this point. We had tickets that proved we had flown here and boarded the Costa Concordia in Barcelona, with a seven day cruise itinerary that was only five-days complete when the ship sunk. But they still needed a police report? Ridiculous.

"In an hour?" I replied. "That's not enough time."

"It'll be fine," said Emily. "There's a police station right next door. I saw it this afternoon when we got back from the embassies."

"Okay, but still…" I said. "Even if we walk over there and find somebody to take our report, I just don't think an hour is enough time. The Italians aren't exactly masters of efficiency."

Emily smiled. "That's exactly my point. I didn't say we should go file a police report. You're right; there's not enough time for that. I just said we should *try* to go file a police report. But if I know anything about Rome, I know that they'll make some kind of excuse and send us away without doing anything. Let's just try it and see what happens."

"Good point," I chuckled, shaking my head at the sad truth.

Emily went on, "In fact, I bet you five bucks we can walk

over there and ask to file a police report — which they will refuse to do — and then we can be back here and ready to go before Jim and Nancy even arrive."

"No way." I replied. "You're absolutely right, which makes that a terrible bet."

"So you agree?" she asked. "You'll do it?"

"Yeah, sure, let's do it!" I answered.

We walked out the front door of the hotel, and within five minutes, we had walked through the front door of the police station. There was nobody at the door or in the entrance corridor, so we took a few pictures (with my phone) of Emily standing next to the big police placard by the front door with the station number in the bottom corner.

"It's just a big hallway in here," said Emily. "Where do you think everybody is?"

I guess we were imagining the kind of police station from TV shows, where all the cops have desks in a big open room. This looked more like the winding back-hallway of a shopping mall. Just grey concrete-block passageways and scuffed linoleum floors.

"I don't know," I said. "Let's just keep walking till we find someone."

So we kept walking, peering into open doors whenever we saw them. Eventually, behind one of those doors, we found a small table where four uniformed police officers sat, playing cards. When they saw us peek through their door, one of them stood up and approached us, leaving the little room where he had been sitting and joining us out in the hallway.

"Please excuse us," said Emily, carefully articulating every word. "We are survivors of the Costa Concordia shipwreck."

I held up my Costa card for the officer to examine. He glanced at it and then back at us again. For a brief moment, there was a look in his eyes of understanding. Not understanding of our plight or understanding of his duties, but understanding that this was going to be an annoying hassle, which might take some time and effort and distract him from his poker game with his buddies. But then that moment passed, and he shook his head and waved us toward the exit. "No English. No English."

"Please... please..." said Emily.

"We need to file a police report..." I pantomimed picking

up a pencil and writing on a sheet of imaginary paper. And with my best fake-Italian, I said "*Per favore... una reporta di polizia...*"

He shook his head. "No no no no no no no..." And then realizing he wouldn't be able to communicate with us, he stepped back into the little room and fetched one of the other officers from around the little poker table.

"Yes, you are from Concordia?" said the new officer with an annoyed sigh, as he stepped out into the hallway.

"Yes, please," said Emily. "We need to file a police report."

"Why?" asked the officer, suspiciously.

"We lost everything. All our clothes and money and passports were on the ship..."

"This is not my problem," he interrupted. "You must talk to Costa Crociere."

He started to turn back toward his poker game, but Emily stopped him, reaching out her hand to touch his sleeve. "We have travel insurance, but when we called them to make a claim, they said they won't pay for our lost luggage unless they have a police report. We *must have* a police report."

"Hmmmmm..." The officer scratched his head for a moment, then mumbled a few words back and forth with his colleague. "One moment please."

The two officers turned back to the little room with the little poker table, and the four men huddled together for a few minutes of hushed conference. The English-speaking officer returned with a smarmy smile on his face — the three other cops barely concealing their own snickering in the background — and said, "Costa Crociere is owned by Carnival, which is an American company."

"Yes, that's true," said Emily. "But what does that have to do with this police report?"

"You go home now and make police report in United States." He gave us a smug, withering look. "It is not for us to do here. It is not our job."

"Okay, thank you so much!" I exclaimed, giving Emily a knowing glance. "But before we go, can I please have your name and phone number?"

He looked at me suspiciously, "Why?"

"When we finish with our police report in the United States," I replied, "I will send a copy of it back to you, at this office."

He thought about it for a moment and then nodded his head, ducking back into the room with the poker table for a moment and returning with a sheet of paper. Looking closely, I saw that it was an official letterhead of the Italian police, and a smile spread across my face as he scratched his information across the page.

"You need email address too?" he asked.

"Yes, please." I replied. "That would be very helpful."

When he finished, Emily slid the paper into her plastic bag, and we shook the officer's hand.

"Thank you so much for your help," Emily said.

"I don't know what we would have done without you," I concurred.

Then we walked out the door. Sure enough, we were back at the hotel in less than an hour, long before our appointment with Jim and Nancy. Emily had been right about that, and I'm glad I hadn't accepted her little wager. But at least we had proven to ourselves that the police would be useless.

"Nobody in this country seems to give a shit about anything," said Emily as we walked through the front door of the hotel and into the lobby.

"I know, right?" I replied. "At first I thought it was just Costa. But then I saw the same thing with some of the people at the hotel. And then the embassy people, and now the police too."

"I just don't get it," said Emily. And then after a second, she whispered, "I want to go home."

42

Jim and Nancy were running late. Traffic in Rome is terrible, and it's nearly impossible to get anywhere without getting stuck in traffic on your way.

I used the extra downtime to respond to some new friend requests on Facebook — the American castaways I had approached at the embassy were already starting to connect with me — and check on my email inbox. One particular email caught my attention:

Benji,

My name is Joanna and I was on the ship. I am at the Hilton hotel. We have organized a meeting with Americans at our hotel at 6 pm tonight. We are trying to get as many Americans together as possible. Please no media. We have probably 40-50 and have contacted both our hotel and the Hilton garden and spread the word. Are you at the Marriott or somewhere else?

You can spread the word. All Americans are invited but again no media. We also have the paperwork from Costa for declaring lost items, but not everybody has gotten it yet. Hopefully you can come if you get this message. Look forward to meeting you.

We also are making a master list of everyone that comes to the meeting, with names and emails.

Thanks, Joanna

Interesting.

Without a second thought, I replied:

We'll be there.

I showed the message to Emily and told her about the meeting.

"Maybe we can get Jim and Nancy to drive us over to the other hotel when they get here," I suggested. "We can go to the meeting and then eat afterwards."

But Emily is smarter than me.

"What do they think they're going to accomplish?" she asked. "It's one thing for us to exchange email addresses and promise to keep in touch, but calling a meeting is crazy. Totally insane."

When I gave it a second thought, I realized she was absolutely right.

It was almost guaranteed that a meeting like this would turn contentious. Less than twenty-four hours after a traumatic life-threatening catastrophe, it's probably a bad idea to put a hundred Americans into a room together and expect them to self-organize into stable, effective, logistical subcommittees.

In all likelihood, they were going to strangle each other competing to be president of the castaways' association. Emily and I didn't want to get sucked into that whirlpool, so we decided to skip the meeting after all. We definitely wanted to keep in touch with everybody, but attending this particular meeting sounded like bad news.

About an hour later, Jim and Nancy arrived, looking stressed and disheveled and fast-walking apologetically into the hotel lobby. Both of them were taller than I expected: Jim was at least six feet tall with a mop of curly brown hair and a pair of wire-rim glasses with perfectly circular lenses. Nancy stood at probably five-ten with a head of bouncy blond locks that looked like they were usually kept in place with a pencil.

I waved at them. "You must be Jim and Nancy?"

"Yes, yes! I'm so sorry we're late," said Nancy. "The traffic in Rome is always terrible."

"And you must be Benji and Emily," said Jim, shaking our hands. "It's a pleasure to finally meet you, after all we've heard about your ordeal."

"I just can't imagine what you've had to go through," said Nancy, pressing her hand against her chest and tilting her head to one side. "It's just more horrible than I can imagine."

"We're just happy to be alive," I said.

"Well, let's get you out of here," said Jim. "This whole neighborhood is just like one giant strip mall."

Nancy continued, "We'll take you someplace truly amazing, right in the middle of the city. Have you even had a chance to look around yet? Or have you guys been stuck out here by the airport? Everything out here is so dismal and dreary, but if you're willing to go for a quick drive," her eyes twinkled and her lips parted into a wistful smile. "we can show you *Rome*."

Suddenly, I felt overcome with hunger. We hadn't eaten anything since this morning at breakfast. And even then, we had only nibbled a few pastries from the complementary breakfast before heading out to the embassies. Suddenly, my body felt empty and depleted of energy, but it wasn't just for lack of food. The idea of getting in a car and driving to a nice restaurant in Rome sounded exhausting and overwhelming.

I looked at Emily for reassurance, and I could see the exact same feeling in her eyes.

Neither of us cared about eating amazing food at an amazing restaurant with an amazing view. We didn't care about getting the full Rome Experience. Dressed in our refugee fleece jackets and thrift-store sweatpants, we had weightier concerns than tasting the world's finest *ragù alla bolognese*.

"Can we just stay here?" I asked. "The food is pretty good. And we're not exactly in love with Rome anyhow."

Jim and Nancy looked confused, but they didn't argue with us. Instead, they reluctantly followed us into the little hotel restaurant and sat down across from us at one of the long narrow tables.

A waiter approached us and said "Excuse me, sir. I am very sorry, but dinner will not be served until after seven o'clock."

"Can we just sit?" Emily asked.

So we sat.

Jim and Nancy ordered a bottle of wine while Emily and I started telling our story.

43

A few minutes after we sat down with Jim and Nancy, before we had a chance to get too deep into the narrative, a woman in a business suit and heels stepped into the restaurant. She was young and beautiful, looking smart and stylish and sophisticated, with a cute dimpled smile and an enormous diamond ring.

At the moment, her attention was entirely focused on her BlackBerry. She held it in both hands, gazing into the screen and thumbing at the tiny keyboard with all her might. After a few moments, she pursed her lips and stuffed the BlackBerry back into her handbag.

Since dinner wouldn't be served for another half hour, the dining room was still mostly empty. She scanned the room and spotted the four of us gathered around our table. She met our eyes with a smile, her eyes twinkling and friendly.

"Hey guys, I'm sorry to interrupt, but do you have any photos or videos of the shipwreck? I'm willing to pay up to five hundred dollars apiece!"

I smiled back at her. "No thanks. We actually have a pretty good collection of photos and videos, but we're not interested in selling them."

Her face sunk. The smile disappeared. "Well, if you show me what you've got, then I might be able to negotiate a slightly higher price, but it really depends on whether…"

I interrupted her. "Sorry… What I meant to say is that we don't want to *sell* our photos and videos, but we might be willing to give them to you for free."

She breathed a deep sigh of relief, and the cute flirty grin returned to her face. At the same time, she reached back into her handbag for her BlackBerry.

"Okay... okay..." she nodded her head at us distractedly.

I continued. "We just want to make sure our story is told. And told well, by a real journalist who really cares about this story. But so far, we're not very impressed with the caliber of reporting we've seen."

"Absolutely." she nodded her head, glancing up at us for a moment to make eye contact, but still mostly focused on the BlackBerry. "I totally understand."

I went on. "So, if you'll sit down with us for 30 minutes and listen to our whole story, then we'll show you our photos and videos. If you're interested in using them in your broadcast, then we'll listen to your pitch about how you plan on telling the story. Not just in this particular broadcast, but over the coming weeks and months. If we like your pitch, you can use the photos and videos for free. If we really like your pitch, we might even agree to an exclusive arrangement, declining all future interview requests from other news outlets."

"That sounds perfect." A sweet smile spread across her face as she pocketed the BlackBerry again. "Let me introduce myself."

She handed me a business card.

"My name is Jenna McJournalist, and I'm an associate producer for The Newsy Newsy News Show, on the XYZ Television Network." She held out her hand for each of us to shake. "You know what's funny? I was actually in an Italian class when the news director called me and told me to get on the next plane to Italy."

(Dear Reader, I probably don't have to tell you this, but that's not her real name, or her real job. It's not a real show or a real network. But don't get me wrong; she's an actual real person, not just a fictional character. In reality, I immediately recognized the name of her show and her network. A topnotch show, on a premier international network, with some of the most respected journalists in broadcasting. I was duly impressed. *Duly*. The reason I changed her name will become clear as the story progresses.)

"Nice to meet you, Jenna." I stood up from my seat and shook her hand. "I'm definitely familiar with your show, and I think it'd be a great place to tell our story."

"Thanks. We're very proud of the work we do."

I continued. "Let me introduce you to our little group. My

221

name is Benji, and this is my wife Emily. These are our new friends Jim and Nancy."

Jenna froze, cocking her head to the side. "Wait a second… You're Benji? Benji *Smith*?"

How strange. She knew my name off the top of her head, without having to look in her BlackBerry or consult her notes.

"Yeah. That's me."

"I saw your CNN interview last night. You did a great job. Really articulate, with lots of details. I felt like I was there."

"Oh, okay. That makes sense. You caught me off guard there for a minute."

"My boss specifically told me to come here and find Benji Smith." She pulled up a chair at the end of the table and sat down. "So how did CNN get in touch with you guys anyhow?"

Emily shrugged her shoulders. "They didn't find us. We called them."

She wrinkled her nose, feigning disgust at the very idea of CNN.

"Here's what I want to know: why would you call CNN first, when you could have called us?"

We reminded her that we had just gotten off a sinking cruise ship and were not interested in her silly network rivalries.

For the next hour, Emily and I told our story, taking turns unfolding the details of the past two days, starting when the ship hit the rocks. We talked about the deceptive announcements over the ship's PA system and the botched evacuation. We talked about the crew's failure to deploy the lifeboats and speculated about whether the lifeboats themselves were inoperable or whether the crew was just too poorly trained to operate them.

We talked about our own escape route, rappelling down the ropes from deck to deck and then down the hull of the ship. We talked about the moment we held hands and said goodbye, just in case we died on that honeymoon cruise.

But we tried not to spend too much time talking about the escape.

That's the sensationalistic part of the story. All the news organizations were already covering that part of the story and didn't need our help.

Instead, we focused on the chaos that followed the rescue. We talked about the near-riot conditions between Giglio and

Rome, on the island and back on the mainland. We talked about being dumped at a random hotel without reservations or any explanation. We talked about the indifference of the U.S. Embassy and the Chinese Embassy, and the refusal of the police department in Rome to file a police report.

Throughout the whole conversation, Jenna never quite fully disconnected with her BlackBerry. Although she made eye-contact with us and listened to our story, there was always a portion of her attention focused on the chat conversation she was having with somebody else. Presumably her senior producer in New York. And twice, she excused herself to take a phone call. I can only imagine the content of those conversations. Probably something like "I've got them. And they don't even want any money for their videos!!"

As we finished telling our story, I finally came to the important theme. The reason we wanted to have our voices heard in the first place.

"After you get past the individual details of the shipwreck and the captain, which are shocking and interesting in and of themselves, we believe the heart of this story is really about the failure of elite institutions to care for the people under their responsibility. It's a story about companies and governments that exploit their customers and citizens, focusing on profits and politics and optics, rather than on the well-being of the people who trust them."

"When you understand the failure of those institutions, you start to see that the institutions really only serve the elite who own and control them, and that they treat the people like animals, who can be thrown away when they're no longer valuable or when they become a nuisance."

I took a deep breath.

Jenna smiled. "We can tell your story."

44

I felt a jolt of euphoria coursing through my body. This was going to work. We were going to make this happen. I looked over at Emily and squeezed her hand.

Jenna pulled her chair closer to the table. "Now let's take a look at those photos and videos!"

We started with the photos: crowds of people struggling to stand up straight on the ever-more-slanting deck. Emily and I in our life jackets, arms wrapped around each other.

When we finished with the photos, we played each of the videos, one by one. In the first video, Emily and I were already perched on the hull of the ship, holding onto the rope. We shot that video to prove that we had been left behind in the failed evacuation.

We showed her video of us on the side of the ship, holding onto the rope, and video of us jumping down into the lifeboat as it crashed against the ship. We showed her footage of the masses of people on Giglio island congregating at the marina and huddling in the little church at the top of the hill.

As we watched the videos, Jenna's smile widened. "This footage is incredible, you guys…"

I could see the hunger in her eyes. She wanted those videos.

When we finished watching the last video, I closed the lid on the laptop and turned to face Jenna again.

"So, now you've heard pretty much everything we have to say, and you've seen all our photos and videos. What do you think? Can you help us tell our story?"

She nodded her head and smiled.

"First of all, let me just say that our show can bring your story to a huge primetime news audience. I don't know if you're familiar with our ratings, but we have excellent reach.

And as the story grows and develops, we can use the power of our international news network to amplify the story, giving you the megaphone that this story deserves. That includes nightly news shows, investigative journalism, magazine shows. We have a substantial broadcast presence, as well as cable and online… I mean, I could go on and on, but I think you get the point."

I frowned. "That sounds great. Really. But at this point, we're more interested in the actual details of the story rather than just the size and scope of your news organization. So far, all the news shows are focusing on sensational details."

"Like that stupid rope," said Emily.

"Exactly." I continued. "They're reporting about the rope. And they're reporting about the captain. But where are the stories about the evacuation? Or the total indifference of the police? What about the U.S. Embassy?"

Jenna nodded. "I completely agree. There are all these amazing stories to be told. And I want to help you tell them. But first, we've gotta cover the events on the ground. We have to tell the story of the broken lifeboats and the captain abandoning ship, and the story of you guys making a rope-ladder. Those are incredible stories. *Incredible*. But that's just chapter one. After we tell that part of the story, we can dig in deep and tell the big-picture story. All in due time. First things first, though."

I bit my lower lip and considered her pitch.

I turned to Emily and looked into her eyes. We didn't have to say a word to communicate exactly how we each felt about this proposal. It sounded good. Very good. This was a serious producer working for a serious show on a serious network.

But something wasn't quite right, and we didn't know why.

Jenna continued, "The on-location anchor is in Giglio right now reporting on the search and rescue effort, and he won't be here until late tomorrow or possibly Tuesday morning. When he gets here, we'll tape an interview at our studio in Rome."

She shrugged her shoulders. "But in the meantime, tonight we can take you back into town and put you up in the Marriott Grand Hotel, right around the corner from the embassy. It's a *gorgeous* five-star hotel with marble tile in every room. They have an amazing spa and a rooftop restaurant overlooking the park. It's very romantic. This is actually where Hillary Clinton stays when she's in town."

Emily and I both laughed out loud.

Emily said, "We've been wearing the same clothes for three days. We smell bad, and we're exhausted. I think it's safe to say we're not really in a touristy mood anymore. And we don't care which hotel has Hillary Clinton's favorite spa. We just want two things: to tell our story, and to go home."

Jenna looked at us like we were crazy. "Well at least you'll be close to the embassy, right?"

I answered, "Actually, we finally managed to get our passports, so I don't think we need to go back to the embassy. At this point, being out here, close to the airport probably makes more sense. Why don't we just stay here at this hotel? We can have dinner with Jim and Nancy, and then in the morning you can send a car to take us back to your studio."

She looked confused, as though she couldn't understand why we weren't interested in her luxury hotel offer.

"Actually, Jenna..." Emily said, "There's something else you could do for us that would make a huge difference."

I glanced at Emily, locking eyes with her for a split second. And in that moment, I immediately knew what she was going to say. And I loved her for it.

"Our travel situation is still completely unknown." Emily said. "We have no idea how we're going to get home. Supposedly, Costa will make travel arrangements for us, but nobody has given us any details yet. We don't know how long we'll have to stay in Rome before somebody from Costa books us a flight. And quite frankly, Costa just sunk our honeymoon cruise ship, so we don't exactly trust them with our travel logistics."

Jenna frowned. "So... what are you asking for?"

Emily measured her words. "I'm asking for a promise that you won't let us get stranded here."

I nodded my head. Both of us looked at Jenna.

"I think Emily is exactly right." I said. "The flight arrangements from Costa will probably work out just fine, and we'll probably get home safely in a day or two. But there's a chance that we might be stranded here for days or even weeks. We don't want to stay in a five-star hotel or eat at a gourmet restaurant or indulge in any spa treatments. We just want to go home."

I took a deep breath.

"Talk to your boss. Tell him we'll give you all of our photos and videos, without compensation. We'll agree to an exclusivity arrangement with your network. We'll do whatever interviews you need for this show, and we'll make ourselves available for follow-up interviews on other shows. When we do get home, we can come to your studios in New York for a follow-up, if you need us. Nobody cares more about telling this story than we do. We don't want any money. We just want your help in making sure we don't get stranded here."

"I don't know, you guys," Jenna shrugged, "This is way above my pay grade."

"That's our offer, though. That's the deal." Emily said. "If you can't promise to help us get home, then we can't do the story."

Jenna frowned and nodded her head slowly for a few seconds. "Okay... Okay, we'll do it. It's a deal."

I took a deep breath. This looked really good.

We were going to have our story told, our way. We were going to work with a real team of top-notch journalists. And most importantly, these people actually cared about us. We were not just some disposable news source for their faceless news machine.

I squeezed Emily's hand.

Jenna retreated to a distant corner of the dining room to make her phone calls, pacing back and forth between the tables and chairs.

I had only had one glass of wine, but with an empty stomach, I was starting to feel a little woozy and light-headed. Or maybe it was the euphoria of the moment. Or dehydration. Emily and I had been running around Rome all day without much to drink.

At the tables behind us, the rest of the shipwreck survivors had already finished eating. (By contrast, we had been so consumed with our conversation with Jenna that we hadn't even ordered food yet.) It was past nine o'clock now, and they had all come back from their meeting at the Hilton. I hadn't even noticed their arrival, but they had definitely noticed us sitting at a table having a long conversation with a journalist. After all, they had just come back from a no-reporters-allowed meeting, and I'm sure our absence at that meeting had been conspicuous. Even now, they were staring at us with sidelong glances and upturned noses.

"Have you gotten your tickets yet?" asked one of the American survivors from the next table.

"Wait… What tickets?" replied Emily.

"Somebody from Costa dropped off a bunch of plane tickets at the hotel." He looked down at a sheet of white paper. "Or… maybe not tickets, I guess, but at least they brought us our itineraries."

"You got this at the front desk?" asked Emily, and without waiting for a reply she said to me, "Go check it out. See if they have our tickets. I'll stay here and wait for Jenna."

"Okay," I said, quickly turning toward the lobby. "I'll be right back."

I jogged over to the front desk and flashed a quick eager smile at the girl behind the counter.

"Hello. I heard that you might have flight information for us?"

"Yes. What is your name and room number?"

"Benjamin Smith. Room 330."

She ran her finger over a handwritten checklist. "Yes, yes… Ah, here we are, Mr. Smith. Your travel arrangements have been made. There is an envelope in your room, slid underneath the door."

"Perfect," I said, turning toward the elevators before the word had fully escaped from my mouth.

"Excuse me, Mr. Smith. Just a moment…" a young man at the front desk called out to me. I turned back around. "There is a phone call for you."

He handed me the phone.

"Hello?"

"Hello, is this Benji Smith?"

"Yes, it is. Who is this?"

"Wow. I'm surprised to actually talk to you. I was just asking for your room number at the front desk. Anyhow, my name is David Abel, and I'm a reporter for the *Boston Globe*. I understand you're a Bostonian?"

"Yeah, actually. My wife and I are both from Boston. We were here on our honeymoon cruise."

"Wow. I'm sorry to hear that. But I'm glad you're safe. Do you have a few minutes to talk? We're trying to put together a piece for tomorrow's paper, and we'd love to hear your story."

"Thanks, David. I appreciate that, and I'd love to work with you on this story, but I'm actually in the middle of a million different things right now. But if you call back in about forty-five minutes, I think I can take your call. Room 330."

"Sounds good. I'll try again at ten thirty. Thanks a bunch, Benji."

I hung up the phone, dashed over to the elevators, and then sprinted the length of the hallway to our room. Emily and Jenna and Jim and Nancy were all waiting for me back down in the restaurant.

When I opened the door, there was a plain white envelope sitting on the floor in front of me. Without even letting the door close, I picked up the envelope and turned back out into the hallway and down the elevator.

Back in the restaurant, we opened the envelope and looked at the flight arrangements.

It was a disaster. Everything was wrong.

Emily's name (her official Chinese name) was misspelled, almost to the point of being unrecognizable. And the flight details didn't make any sense. According to this page, we were supposed to fly from Munich to Boston. Tomorrow.

Munich? How were we supposed to get to Munich?

"This is bullshit." I said. "They can't even book a flight without screwing it up. This is exactly what we said would happen. Jenna, this is exactly why we need your help."

"Let me take look." Jenna looked at the page. "There's probably just a missing page. You probably fly from Rome to Munich and then just change planes."

"Maybe." I frowned. "I'll check at the front desk and see if they know anything."

Nobody at the front desk knew anything. They had just delivered whatever details were given to them by Costa, and there were no extra pages anywhere that might fill in the gaps in our itinerary.

They said we could double-check the flight details in the morning. Someone from Costa would be there, and we could straighten out the confusion then.

But if history was any guide, the people from Costa never knew anything about anything. Their information was always wrong. Names were always misspelled. Details were always missing or contradictory.

And what if the Costa representative got to the hotel too late? What if our flight to Munich left early in the morning?

Insane. Unbelievable.

I came back to the restaurant and reported my findings.

"The front desk doesn't know anything about our flight." I said. "And since we obviously can't get to Munich on our own by tomorrow afternoon, we definitely need your help, Jenna."

"Actually, I have good news!" she replied. "My anchorman is going to just stay in Giglio, focusing on the captain and on the ship itself. So we can save a lot of time by just shooting the interview right here tomorrow morning, and then you can go catch your flight."

I frowned. "Our flight from Munich?"

She shrugged "I'm sure it's just a miscommunication. It'll be fine."

Emily was not pleased. "Benji, can I talk to you for a second in private?"

"Yeah, of course." We walked together out into the lobby.

As soon as we were out of Jenna's earshot, Emily turned to me, took my both my hands in hers and asked "Do you trust me?"

"Yes. I trust you."

"Okay. Here's the thing." Emily took a deep breath. "I think we should call off the whole interview. I don't like Jenna. I don't trust her. She promised to help us get home, but now she's trying to weasel out of it."

"Okay," I said, immediately. I didn't even have to think about it for a moment.

"You're right. Let's call the whole thing off."

Emily squeezed my hands. "Thank you. I'm so glad we agree."

We make a great team.

From the outside, it's easy for other people to get confused and think I'm the spokesperson for our little family unit. Or that Emily holds the negotiating power. But we almost always see eye-to-eye. When it comes to storytelling, Emily usually steps aside and gives me the stage. But she's a much more savvy negotiator than I am. When it comes to business, I usually step back and let her take control.

And thank god for that. When you're fighting for your life or fighting to get home, it helps if your spouse is a good team player.

We held hands as we walked back into the restaurant.

"The deal is off" I said to Jenna, as soon as we got back to the table.

"Wait… What do you mean?" She was not expecting this.

"You said you'd help us out. You said you'd make sure we didn't get stranded here. But now seems like you've changed your mind."

"I'm sorry," she said, not actually sounding very sorry, "but I can't just spend thousands of dollars to fly you home."

"But that's what you promised, isn't it?" For the first time in this whole ordeal, I was starting to get really angry. "Or maybe you only made that promise when you thought you wouldn't have to actually do anything. When you thought our plane tickets would be good, and we'd be able to get home on our own anyhow."

"You guys, that's not fair… I never promised to fly you home."

"No, but you promised you wouldn't let us get stranded. And now you're going back on that promise. You're trying to finish up with us as quickly as possible so that you can wash your hands of us."

"Exactly," said Emily. "She was only willing to help us when she didn't think she'd have to do anything. Now that we might actually need her help making sure we can get home, she's just going to leave us high and dry."

"But you guys…" Jenna was starting to panic. Tears were starting to well up in the corners of her eyes. "You guys… We were going to tell your story…"

"You're not qualified to tell our story," I said. "Our story is about being left behind to die on a sinking ship, abandoned by a company that cared more about its profits than about our safety. You're not qualified to tell our story because you work for one of the world's largest media organizations, worth tens of billions of dollars, and yet you're not willing to go out of your way to help us get home. You're part of the problem. You'd rather collect our photos and videos and then leave us stranded here."

"That's not fair," Jenna said. "It could cost thousands of dollars to fly you home. It's just too much money."

"And how much did your network spend to get you here? How much did it cost to put you and your anchorman and your camera crew, and all of your equipment, on the next flight to Rome? How much did it cost for them to put you all in a five star hotel?" I was starting to shout at her. "When you first got here, you thought it worth paying us $500 a piece for our photos and videos. You thought it was worth putting us in a five-star hotel too. But we just want to go home. We're not even asking for you to buy us any plane tickets. It probably won't cost you anything. We probably have legitimate tickets already, if we can just figure out how we're getting to Munich. But, yeah, there's an off chance that those tickets are bullshit, and it'll cost your network a few thousands dollars to fly us home."

There was silence, while we looked at each other for a moment. Then I went on, "If that's too much to ask, then I'm sorry, but… we don't want to work with you. Because you don't really understand our story to begin with."

Now she was really starting to cry. "Maybe I could see if the network could pay for your change fees… If you have to pay for switching your flight…"

"It's too late, Jenna," I said, quietly now. A sense of peace and calm was finally coming back to me. This was the right thing to do. "You lost the story."

45

I told Jim and Nancy that we'd be back in a few minutes, and then Emily and I left the restaurant. Jenna had broken down in tears, and she was having a hard time believing the *disaster* that was happening to *her*. She couldn't believe that we would really cancel the interview or that we would put our photos and videos back under lock and key. She couldn't believe that we would take this story away from her.

We cleared out of the restaurant, giving her a few minutes alone so that she could cope with this great loss.

While we waited, Emily and I sat outside on a bench and enjoyed the fresh air. A cool winter wind blew through our thin fleece jackets, reminding us of the sea breeze we had felt just two days ago from the deck of the cruise ship. The open air helped clear our minds after the heated argument inside.

When we returned to our table, Jenna had gone.

We realized we still hadn't eaten anything, and it was getting really late. Suddenly, we were overwhelmed with hunger.

We finally ordered food. And what the hell, we'd have some wine too. We could use the stress relief. We needed something to help relax.

When our food arrived, I realized that I had blown off the reporter from the *Boston Globe*.

Shit.

I felt bad about dropping the ball. This was our hometown newspaper, and in fact, we really did care about helping real hard-working journalists tell this story. But on the other hand, neither of us had the energy to interact with another journalist tonight.

The dinner was delicious. Roast chicken in a thick, rich, buttery, garlicky sauce. After a few bites, I felt my body returning to a normal blood-sugar level, and I realized we had basically eaten nothing all day. Except maybe a few pieces of bread for breakfast.

With this renewed energy, I suddenly realized how bereft the day had been, and how we'd been running around frantically the whole day with no significant source of nourishment. We had been running on fumes all day but didn't even know it.

Then I saw Jenna, sitting by herself with a glass of wine at the far end of the lounge area.

"I'll be right back in a minute," I told Emily and Jim and Nancy, getting up to walk across the room.

As I got closer, I could see the skin around Jenna's eyes was red and puffy, though the tears had gone. I smiled weakly at her.

She looked at me with a wounded expression.

"Hi," was all she said.

"Hey, I just wanted come say I'm sorry that things didn't work out. And I know you were just going after your story. You worked really hard, and I recognize that. You're doing your job. But in the end, you're not the right team for this story."

"Why? Why aren't we the right team." She really didn't get it.

"I'm sorry." I said. "You just don't understand this story. Not from our perspective anyhow."

There wasn't anything else to say.

So I turned and walked back to our table.

The rest of our dinner was actually really nice. We finally got to know Jim and Nancy a little better. Since they had already heard our whole story, Emily and I could take a much needed break while Jim and Nancy did most of the talking.

"So, what brings the two of you to Rome?" I asked. "I've been told you have diplomatic status. Does that make you diplomats?"

"No, we're not diplomats." Jim chuckled. "I'm a veterinary epidemiologist, and technically I'm employed by the Centers for Disease Control, but right now I'm on loan to the United Nations Food and Agriculture Organization."

"So you're a scientist?" I asked.

"Yes, actually," he replied, his face lighting up. "You see, there's a delicate interface between humans and animals and crops — the whole food supply is a vast interconnected network of organisms — and infectious diseases can travel through that network surprisingly fast, even jumping from species to species. We monitor the health of that network and when we find weaknesses, we set up reinforcements to make it strong again. We're trying to keep the whole ecosystem healthy, from top to bottom."

"He does a lot of work with cows," said Nancy, with a wry smile.

"Yes, that's true," said Jim. "It's one of the more glorious and enviable aspects of my profession."

"What about you, Nancy?" asked Emily. "What do you do?"

"I'm on the board of directors for an interdisciplinary arts organization in Rome," she replied.

Emily swooned a little, "This must be an amazing city for the arts. Do you have a gallery?"

"Actually, we're more focused on the city itself as a work of art," Nancy said. "And in the center of the city, the great Tiber River winding and flowing between the flourishing city streets… filling the ancient viaducts, feeding the fountains, and fostering an entire civilization for 2500 years."

Her words floated through the room with passion and magic — like an incantation or a mantra — painting a verbal picture and then vanishing into the brushstrokes.

"But by and by," she continued, "the Romans forgot about it, building bridges and channels and canals. Now it's almost completely isolated from urban life… disconnected and abandoned. We're building a new piazza and bringing the Romans back to the river banks, creating open community spaces and open-air art installations."

Her gaze focused inward, as she admired the revitalized river in her imagination. But then, slowly her expression changed. She frowned and blinked her eyes and said, "I don't think you guys should take this flight. I have a really bad feeling about it."

"What?" I asked. "Why not?"

"I just have this feeling," Nancy said, "This is too fast. It's too soon… It's like Costa is trying to get you out of the country as fast as possible."

"What's wrong with that?" I asked.

"We really just want to go home," said Emily.

Jim rubbed his chin and stared into space for a moment. "We've been in Italy for almost three years. It's a good place, and we love it here; don't get me wrong. We have diplomatic status, and we have a good relationship with the embassy, so we've really seen this country in the best possible way. But we also know a little bit about its faults. And… nothing happens this fast here. Nothing. The shipwreck was on… what, Friday night? And now today is Sunday, and they're already going to put you on a plane? Tomorrow morning?"

Nancy bit her lip. "Yeah, if you ask me, they're trying to get rid of you as fast as possible."

Jim continued, "Given the usual speed of Italian bureaucracy, it's somewhat astonishing that they've already booked your tickets."

"But if *they* want you to go home so badly," said Nancy. "then I think it makes sense to stay for a few more days. There's no sense rushing home. You can maybe talk to a local attorney or something. You can file a police report. You can go to the American Embassy."

Emily and I rolled our eyes.

"The embassy was completely worthless," I said.

"Give them another chance," said Jim. "You guys hit the embassy on a holiday weekend. It's not ideal, I know, but they just weren't prepared to help you. Not on a holiday weekend. That's just not how Italy works."

"Italy has been so corrupt for so long, the people really don't expect anything from the government or the police, or from a big business." Nancy leaned back in her chair and looked up at the ceiling. "They just want to eat good food and drink good wine, and have great sex and hear great music. They want to see the most amazing art in the world. The want to take naps in the afternoon and stay up late at night and watch football and eat great food and drink wine. That's just how the people are. They don't expect to get rich, and they know the government is corrupt. So they don't kill themselves working for a living, like Americans do. They just try to enjoy the little things in life, because the big things are so fucked up."

"And they definitely don't work on holiday weekends," Jim reminded us.

Emily considered this. "So you guys think we should stay? For how long?"

"Just a couple of days," Jim said. "If there's nothing else for you to do here, then you can always go home. But if you go home too soon, it's going to be real hard to come back next week."

"And you can stay at our house!" Nancy clasped her hands. "We would be so happy to have you."

Jim nodded. "Our house is right on the river, right in the middle of town; you're going to love it. You can see Rome the way a person is truly supposed to see Rome."

"Too late," Emily said.

And then we all laughed.

This whole experience was ridiculous. And terrifying. And hilarious.

But knowing we had friends here made all the difference in the world. Friends who we had just barely met a few hours ago but who would open their home to us and feed. It was almost overwhelmingly wonderful.

Still though, we wanted to go home.

We told Jim and Nancy that we'd think about their offer. If we decided to stay in Rome for a few more days, we'd definitely call them and take them up on their offer. But maybe we'd just go home as soon as we possibly could.

We thanked them for coming all the way out to our remote airport hotel to meet us. We thanked them for their hospitality, and we gave them humongous hugs and said goodnight and went upstairs to sleep.

46

Moments after we returned to our hotel room, the phone rang.

It was David Abel, from the *Boston Globe*.

I had forgotten about him, but he had not forgotten about me. I wondered whether he had been calling this room, continuously, for the past hour and a half.

"Hey, David. Sorry I dropped the ball earlier. It's been a crazy day."

"No problem, Benji. I know how it must be for you guys, so I'll try not to take too much of your time."

"Sounds good, David. I'll do my best. Can we keep it down to fifteen minutes or so? Interacting with journalists is really starting to take its toll on us."

He laughed. "I completely understand. I spend a lot of time around journalists, and I feel exactly the same way."

He had a kind voice, and I thought he probably looked like Steve Carell.

We spent fifteen minutes on the phone, and I told an abbreviated version of the Benji and Emily Shipwreck Story.

While I talked, Emily sat at the desk in the corner, organizing all of our logistical information. By now, we had more weird little scraps of paper with phone numbers and addresses and email addresses than we knew how to keep track of. We had contact information for Jim and Nancy, the American and Chinese Embassies, the Mormon Missionary Headquarters, and a half-dozen different reporters from just as many different news organizations. We had names and phone numbers for attorneys in Rome, Boston and Miami suggested by our friends and most of whom we still needed to cold-call. We had befriended many of the other surviving cruise ship passengers too, so we had their names and email addresses written down here too.

Emily consolidated all this information onto a fresh new sheet of green paper, organizing all the people into different categories (friends, journalists, lawyers, etc). On the top of the page, she wrote the word "iPad" and for the rest of our journey, whenever we had to write down an essential piece of information, we'd make sure to put it on the iPad.

While Emily organized the iPad, I finished talking to David the *Boston Globe* reporter.

I hung up the phone and leaned my head back onto a big pile of hotel pillows and thought about Boston.

It was winter now in Italy.

For a moment, I wondered what the weather would be like in Boston when we got home. I hoped it was summertime in Boston now. It would be so nice to get off the plane and step out into the sunshine. For a split-second, I sincerely wondered what month it was in Boston now... but then I suddenly realized... We had only been gone for two weeks — not two years or two months — and nothing about the Boston weather would be any different than the day we left.

"I've got to get some sleep," I told Emily. "I can't even think straight anymore."

"Oh okay," said Emily. "I'm going to stay up a while longer and make some phone calls and write some emails."

"Are you sure?" I asked, glancing at the clock. "It's after midnight, and we only got six hours of sleep last night."

"No, that's okay," Emily replied, "I feel great, like I'm actually *full* of adrenaline."

I shrugged my shoulders and put my head down on the pillow. "Suit yourself. But if you start to feel sleepy, come to bed, okay?"

"Okay."

I dug into the blankets and curled up a fetal position and closed my eyes, but I couldn't fall asleep.

I just kept thinking about Boston and how it was exactly the same as when we left it, and that only two weeks had passed. I thought about everything that had happened to us over the course of these two weeks, and my memories were so dense with images and sounds and emotions, it felt like our life at home had been nothing more than a distant dream from the distant past, the chimeral images now hazy and incomplete. The dream world had become more real than the real world, and this bizarro world, this apocalyptic shipwreck nightmare world had overshadowed our former lives and selves.

There was one other fact about life back at home that eluded me. There was something else important about our former life that seemed important, but I couldn't quite figure out what it was. I had called my mom and dad. I had sent my brother to check up on my kids. What else could there be?

And then I remembered that I had a job. A brand new job.

I was supposed to be home tomorrow night, and back at work the day after that. But I hadn't gotten in touch with anybody from the office yet to let them know that I might need to burn a few extra vacation days since my honeymoon cruise had sunk into the sea. How do you even start writing an email like that?

I got up out of bed to find Emily at the laptop, her fingers dancing across the keys.

"What's up?" asked Emily. "I thought you were going to sleep?"

"I just remembered I have a job," I told her, rubbing my eyes, "and I think I need to call in sick this week."

"You're supposed to be at work tomorrow?" Emily gasped.

"Not tomorrow," I replied. "But the next day. Scoot over, and let me type for a minute."

I sat down at the computer and started typing:

Hey guys…

It was as good a beginning as any.

I just wanted to let you know about this disaster…

And then I pasted a link to the CNN video website, where my interview from last night was posted. Rather than trying to explain the disaster to my boss in my email message, it would make much more sense to let them watch me on the news explaining it to the whole world.

I'm not sure yet when I'll be home, so I appreciate your patience. Please post this article to Facebook and share it

240

with everyone you know. The cruise company is trying to cover up the magnitude of this disaster and their culpability at every level.

I hesitated before moving on to the next paragraph. This was starting to read like it had been written by a crazy person who can't stop talking about their insane conspiracy theories.

This was a new job. I had just met these new co-workers. And I didn't want to be end up being *that guy*. But I was too tired to worry about it right now, so I just left it alone and kept writing.

Also, if anyone has contacts in Italy, we need an excellent attorney. So reach into your professional networks and see if anyone can recommend someone for us to talk to.

Thanks! Hopefully, I'll see you soon!

benji

When I finished, I clicked *send* and got back into bed.
Emily kept working.
First she spent an hour or so talking to an attorney at a big international law firm — somebody recommended by Emily's friend Roy Niederhoffer, who runs a successful hedge-fund in New York City — and she gave him the whole narrative summary of our ship hitting the rocks and our lifeboat failing to deploy. She told him about climbing down the rope and waiting for three hours for the Coast Guard to rescue us. She told him about how Costa never spoke to any of us, but instead just dumped us off at a random hotel. And she told him about our miserable experience with the American and Chinese Embassies.

I couldn't hear his questions, but I could hear Emily describe every moment of the ordeal, and as much as I tried to sleep, I couldn't help but listen to her tell those stories.

I could see all those events unfolding again, projected onto the big movie screen in my mind, as Emily narrated each story.

I closed my eyes tighter and tried to sleep, but I couldn't stop thinking about the people throwing up on the lifeboat or shitting on the side of the road in Giglio. I imagined myself yesterday morning, wrapped in a blanket and shivering with fever. Had that really just been yesterday?

Emily had finished her phone call with the attorney. He would go conduct some research, and then he'd call us back with a preliminary report as soon as possible.

Meanwhile, throughout her whole conversation with the attorney, Emily had also been responding to a sequence of emails from the CEO of the online travel company (*AffordableTours.com*) where we had bought our cruise tickets.

"He says he just discovered this morning that his company sold us those tickets," Emily told me, "and now he wants to know if there's anything at all he can do to help us out. He offered to wire us some cash."

"Wow, that's really generous," I said, my eyes still closed, though I hadn't yet slept a wink.

A minute or two later, her voice suddenly giddy with excitement, she exclaimed, "He's also offering to fly us home!"

I opened my eyes.

This changed everything. If we accepted his offer, then we wouldn't need to worry about how to get to Munich or whether the ticket Costa had arranged would actually materialize. We could stay in Rome for a few days like Jim and Nancy suggested, we could visit the embassy and get a police report and some paper documentation.

Emily got on the phone and spoke with him. He was so nice and so apologetic. We got the same basic feeling from him that we got from the innkeeper in Giglio, or from Jim and Nancy. Their overwhelming kindness and generosity reinforced our faith in humanity. In spite of senseless selfishness we had seen from so many different directions, these guys gave of themselves without hesitation.

Before Emily got off the phone, he reserved and purchased our tickets, for Wednesday morning. Emily thanked him profusely and said goodbye.

We had our tickets home.

We raised our hands in the air, celebrating this great triumph. We threw our arms around each other and squeezed. We laughed and smiled and fell back onto the bed.

"You think you can sleep now?" Emily asked.

"No way." I said. "I'm wired."

"Want to go down to the front desk and get something

to drink?" she asked. At home, I'm the designated go-down-three-flights-of-stairs-to-the-kitchen-in-the-middle-of-the-night cocktail waitress. I don't mind. "Maybe a bottle of water and an orange juice?"

"Yeah sure." I smiled, putting on my clothes again. "I'll be back in a minute."

The hotel had given us free access to their grab-and-go snacks, so we could have a bottle of water or a can of Coke just by making a tick-mark on a sheet of paper next to the items we were taking.

It was past two o'clock now, so the lobby was empty except for the girl behind the counter. I grabbed a liter of water and a few small bottles of orange juice from the glass case and then stopped at the desk to make my tick-marks on the sheet.

"What room number?" asked the girl at the desk. Over the past 24 hours, the staff at the hotel had gotten progressively more personable and gracious with us. At first, I think they were annoyed with our sudden rude entry into their hotel, with no money or reservations. But it quickly dawned on them that we were basically homeless and helpless, and when they realized that, they were very generous and understanding.

"Room 330," I said.

She gasped and put her hand to her breast. "Mr. Smith!"

"Yes, that's me." I said.

"You have so many phone calls tonight. I'm so sorry to keep you awake."

"It's okay. We're awake. Keep sending us the phone calls."

"Oh okay," she was relieved. "Well... have a good night."

"Thanks."

By the time I got back up in our room, Emily was on the phone again. It was an associate producer from ABC News, asking if we'd be willing to appear on Good Morning America tomorrow.

Emily said that we were getting a bit overwhelmed with journalists, and that we had had a particularly nasty encounter with a journalist at dinner tonight. But still, we wanted to tell our story to a broad audience and we truly believed in the importance of the story. So we'd be willing to spend some time talking with the segment producer. If that producer could earn our trust, then we'd be willing to meet up with their local on-the-ground producer from the associated press. And if we liked him, then we might agree to the interview.

The segment producer called us back, and Emily spent about an hour telling him our whole story. Every little detail, from beginning to end, including the parts about the American and Chinese Embassy and the Italian police department refusing to take a police report. We told him about our experience getting burned by Jenna McJournalist, and how our trust for the media was rapidly waning.

He was a great listener, reacting with genuine compassion to each twist and turn of the story.

"Is there anything we can do to help? Do you still need a flight home?" He had a kind voice. I imagined that he might have a beard, with salt-and-pepper coloring thanks to his many years of dedicated service to the network.

"No, actually, our flight home has been taken care of. The CEO of the travel agency that booked our cruise offered to fly us home. We actually just got the arrangements settled within the past hour."

"That's wonderful," he said. "Well, if there is anything else we can do for you, please let me know immediately. I want you to know how much we care about this story, and how much we care about the two of you guys getting home safely."

"Thanks, but at this point, we just want to make sure our story gets told, so that's the only thing we ask of you. If you're going to do this story, it's absolutely essential that we talk about the failure of the embassies to help out their own citizens."

"Yes, absolutely. I couldn't agree more. That's what I'm here for."

Of course, he asked how CNN had originally found us, and we said that we called CNN ourselves.

Half-jokingly, he said, "I guess I'll forgive you for calling the other guys first, now that you've made things right by talking to ABC News."

We rolled our eyes. Though I guess he couldn't see that.

We said goodnight and agreed that we'd meet the local AP reporter in the morning. But we needed to get some sleep. It was after 3 am, and we were starting to get delirious from stress and lack of sleep. We asked if they'd wait until after 7 am to call.

And then, finally, we slept.

47

We woke at about 7:15 to the sound of the phone ringing. It was another ABC News producer, setting up the logistics for our morning meeting with the AP producer. His name was Jamie Walker, and he would be at the hotel to meet us by eight o'clock.

At least they had kept their end of the bargain by not calling us until after 7. But we had gotten less than four hours of sleep, and we could feel it.

Groggy-eyed, Emily and I stumbled down to the restaurant. In a few hours, we were going to be on television in front of millions of people, so we needed to drink enough coffee to overcome the zombie-like pallor that had descended upon our faces sometime during the night.

We filled our cups with coffee and our plates with fresh fruit and perfect little pastries. I don't know how we didn't notice it yesterday, but these were some of the best little croissants we had ever eaten. Big and flaky and saturated with butter.

In the dining room, all the shipwreck survivors were hugging each other and saying farewell. Everyone had their tickets from Costa, and everyone was going home. When we told people that we were staying few extra days, they looked at us like we were crazy.

The hardest goodbye was with John and Apple and Erik and Chui Lin. I know I haven't given them a deep and detailed treatment in this book, partly because the constant English-to-Cantonese translation is hard to represent on the printed page without seeming tedious. But over the past few weeks, we had developed a sort of pidgin pantomime form of communication that brought us together. And anyhow, we had all just been through a ridiculous surreal life-changing experience together. We had all held onto the same rope, and we were bound together by that experience. We were all family.

Like Emily and I, they had made their own alternate travel arrangements, rather than accepting the itineraries Costa had arranged. But in their case, they bought the tickets themselves — with the help of some friends back home in Hong Kong — yesterday afternoon, when they had lost their patience with waiting for Costa.

At around seven thirty, after sitting with us at breakfast for a half hour or so, they got into a cab and left for the airport.

We gave them great big hugs goodbye. Apple cried a little bit. When she hugged me, she said "You are a good man. A *very* good man." Even John shed a few tears, which was weird because I've never seen him without a calm peaceful smile on his face.

Then we walked the to the front driveway of the hotel and watched as they got into a taxicab and drove away.

After they were gone, Emily and I sat on a bench in front of the hotel and waited for the Associated Press reporter to show up. He was running late, and apologetically arrived at about 8:15. (Everyone in Rome is always late for everything. That's just how it works here.)

Jamie was from London, and he was primarily a documentary filmmaker, although he worked in TV news from time to time as a freelancer. He had been living and reporting in Italy for years and years now, and had learned to tolerate the particularities of life in Rome. He was tall and handsome, maybe forty-five years old, and he wore a weathered tweed jacket and jeans.

Unlike the other news reporters we had interacted with so far, Jamie wasn't in a manic self-important rush all the time. He didn't have a BlackBerry, and he wasn't constantly on the phone making deals or trying to seem important. He wasn't a fast-talker or a narcissist. He was, in fact, the polar opposite of the TV news media people we were familiar with so far.

He was a gentleman. The kind of gentleman that wears a tweed sport coat out on his daily business. We liked him immediately, and started telling him our story as we crossed through the lobby on our way to the elevators.

But before we could get to our elevator, Jenna McJournalist stepped out of the restaurant door and into the lobby. She was lost in thought for a moment and took a few steps toward the elevator. But then she noticed us and stopped. I could see the look of recognition on her face as she realized that we were now meeting with another reporter, and I could see her shame and embarrassment at losing the story.

Then she turned and walked away in the other direction, and we never saw her again.

For the next hour, we told Jamie our story and showed him our photos and videos. Throughout this conversation, we continued to stress the importance of the American and Chinese Embassies in the telling of our story. We told Jamie that these details were more important to us than the details of the ship sinking or of our escape.

"It's bloody ridiculous," he said, "that these embassies would just turn you away. Nothing but the clothes on your backs, and they're criticizing you for coming in on a weekend? Unfathomable."

Emily reminded him that the Chinese Embassy had sent us away on Saturday because they were busy having a party.

He was incredulous.

When we felt like we had told all the important parts of our story, Jamie phoned the segment producer back in New York (the guy we had spoken with in the wee hours last night).

Finally, Emily and I gave our official acceptance to the producer in New York. We had been skeptical at first about appearing on Good Morning America, but once we met Jamie, his compassion and professionalism sealed the deal.

"It was very smart of you to send Jamie," Emily said. "Otherwise, if you had sent some other reporter, who knows? Maybe we would have ended up saying no to the whole interview."

"Well, I'm glad you like him," said the producer in New York. "He's the best producer in Italy."

It didn't take us long to pack our things. We still didn't have much stuff. Apart from the clothes on our backs, we had a few sheets of paper and a couple of fleece jackets, a couple pairs of sweatpants (from the Chinese shop), a few extra pairs of socks (from the rescue workers), a couple of toothbrushes (courtesy of the hotel), and a few pens and pencils. We also had John and Apple's digital camera (with all the photos and videos we had taken during our escape) and Jim and Nancy's laptop computer.

But since we had no luggage, all those items were stuffed into a haphazard collection of plastic bags and paper sacks, with Emily and I each carrying two or three small bundles.

On our way through the lobby, we stopped at the front desk and thanked them for their kindness and generosity. We talked to the hotel manager and the girl at the front desk. We poked our heads into the kitchen and said thank you to the maître d' for hosting us. We gave everyone our names and email addresses, and we invited them to come visit Boston in the summer. They could stay with us for free, and we'd show them around the city. One of the waiters from the restaurant seemed especially enthusiastic about Boston and promised to come visit us at home. Maybe next summer.

When we finished saying our goodbyes, and crossed over the threshold to the front driveway, I looked back into the lobby and my heart swelled with joy.

This was a special place, and the people here who took care of us will stay in our hearts forever.

The taxi to the Associated Press studios took about an hour. I was very interested to see the inside of a real TV studio. I tried to imagine what it would be like; surely there would be reporters and technicians and producers. People would be wearing headsets and communicating through glass-walls into studios behind doors with a big red ON THE AIR sign in the hallway.

We were shocked when we stepped inside to discover that it was basically just a closet, maybe a couple hundred square feet, with musty old cardboard boxes stacked up from floor to ceiling, creating a narrow hallway leading to a narrow set of stairs.

There was one person in the office, the cameraman, and he didn't know how to do anything. He didn't know how to get our videos off the SD card or edit them down into broadcast-ready clips. We would have to send all our media files to New York, but didn't know how upload them either.

"There's a computer over there against the wall," said Jamie. "You can transfer the photos and videos to New York, and they'll do all the editing work on their end."

The entire studio had just one MacBook. An old white plastic model from 2008. No other computers.

"Are you sure you want me to do that?" I asked. "Isn't there a technician here?"

Jamie smiled. "Welcome to Rome. This is how we do things

248

here." He took the SD card and looked closely at it before handing it back to me. "I'm quite certain you're the only person here who knows how to operate that device."

I sat down at the computer, and Jamie gave me the username and password for the global ABC News FTP server. The password was the same as the username, and would have been laughably easy for any hacker to guess ("newspub"). I don't mind putting it in print, because maybe that will motivate the ABC News IT staff to come up with some reasonable security.

This is the central server where news reporters all over the world upload photos and videos of breaking news stories for editing and broadcast by the technicians in New York. And they had just given me the credentials. I was dumbfounded. At that moment, I was the foremost expert on computers at the Associated Press Rome Bureau.

But the FTP site wasn't working. We had READ permissions but not WRITE permissions, so we could see all the existing files on the server (hundreds of folders for different news stories) but we couldn't upload our own media files videos.

For five or ten minutes, we puttered around, trying to upload the files to a free online file-sharing account, but we soon discovered that the internet connection at the AP studio was too slow. Embarrassingly slow. The progress bar told us it would take another 13 hours to finish transferring the files.

And the clock was ticking. We were supposed to start shooting our interview in a half an hour, and here we were stressing ourselves out trying to send these goddamn videos. It's 2012. You'd think the Associated Press would have figured this stuff out by now.

So Jamie took us upstairs to the ABC News Rome Bureau office, and I thought we'd finally see a real technician. Instead we met with a nice lady named Pam. She didn't know how to upload files, but she figured she could probably email them. Of course, these were high-resolution photos, so she could only attach a few of them to each photo before hitting the limit on attachment size, and she had to send five or six emails. The high-definition videos were way too big to attach to an email, so the videos never actually got sent to New York.

That kind of technology was just too tricky for ABC News.

"Hey you guys, I'm starting to get really light-headed," said Emily. "Is there anything to eat or drink here? I think I can actually feel my blood-sugar dropping."

There was nothing to eat in the studio, so Jamie went downstairs and hunted for a cafe or sandwich shop. Ten minutes later he was back, with a panini sandwich for each of us and a bottle of coffee. (He had bought bottles of juice but poured out the juice and filled the bottles with coffee, since the cafe had no concept of "coffee to go")

Then we went into the actual studio room. It was about as big as our living room at home, with the camera and sound equipment on one side of the room and a few chairs on the other side. Emily and I sat in the chairs. Behind us, a backdrop of the Colosseum. The cameraman gave us microphones, helping us thread the wire up through our shirts and then pinning them on the inside of our collars. He also put a tiny speaker in each of our ears.

For the next twenty minutes, this speaker seemed only capable of producing static.

Jamie and the cameraman made phone calls to New York, and they pushed buttons and adjusted cables, but it didn't seem to make much difference. And then finally, we heard something. A prerecorded voice:

"This is the IFP loop for ABC News..."

And then nothing but static again. Every few minutes, the line would clear up and we'd hear something, but after a few seconds it would deteriorate into static again.

Eventually, they managed to get a signal, and we could hear the voice of the anchor in New York, but the static was still strong and it was almost impossible to understand what she was saying.

"This is Robin Roberts. Benji and Emily, tell us about..." and then more static.

We couldn't hear more than a few words at a time.

How was it possible for them to get perfect picture and sound from our end, while we were unable to hear the anchor in New York for longer than five seconds?

We listened as well as we could.

"I understand that you fashioned a rope out of bed sheets?" asked Robin Roberts from New York.

Bed sheets? Are you kidding me?

"No, that's not right." I said. "We didn't make a rope out of sheets. We were on a boat, so there was rope everywhere. We took one of those ropes and tied knots in it to make a rope ladder. Then we tied that rope to the railing and climbed down to the next deck."

This idiotic line of questioning got me sidetracked into a long, complicated discussion about the rope. But that wasn't why we were here. We wanted to talk about the embassy. And the police!

This is why politicians ignore the questions they're asked and just yammer on about whatever they want. Because if you answer the interviewer's questions, then the interviewer is in charge of the conversation. But if you just ignore their questions and recite your own little speech, there's basically nothing they can do about it.

But Emily and I hadn't learned that lesson yet, so we tried our best to answer the questions we were asked.

The hiss of static was occasionally broken for a moment or two, so that we could hear a list of nonsense questions from an interviewer who had clearly shown up with no preparation about the facts of the story. We had already spent more than three hours talking to producers for ABC News, and the anchor shows up to an interview asking left-field questions about making ropes out of bed sheets?

What happened to the substantive questions about the lack of help from the American and Chinese embassies? Or the questions about institutional failures in the Italian police department?

These were not the questions we agreed to answer. This was not the story we were here to tell.

I was so annoyed and so caught off-guard by the shoddy equipment and the static in my ear and the bad questions, I stuttered and stumbled my way through the interview. Any clarity of thought I might have enjoyed on Saturday during my CNN interview was gone. In this interview, I sounded like a person in shock, who had just stepped off a sinking ship and hadn't gotten a good night's sleep for four days, muttering and mumbling, speaking in fragments and tripping over my tongue. Every other word was an "umm" or a "uhh" or a "well".

But then, abruptly, the interview was over.

"Benji and Emily, thank you for sharing your story with us." said Robin Roberts, from across the ocean. "We're glad that you're safe and that you're coming home. Please take care."

251

Wait, what?

We're not finished.

What about the rest of the story? What about the chaos on land? What about being dumped at the hotel? What about the *embassies*? What about the story of institutional failure that we all agreed to tell?

This was not the story we agreed on.

We got on the phone with the producer in New York.

"Hey, you guys! That was fantastic. We're really happy with everything. The part about calling the captain a coward was awesome. Back here in the control room, everybody's jaw dropped. It was great!"

"We're actually pretty upset," said Emily. "I thought we made it clear on the phone last night that we wanted to focus on the embassies and the police and the post-evacuation story. Why did we spend the whole interview talking about the stupid rope again? Or the captain?"

The producer was dumbfounded that we could be so upset. "This was a great interview, you guys. You should be really happy with this. Seriously."

"But everything we said was just a rehash of stuff we've already said before on CNN or Al Jazeera." Emily was fierce and relentless. "There's nothing new here. We're just repeating ourselves! Don't you think we have better things to do than just repeating ourselves over and over again so that your network can own a sound bite? I thought we were here to report the news."

For the next fifteen minutes, Emily argued with the producer. He insisted that the interview was great, and that we were the ones with unrealistic expectations about the media.

He told us that the shipwreck had happened on a Friday night, and most Americans don't watch news shows on the weekend, so the basic details of the story were still unknown to most viewers. In fact, he said most news organizations have a whole different crew over the weekend, and the regular weekday news reporters were just now learning the rudimentary facts about the story.

Slowly, gradually, we started to understand.

It had only been two days.

Which seemed impossible, of course. So much had happened, and we had been on such an emotional roller-coaster, our perception of the passage of time had begun to badly malfunction. To us, it felt like the shipwreck had been months and months ago, and we had been stranded in Rome for ages, homeless and desperate, with only the clothes on our backs.

The room started spinning. Darkness flooded into the corners of my peripheral vision, and I felt like I was going to collapse. I steadied myself against a filing cabinet in the corner of the studio and tried to breathe deeply.

48

Jamie walked us from the AP studio down to a nearby taxi stand.

We talked about his documentary projects and about the state of journalism and news media. He said that we had done a good job, and he repeated that the people in New York were happy with our interview.

"You should feel good about it. You should feel proud," he said.

"Yeah," I said. "It's hard, though… We're just…"

"You'll feel better soon."

While Jamie gave the cab driver directions to Jim and Nancy's house and paid him in advance for our ride, Emily and I stood on the curb. All around us, cars rushed by. The air smelled hot and dirty.

For a moment, we set our belongings down on the ground. We found the green sheet of paper with all our most important information (with the word "iPad" at the top) and wrote down Jamie's contact info. We had two small white plastic garbage bags stuffed with our donated fleece jackets and our five dollar sweatpants. There was a green plastic bag filled with important papers. And a brown paper sack with our free hotel toothbrushes and other miscellaneous stuff.

We were bag-people. Refugees.

We thanked Jamie for all his help today, and for buying us food when we were hungry, and for helping us tell our story to the world.

"But mostly thanks for just listening," said Emily. "It's nice to have someone listen."

Jamie gave us each a hug. Kind of a semi-formal British sort of a hug. But we could tell that he cared about us and hoped we'd see happier days soon. Then we took a few photos together, and we thanked him for his work and his kindness.

Then he loaded our bags into the cab, and we drove away.

The afternoon sun shone in through the window, and I squinted my eyes.

I felt dizzy. And I couldn't quite catch my breath.

Next to me, Emily talked about the interview we had just done. She talked about her experience as musician and how she had been able to overcome her stage fright very young. So when it was time to be interviewed on TV, she didn't get nervous or afraid.

As she spoke, I started to lose track of what she was saying. I could hear the words, but I couldn't understand what she was talking about. I could look into her face, but I didn't know what was going on.

I felt like I was losing touch with reality.

I felt like I was having a stroke.

A sensation overwhelmed my consciousness, as though my mind had been seized by a high-voltage current and sparks were jumping all along the ridges of my cerebrum, my brain a twitching ball of electric spaghetti.

I felt pathetic and small and broken and humiliated, disoriented and powerless in the back of a taxi I couldn't pay for, lost and abandoned in a foreign country.

I looked at the plastic trash bags holding our refugee belongings and felt like a failure.

"Did you hear what I was saying? Are you okay?"

Emily was asking me questions, but I couldn't answer them.

"Are you okay?"

I couldn't even answer.

I wanted to say, "yeah, I'm okay. I'm always okay. I'm not the kind of person who isn't okay."

But I couldn't muster the words. I couldn't figure out how to form a sensical sentence. I tried to say something, but I just couldn't spit it out.

"No," was all I could reply.

No, I'm not okay.

And that was all it took to open the floodgates.

My eyes filled up with tears, and then they poured down my face in cascades. I could feel all the fear and frustration and panic and confusion tumbling out of me in waves. I cried and cried until my shoulders shook from sobbing.

Emily said things to soothe me. She put her hand on the back of my neck and whispered, "it'll be okay."

I nodded my head and buried my face in her hair.

And then I cried and cried and cried.

Eventually, the taxi pulled to the curb and we got out.

"This is it," said Emily. "This is Jim and Nancy's house."

We gathered our garbage bags and got out the cab. I stood, trembling on the sidewalk. I closed my eyes and tried to breathe deeply, but my brain was still short-circuiting, and the things that normally serve to calm me just weren't working.

Emily rang the bell.

We stood and waited and held our bags. It wasn't raining, but it felt like it was. I felt the pathetic defeat of someone standing in a downpour, not even bothering to cover my head with a newspaper but resigned to the onslaught of rain, buried in the downpour.

When Nancy opened the door, she had a smile on her face.

"Hello hello," she said, "Come on in."

But then she saw my face, saw the tears and mucus pouring out of my eyes and nose, and her smile disappeared.

"Oh my God, Benji, are you okay?"

I couldn't talk.

I shook my head.

Emily put her hand on my back and said, "He's had a really rough day."

"Well then, come on in and let me take care of you!"

We walked in behind Nancy and watched as she fluttered like a bird, flitting from room to room and looking for all the little things she could find that might calm us and comfort us.

"Do you need a change of clothes? I was thinking we could watch a movie tonight. Are there any movies you want to see? But what am I thinking? First, let me get you some food. Would you like a sandwich or maybe some soup? You just sit down over there and I'll get you something to drink. I've got milk and orange juice and soda. And water! Of course, I have water. Or maybe tea. Yes, yes. I'll make you some tea. Sit down right here and let me make you a cup of tea."

I just stood there. It was too overwhelming.

Nancy stopped for a second and looked at me. She could see I needed help, and she wanted to do *something*, but she couldn't figure out what I needed. With no idea what else to do, she just smiled a sweet and sympathetic smile.

It was such an earnest smile. So sweet and nurturing. It made me think of my mom. And then I thought about how my mom would have felt if she had seen Emily and me, climbing down the rope. What if she had heard me and Emily saying our goodbyes?

I broke down again, the tears stinging my eyes and burning my cheeks.

Nancy's sympathetic smile curled downward into a concerned frown. "Are you sure I can't get you some tea?"

I shook my head and concentrated on forming the words I wanted to say. "I just want to go to sleep."

"You can curl right up over here, on the couch." She opened a closet and started fussing over blankets and pillows, stopping suddenly to ask "Or would you rather sleep in Zoë's bed? It'll be quiet and dark in here, and you can get some good rest. I think that'll be just perfect. It's only a twin bed, but it's very comfortable."

"I don't know," I said softly, underneath the tears. I don't know if anyone heard.

Nancy led us down the hall and into a teenage girl's bedroom. Once we were there, she scanned her eyes over the room and seemed to find it wanting. "Or maybe you'd be better off in our bedroom. It has a king size bed, and…"

"This will be just fine. Really. Thank you." said Emily.

"Of course. How silly of me." she shrugged her shoulders. "Let me just get you some clean sheets."

She turned to get sheets, but before she could turn back around again, I had already climbed into the bed and started pulling the blanket up over me."

"Oh. Okay," said Nancy, turning back toward me. "Are you sure you don't want some fresh clean sheets? It'll just take a minute."

"It's okay," said Emily. "Let's just let him sleep."

Nancy nodded her head.

Together, they tiptoed out of the room and left me alone.

49

When I woke up, it was evening.

I stretched my arms and opened my eyes.

The sun had set, but there was still light in the sky. The tiny bedroom I was in had filled with this dusky illumination, and it created an otherworldly glow.

I felt like a normal person again.

I felt calm. I felt stable.

I yawned and stood up and walked out into the hallway. There were three wire cages on a table in the center of the hallway, and in each of those cages, there was a hamster.

They were holding onto the bars, pointing their noses up through the wire and looking at me, sniffing at me.

"Hello hamsters," I said, and walked further down the hallway into the living room.

Emily was sitting at the dining room table with a laptop and a phone. There was a plate of food sitting next to the laptop, but it looked completely untouched.

"Hey," she said, when she saw me. "How are you? Did you have a good nap?"

"Yeah. I'm actually feeling much better," I said. "Like myself again."

Her shoulders were slumped. Her eyes looked tired.

"Good, I'm glad," she kissed me. "I was worried about you."

I looked over her computer. She was reading news stories about the shipwreck online. There were at least three different articles open on her screen. Plus a few different Facebook windows, email, chat, some other web pages I didn't recognize.

Next to the computer was our sheet of green paper with our growing list of names and phone number and email addresses. The iPad.

"I just got off the phone with a reporter from The Cambridge Chronicle," Emily said.

We live in Cambridge, Massachusetts. Our house is about a half-mile from Harvard, on a cute little tree-lined street, in a neighborhood with more per-capita PhDs than just about anywhere else on earth. The local newspaper has been published for 166 years, but it's just a simple little weekly paper.

"The Cambridge Chronicle?" I asked. "Do they have investigative journalists now?"

"His name is Scott. He seems like a nice enough guy," said Emily, closing her eyes and putting her head on the table. "I don't know how it happened, but I spent an hour on the phone with this small potatoes reporter. I don't know why. Maybe because it seemed like he cared about us."

Quietly, she started to cry.

"Benji, I'm so tired. I can't do this anymore."

I ran my hand through her hair. She was trembling.

I knew exactly how she felt.

Maybe this was how things were going to be from now on, the two of us breaking down in a sequence of alternating panic attacks.

"Here sweetheart, you haven't eaten anything," I said. "Here, have a bite of this pasta."

I lifted the fork to her mouth, and she took a bite.

"I don't want to talk to anybody but you," she said.

"I know," I said, bringing the fork back to her mouth again. "You don't have to talk to anybody else. Let's just get some food in you, and then I think you can take a nap. It's been a long day."

She sniffed. "Can I take a shower first? I feel so gross."

"Yes, of course. Let's get you in the shower," I said. "I'll go get some towels from Nancy."

I found Nancy in the next room and asked her about taking a shower. She came buzzing back into the living room and gave Emily a hug "Oh hey, sweetie, let's get you into a nice hot shower, okay? Did you get some food?"

"I helped her out with a few bites," I said.

"I'm not very hungry," said Emily, struggling to talk through her tears. "I just want to take a shower."

"All righty then!" said Nancy squeezing Emily's shoulders, "You guys, follow me, and I'll get you some towels."

We followed her down the hall and into a big walk-in closet.

"Here are a couple of towels for you. And some washcloths. You can use whatever shampoo and soap you find in there. Do you use shower gel or just regular soap? And maybe instead of a washcloth, you can use this loofah."

I carried the towels and the washcloths and the loofah. Nancy bit her lower lip and opened more drawers, hunting for more things to give us.

"I put all your clothes into the wash earlier," said Nancy, "but the washing machine door got stuck and your clothes are all trapped inside, so I'll have to find some stuff for you to wear."

"Here's some underwear. And some socks."

Now Nancy was digging through a laundry basket. "There are some tee shirts in here, and some sweatpants. You can look through here and find everything you need. Or if you want to wear a dress, I can find some of Zoë's things…"

"Please don't ask us to make any decisions," I interrupted her. "We can't do it."

Nancy stopped. I could so see so much love and concern in her eyes. She really wanted to take care of us.

She moved around like a mother hummingbird, flitting from flower to flower and gathering nectar for her tiny little helpless chicks. Emily was still crying.

"If you just pick some things out for us, that'd be perfect." I said. "It doesn't matter what it is. But we can't even really think straight right now."

This seemed to give her focus. She picked out a pair of underwear and sweatpants and tee shirts and socks for each of us, and we retreated to the bathroom.

I helped Emily take off her clothes and climb into the shower. It was a narrow glass closet, with only just enough room for one person, so I stood on the outside and reached in.

Emily just stood and cried, while I washed her body.

As the water showered down on her, I sang another anniversary song:

Well, it's been
eighteen days
since I
held your hand
and said "I do."
I'm grateful that
I was lucky enough
to get married to you.

"Happy eighteen-day anniversary," I whispered.

"Wash my hair," she asked softly.

I lathered her hair and massaged her scalp, then tilted her head back and rinsed the bubbles away, running my fingers through the long flowing black strands.

When we first met, her hair was short. A cute bob cut with locks of hair tucked back behind her ears. But she knows I like it long, so she grew it out for me.

I thought about the little wooden comb I had bought Emily just a few months ago, hand-carved by a woman in a thousand year old village near Shanghai. When Emily was sad or upset or frazzled, I'd sit behind her and comb her hair, and it would make her happy.

"I wish I had that comb right now," I said. "I wish we could sit on the edge of the bed, and I could comb your hair until you fall asleep."

My voice cracked, and my eyes watered. "But that comb went down with the ship. We lost it."

And at the thought of losing that comb, I cried again.

And when Emily saw me crying, she cried too.

"Can we go back to that little village again? And buy another little wooden comb?" asked Emily.

"Yes, absolutely," I said. "I promise."

50

After the shower, Emily took a nap for a few hours.

Now it was my turn to read the news.

The search and rescue crews had found five more bodies, bringing the official death toll to eleven now, with twenty-four people still missing. All five of the bodies recovered today had been adults, wearing life jackets.

One of them was Sándor Fehér, the 38-year-old Hungarian violinist who had played for Emily and me, just a few nights ago. He had been helping a group of children put on their life jackets. And then, after he had gotten all those children safely aboard the lifeboats, he went back to his room to pack up his violin.

He was never seen again.

I closed the news story and stood up.

Someone we had known on the ship was dead. Someone we talked to. Someone who had played music for us. A living breathing person who had touched our lives just a moment ago.

And now he was dead.

I took a deep breath and wiped my forehead. Droplets of cold sweat had formed along my brow.

I logged into Facebook and browsed through the messages my friends had posted.

The CNN interview had been re-posted by at least fifty of our friends, and we had started getting a few private messages from people offering logistical help in Rome or offering to find us a good attorney.

Next, I created a new Facebook group called *Costa Concordia Survivors*, inviting all the people I had met so far to join. Most of them were probably just getting off a plane — or they'd be landing soon enough — and I wanted to make sure we didn't lose touch with them.

I was also starting to get a lot of new friend requests from people whose names I didn't recognize. Most of them were probably other survivors, but some of them were definitely journalists.

I updated my Facebook page with a new status message:

NOTE TO JOURNALISTS: I am currently accepting all incoming friend requests because I'm working on an effort to mobilize all Costa Concordia survivors into Facebook groups, so that we can stay in touch and coordinate our actions. I will also accept friend requests from journalists (because I can't reliably figure out who was or wasn't a survivor). Emily and I will do our best to make ourselves available to the press, but we're getting pretty exhausted. It's a lot of work. To make things easier for us, don't send interview requests via Facebook. Instead, I expect all interview requests and other media logistics to be sent to my email account: benji@benjismith.net

"Hey, husband, whatcha doing?"

I looked up from the computer to see Emily standing in the doorway. Two hours had passed, and she looked like she had been completely recharged. The sparkle had returned to her eyes.

"I read the news and wrote some emails and did some Facebooking," I said. "But I think I'm finished. Wanna sit and hang out with me for a while?"

"Yeah, skooch over," she said and sat down next to me. "I don't think I can read the news anymore. It's too emotional. Did you read about the violinist?"

"Yeah, I did."

"He went back to get his violin, and then he never came back." said Emily.

"I know," I said, "It's totally crazy. I can't believe he'd go back to his room to get the violin."

Emily shook her head. "No. Every single musician I know would have done exactly the same thing. You *never* leave your violin behind. For a real musician, it's like an extension of your own body."

263

"Wow. That just… blows me away." I continued. "I just can't believe we heard him play less than a week ago, and now he's dead. It's very surreal."

Emily stared into space for a second, lost in thought. And then suddenly, she took my hand.

"Let's take a break for a few days. Disconnect from the whole news media thing, okay? This is just getting too overwhelming."

"Yeah, okay." I replied. "It'd be nice to have a day or two with no nervous breakdowns."

Emily took the laptop and updated both of our Facebook pages with a new status:

we are broken. can no longer be in touch. take care everyone, for a while.

"Let's just hang out with Jim and Nancy," said Emily. "And let's talk about anything *else*, other than the shipwreck. Everything is so intense all the time. I just want to have a normal conversation, like a normal person."

"Okay," I said. "That sounds perfect to me."

So we turned off the computer, and we put away the phone.

51

Nancy brought us a late dinner.

"It's comfort food," she said. "Roast chicken, mashed potatoes, and string beans."

"Looks delish," said Emily.

"Starchy and good," Nancy winked at us. "Makes bellies happy."

Together, the four of us stuffed ourselves full of Nancy's best starchy-sweet belly-happy comfort food. And instead of talking and obsessing and stressing about the shipwreck, we talked about art and music and science. We talked about psychology and philosophy and spirituality, and eventually we talked about our unlikely shared connection.

"So, here's one thing I still haven't figured out," I said. "How do you guys know Daryn anyhow?"

"Actually, we don't." said Jim. "He's a friend of a friend of a friend, I suppose."

"The story is pretty amazing," continued Nancy. "Two months ago, I was back in the states, attending an arts workshop in Chicago. At the end of the workshop, one of the locals was having a party at his house."

"This is Sean we're talking about," adds Jim.

"Right. His name is Sean Kaplan. So, Sean has a party at his house for all the people at the workshop, and like everybody else at the workshop, I went to the party and mingled around for a few hours. And then I was actually going to leave early. I was really tired and just wanted to go back to my hotel and sleep. But then my car broke down, and I was stuck at the house with the party. A bunch of us ended up staying all night, and we all got to know each other and had a really great, really amazing time, building all these fantastic friendships. And then afterwards, we all stayed in touch with each other. And so that's how I became friends with Sean."

She went on, "And of course, Sean is friends with Cam Deaver through the Chicago theatre scene. And Cam knows Daryn from back at BYU, I guess."

"Actually I know him too," I said "He goes by 'Cam' now? Back when I knew him, he was 'Cameron', and he was actually the director of a play I was in. Henry IV."

"See, I don't really know him. Not at all." replied Nancy, "So I don't know whether he goes by Cam or Cameron. That's the crazy thing though, right? I mean, just two months ago, I had never met Sean, and I had never even heard of Cam or Daryn. I would never have met Sean if I hadn't gone to this workshop in Chicago. I never would have really become friends with him if I hadn't gone to his party, and we definitely wouldn't have kept in touch. Except that my car broke down."

Jim jumped in and added, "And then less than two months later, Daryn finds Cam, and Cam finds Sean, and Sean finds us. We get a random phone call one day from Sean asking if we can help out a friend of a friend, who knows a guy who's friends with a newlywed couple on a cruise ship who just got shipwrecked outside of Rome."

Nancy nodded her head and laughed, "The whole story just sounds crazy, but here we are. I mean… it's just too crazy to be a coincidence, right?"

Emily was nodding vigorously, "Yes. Exactly! It's too perfect to be a coincidence. What are the chances of all those connections just happening? Randomly?"

"That's what I'm talking about," said Nancy.

"It would be impossible," Emily finished.

I leaned back in my chair and took a slow breath. "I don't know… If there was some kind of cosmic force bringing us together, then wouldn't it also mean that the same cosmic force was responsible for sinking the ship in the first place?"

"So you think this was all just random?" asked Emily.

"No, not like that," I said. "I just think there's a middle ground between random chance and magic."

Everyone sat back in their chairs and listened, giving me a look that said *this ought to be good.*

"When I posted our help-message on Facebook," I said, "it was broadcast to almost a thousand people. Then Daryn posted the message to each of his thousand friends. And each of those thousand people reached into their own network of connections. We have no idea how many thousands of people might have each spent just a moment of their time trying to find a connection in Rome."

"Okay," said Jim, "I see what you're saying."

I continued. "Yes, it's true... Something almost magical brought the four of us together. It wasn't random, but it also wasn't supernatural. It was just us. It was just human beings acting in tandem to do something special, something none of us could have done on our own. The world is full of phenomena that we'll never untangle and patterns we'll never even notice, let alone comprehend. And it's not because of ghosts or gods or fate. The universe is just too complex, and sooner or later, we reach the boundaries of our ability to understand. Past that boundary, I guess we forfeit truth for beauty..."

"I completely agree," said Nancy.

"When you guys say there's something bigger than us out there," I continued, "I know what you're talking about. I believe in it too. But you guys think that the wondrous magical thing out there — the thing that's bigger and more wondrous than you can imagine — is some *other* thing... something outside of ourselves. I believe in it too, but to me, it's just *us*. There's a magical creature out there with ten-thousand heads who brought the four of us together right now. And the most amazing thing is that *we are* that magical creature."

"Well..." said Emily.

"We don't need some *other* higher power, because the higher power is *us*, acting together as a great big swarm of humanity."

There was silence in the room for a moment.

"...I don't know," said Emily. "I still think there's something *else* out there. Besides just us."

"Yeah, me too," whispered Nancy to Emily with a wink.

Then she continued, "It's like the flow of a river... There's this slow, steady, relentless force moving through the world, connecting us all together and giving us life. We drink from the river, but we swim in it too. It carries our boats and irrigates our crops. And when it leaves our own little villages, it flows downstream and nourishes someone else. It's not *impossible* to swim upstream, but it takes work... I guess it's not exactly *fate*,

267

but it's a guiding force that aligns all of these events and people together and gives them color and texture and *meaning*."

"But I think *we are* the river," I said. "We ride the river, and sometimes we fall into the river, but the river is just us. It's just the sum total of all of us individually doing our own thing. All of our individual decisions add up, and our haphazard wandering seems to have some collective purpose. That's what's so amazing."

"The river has a course," said Nancy. "The river has a direction. Maybe it winds around a little bit on its way there, but if you ride the river, eventually it takes you to the ocean."

"That's true," I replied. "And it makes me wonder… When was this course of events set in motion? When did we hit the point of no return? When did the shipwreck become inevitable?"

"Have you guys heard about the 'salute' maneuver?" Emily asked. Jim and Nancy nodded. "Maybe from the first time the captain saluted Giglio, back in 2010… Maybe from that point on, the shipwreck was inevitable."

"Exactly," I said. "At some point in time, the course of events leading to the shipwreck had been set in motion. We'll never know whether the point of no return came a minute before we hit the rocks or when the captain drank an extra glass of wine with dinner. Maybe this cruise was doomed from the moment it left port in Rome. Or the moment it left the shipyards in 2006. Maybe this shipwreck has *almost happened* a hundred times…"

Nancy nodded. "Some things just aren't knowable. We might never know what truly caused the shipwreck."

"Maybe it was something we did ourselves," added Emily. "A few nights ago, we got into an argument with one of the waitresses, who had mistakenly charged us for a bottle of wine she never delivered. But who knows? Maybe after we yelled at her, she complained to one of her friends in the engine room. And maybe that person was supposed to be listening to the captain's instructions. And then maybe he got distracted, and that's what caused the crash. Maybe we caused the shipwreck… I mean… It's possible, right?"

"Yeah, it's possible," I said.

The conversation carried on for hours. It was so warm and welcoming and wonderful to be in Jim and Nancy's home, wearing their borrowed clothes, eating at their table, and feeling like a part of their family.

After dinner, and after dessert, and after a few glasses of wine, it was time for bed. Emily and I were exhausted (again), but this time, at least our hearts were full with friendship.

"When you guys get home, I really can't emphasize it enough," said Nancy, "but you should really try spending some time with a good PTSD therapist. You've been through a lot."

"Yeah," Emily said. "We're already starting to feel kind of crazy sometimes."

Nancy laughed. "Ya think?"

"Is it that bad?" I asked.

"You're both very thoughtful," Nancy said, "and very articulate. But you've got this energy emanating from you — like this wild urgent manic energy; it's actually very intoxicating, but I don't see how you can keep it up — and anyhow, I just feel like you two could use some re-centering."

I didn't know people could see it from the outside — I didn't know people could see this cloud of buzzing anxiety around us — but now that I thought about it for a second, of *course* they could. We were both acting like lunatics.

"We know a very good trauma therapist," Nancy continued, "and if you want, I can set up an appointment for you tomorrow. He can help you start to make sense of what happened, and make *meaning* for yourselves from all these frantic, horrible, confusing experiences."

"Thanks," said Emily.

"Yeah, thanks for taking care of us," I said. "You didn't have to do that. You didn't even know us."

"You're like our Italian mother," Emily said.

Nancy laughed. "You know, it's funny you should mention that. When our son Jake — he's the one in the middle, sixteen years old, tall and handsome now and getting old so fast — anyhow, when Jake was just a tiny kid — four or five years old — he created an imaginary mother for himself. Not an imaginary friend, an imaginary *mother*, an imaginary *Chinese* mother."

"That's so funny," Emily said. "He must have a very vivid imagination."

"Well, we had just gotten home from years in Africa, back to the United States, where Jake had never truly even lived in

269

his life. Jim was still abroad, and I was nine months pregnant with Zoë. We had just moved into a new house, and he was going to a new school with new teachers and new friends. It was a very overwhelming time for such a little guy. But anyhow, one day, while he was eating his after-school snack, Jake said, 'My Chinese mom jumped out of a tall building last night, and just before she hit the ground she turned into a ball, and bounced and bounced all over the world. She was bouncing down a street and a big truck came by and drove over her and flattened her like a pancake. But then a man saw what happened, and he walked over and picked her up and put her in his pocket and took her home and sewed her into a blanket.' He ran outside and played with his toys and probably forgot all about it two minutes later, but I've been thinking about that Chinese mom for the past twelve years. Where did she go anyhow?"

"Thanks for being our Italian mom," I said. "Even if you're not Italian."

"If you get squashed into a pancake, we'll make a blanket out of you too," said Emily.

Jim set up the sleeping arrangements for me and Emily, reconfiguring a pair of couches into a makeshift bed. With the pillows tossed asunder and the arm-rests pushed together, the couches combined to form a comfortable, roomy, full-sided bed, with high walls all around the perimeter like a crib.

We snuggled up there for the night and finally got a good night's sleep, for the first time since our bed had been sucked into the sea.

52

The next morning, we didn't set an alarm. We didn't have to try meeting up with anybody from Costa first thing in the morning; we already knew how we would be getting home, and our plane didn't leave Rome until the next day.

Probably most importantly, though, for the sake of our sanity: We avoided reporters all day. Although we would read our incoming email, we wouldn't reply to any of the journalists. They didn't know where we were staying in Rome, so there were no phone calls. And since there were no phone calls, there would be no interviews.

And somehow, without the incessant drumbeat of the news media, things seemed a lot less urgent.

We slept in till ten.

Still though, we had a lot of things left to accomplish. In particular, Jim had convinced us that we should really file a police report. Some of the attorneys we talked to echoed the same message: we would be fools to come back home without first filing a police report.

After a lush, syrupy, pancakey breakfast, I called the American Embassy again. On the Embassy website, the emergency phone number for evenings and weekends is listed on its own page, with this disclaimer:

The numbers below are provided for U.S. citizens who are distressed and require emergency services such as assistance with the death, arrest, illness or injury of an American citizen. Routine services such as passport renewals, reports of birth abroad and notarials are not considered emergencies and are processed during regular business hours.

The holiday weekend was over. Regular business hours had resumed.

Which was good, because I had some important, non-emergency business to attend to.

"Hello, my name is Benji Smith. I'm a survivor of the Costa Concordia shipwreck, and I'd like to…"

"Yes, Mr. Smith." the voice on the phone interrupted me. "If you come into our office, you can apply for a free temporary replacement passport, or you can pay $135 for a full permanent replacement passport."

So kind.

So helpful.

"Thank you, but I've already gotten my passport replaced," I replied.

There was a short pause.

"Well then, what can we do for you, Mr. Smith?"

"I'd like to file a police report regarding this incident."

The reply was routine and automatic. Bored.

"You can file a report with the local police."

"I've already tried to file a police report," I answered. "Yesterday, my wife and I visited an Italian police station and attempted to file a report. The officers on duty refused. They shrugged their shoulders and told us to go home."

She was annoyed.

"Well, why do you need a police report?" asked the voice. "The cruise company already has all your contact information."

I felt a rare surge of pent-up rage boiling in my blood, my throat constricting and my teeth clenching.

"What's your name?" I asked.

Her voice was a monotone. "We aren't allowed to give our names out over the phone."

I could barely contain myself.

"Listen to me," I said. "Two days ago, my wife and I got off a sinking ship with only the clothes on our backs. Nobody from the police department or governments of Italy, the United States, or China had taken our names or asked if we're okay. There's no written record that we were here. There's no documentation of what happened to us."

"Mr. Smith, I'm not sure what you want from us."

"I want a translator to accompany us to police headquarters, while we file a written affidavit of the events we experienced during this disaster." I couldn't believe I was having to explain all this. "Someday, somebody is going to do an investigation, and we should probably write *something* down about it all." I was running out of breath. Almost panting. "Right?"

"We can provide the names and telephone numbers of several local translators," said the voice, "though we cannot endorse any of their services."

"No," I said, "that is unacceptable."

There was silence on the other end of the line.

I breathed deeply and lowered my voice. "I refuse to leave this country until somebody, from some government, gives us an official written document describing this disaster, and testifying that we were among the victims. I am a citizen of the United States, and I expect you to provide a translator to accompany my family while we file this report."

There was more silence.

"Just a moment, Mr. Smith."

I closed my eyes and smiled as I held the line, waiting for my insistence to pay off. Finally, I felt like something was happening. I had broken through to *someone*. Somebody cared. Even if it was just the woman who answered the switchboard at the embassy.

"If you come back to the embassy before one o'clock, we will have a translator ready to meet with you." The voice was softer.

"Thank you," I replied. "We'll be there."

Jim and Nancy still hadn't managed to unlock the door of their washing machine, so all of our clothes were still trapped inside. We weren't so disappointed about the refugee fleece jackets, but it would have been nice to at least have our own pants.

Instead, we wore some bottom-of-the-drawer sweatpants from Jim and Nancy's closet. On our way out the front door, we paused in front of a mirror.

"We look like we just rolled out of bed," Emily observed. "In 1992."

Nancy drove us to the embassy, where the translator was waiting for us at the gate. At the police station, we gave our statements. We narrated the events of our escape and listed all the things we had lost on the ship.

When we finished making the list, the translator read it

back to us.

"One wooden comb, made in China."

"No, no, that's not right," interrupted Emily. "It's a one of a kind, hand carved comb, made from green sandalwood by a craft-woman in a thousand year old water village near Shanghai. The only way to replace it would be to go back to that village."

The translator conferred briefly with the police officers before turning back to us and asking "How much is it worth?"

Emily and I looked at each other. Then she looked down at her hands. "We paid about ten dollars for it."

The translator had barely begun translating before Emily interrupted. "But this comb is special to us. It has emotional value."

The translator nodded her head and spoke to the police officers.

"We will call it 'an artistic wood-carving from China'".

For the next two hours, we continued playing this game, assigning individual dollar values to some of our most prized sentimental possessions.

When we finished, they gave us a piece of paper. I guess that's what we wanted.

53

Our other important task for the day was meeting with a doctor friend of Jim and Nancy. Besides being a psychiatrist and a cognitive behavioral therapist and a neurologist, he was also on the faculty of the University of Rome Medical School and he taught yoga classes and had a black belt in some sort of obscure complicated martial arts. He's one of the best trauma therapists in Rome, and luckily for us, he speaks English. He's a slightly eccentric American expat, and he has agreed to make an emergency appointment for us.

We walked from the police station, up the famous Spanish Steps, and down through the little neighborhood on the other side of the hill — peering into the windows of the little shops and cafes we passed on our way through the city's winding streets — until we arrived at the doctor's office at the bottom of the hill.

Along the way, Nancy bought us each a sandwich from a street vendor and we ate as we walked.

The sandwiches were big and greasy and filling, and neither of us could finish more than half the sandwich. But we continued to carry those damn sandwiches anyhow, in a way that only a refugee can. When you've lost everything — when your entire luggage consists of a small plastic grocery bag — and when you're not sure how you'll pay for your next meal, you don't throw away half-sandwiches.

We sat side-by side in the doctor's waiting room.

I can only describe his office decor as "hippie minimalism." In the center of the waiting room, there was an enormous yoga mat — easily twenty feet long in each direction — and hanging on the walls were various interesting artifacts of assorted native peoples from around the world: ceremonial masks and ornamental kimonos and whatnot.

After about a half hour, the doctor appeared in the doorway and waved us into his office. He was tall with broad shoulders and a calming, peaceful smile. The way he carried his body was simultaneously very relaxed and extremely intense, and the paradox intrigued me. I felt like he might bow to us and say "namaste" at any moment, and I immediately liked him.

"Benji and Emily, welcome to my office," he said. "My name is Mark. Have a seat."

We said thank you and sat side-by-side on a couch across from Mark's desk.

"Tell me a little bit about your experience. What happened to you guys? And how do you feel?"

We told him our whole story, and he sat quietly watching us. We told him about the escape from the ship and all the chaos on land. We told him about the embassies and the journalists and the dead violinist. We cried a few times, and we shouted a few times. He nodded his head and took notes in a small book. If it's possible for a person to listen intently *and* intensely, he was doing it. He's an intense listener.

Finally, after an hour or so, and after Emily and I had finished telling all the parts of the story that we wanted to tell, Mark put his little notebook down on his desk and spoke to us.

"The two of you are currently suffering from *acute stress disorder*. I've seen worse, but you need to take this very seriously. If left untreated, this will probably progress into post-traumatic stress disorder — I'm sure you've heard of PTSD — which can mean years and years of difficult therapy."

Emily and I nodded.

I was surprised at my relief. It felt good to hear someone give a name to this crazy manic intensity. I wouldn't expect that to be so comforting, but it is.

"You need to be sure to get lots of sleep and good nutrition. Your brains are both working in overdrive. All day long, you've been making phone calls and sending emails, talking to reporters and organizing your papers and making travel plans. Over the longer term, you'll learn to calm down and relax and cope with the anxiety, but in the immediate future, we just want to make sure you're eating enough food to fuel your brain, and that you're getting enough sleep to give your brain a rest at the end of the day. Seven hours every night, and then three full meals every day. Understood?"

We nodded our heads again. He was absolutely right about us. We had been staying up all night, making phone calls instead of sleeping. We'd eat a few bites of breakfast and then get distracted by a mountain of tasks. When lunchtime came around, we'd take a few ravenous bites from a sandwich before getting sucked back into a whirlpool of logistics. What a mess.

"I'm going to write you a prescription for Clonazepam," he continued. "Here in Italy, it's called Rivotril, but you're probably more familiar with the American brand name Klonopin. You'll get a box of twenty pills, and I want you each to take one quarter of a pill twice a day. Just break each pill into four pieces, and that's the size of dose I want you to take. You'll probably feel a little bit lightheaded at first, but that feeling will go away after a few doses. Mostly, you'll notice that it's easier to get through your day without getting into a frenzy. You'll notice everything is a little less frantic. Ultimately, we don't want you to keep taking these pills forever, but over the next few weeks, this drug will help you recalibrate your nervous system to a lower level of stress. Right now, your autonomous nervous system is in fight-or-flight mode, but we don't want it to get stuck there. This drug is a little bit like a reset button."

Suddenly, Emily burped.

"Excuse me," she clapped her hands to her mouth. "I've been burping for two days. I can't seem to stop."

A wide smile spread across Mark's face. "Don't worry. That's completely normal." And then he told us the scientific name for the condition when a person burps uncontrollably in the aftermath of a severely stressful event… But I don't remember anymore what he called it, and neither does Emily, so we just refer to it as "acute burp-a-topia."

"PTSD is a *chronic* condition," he continued. "By definition, you can't be diagnosed with PTSD until at least 30 days after a traumatic event. What you have right now is an *acute* condition. So go home, and find a good therapist immediately. If you get to work, I think you can beat this thing before it gets worse."

"Finally," said Mark, "I don't know what you believe religiously, and honestly it doesn't really matter. But you need to find some higher meaning in this. You need to take this trauma and create something out of it. You need to make meaning."

We left Mark's office feeling good. Surprisingly good. It felt vindicating to hear a top-notch mental health professional put a label on our craziness.

We walked to a drug store on the next corner, and we went inside to fill our Klonopin prescription. I went to the pharmacy counter while Emily browsed through the aisles.

"Okay, we're all set," I said, when I had finished paying.

"How much did the pills cost?" asked Emily.

"One forty-four," I replied.

Emily's face fell. I thought she might start crying.

"A hundred and forty-four euros?" she said. "We can't afford that! I was hoping we could buy some real jackets. It's getting cold, and these fleece jackets are too thin."

"No, sweetheart," I smiled. "Not a hundred and forty-four euros. *One* euro. And forty-four *cents.*"

Emily looked confused. "For each pill?"

"No, for the whole box. Twenty pills. And since we're only supposed to take a quarter-pill per dose, that's 80 doses. In American money, it ends up being about three cents per dose."

Emily laughed. "Socialized medicine is awesome."

We found a simple little pasta place around the corner and ate lunch again. Sure, we had just eaten those half-sandwiches a few hours beforehand, but now we felt particularly hungry. Baring one's soul can make a person very hungry.

We told the waiter that we had been on the Costa Concordia. He nodded his head, indifferently and said "Yes yes, thank you."

He didn't get it. We explained again, this time with hand-waving gestures to illustrate the concept of a cruise ship sinking into the sea. Suddenly, his eyes got big; he understood. He brought us a big slice of tiramisu and a couple demitasse cups of espresso. When the dessert arrived, we asked him to help us read the instructions for the Klonopin, since it was all in Italian.

"Should we take it with food?" Emily asked, "Or should we take it on an empty stomach?"

With his glasses on the tip of his nose, he flipped through the tiny white booklet included within our pill box. After a minute or two, he said "You must eat this pill with food. But please... Then you must go home. Get a taxi and go home. No crossing streets. No walking on sidewalks. No operate machines, okay? This pill will make your head go…" and then, since he didn't know the right word in English, he pantomimed vertigo, pretending to lose his balance and reaching his arms out into the air to steady himself.

"Dizzy?" asked Emily. "The pill will make us dizzy?"

"Yes!" he replied. "It make you dizzy. You must please go home. It is too much danger."

"Okay," said Emily. "Thank you so much for your help!"

So we broke one pill in half, and then broke it in half again. We each washed our quarter pill down with a drink of water, and then we walked back out onto the streets of Rome.

54

The Klonopin had already started to work its vague fuzzy delightful magic, and we felt the anxiety float away from us, like a family of ghosts had gotten bored with us and floated away to find someone else to haunt. Now, with no cares in the world, we were just roaming around Rome.

Roaming. Hahahahahahaha. ROME-ING!!

We were rome-ing around in Roam :)

It was like walking through a maze, in so many ways. In a crazy hazy daze.

I wondered whether I was dizzy, or if I was just imagining I was dizzy. Doesn't really matter, I guess. Either way, it felt like I was sitting on top of a soap bubble, and that's just fine by me.

Evening descended upon the city, and a dusky electric fog enveloped everything. Above our heads, strands of tiny lights — thousands of them, in white, green, and red — had been strung between all the lampposts, hanging like a ribbon above the city streets, and you could see their reflection shining in every window. Neon signs shined through shop windows and into the streets, and the warm welcoming glow beckoned us in.

Our own clothes still trapped in Nancy's washing machine, Emily and I explored the trendy little boutique shops in Rome dressed in Jim and Nancy's saggy sweatpants.

The entire length of my outer thighs were visible through some kind of weird sweatpants slit that had been deliberately left open by the designer of these bizarre pants.

Ventilation for runners, maybe?

The people in the shops shot nasty looks in our direction and shuffled out of the way when we walked through the aisles. The shop employees didn't talk to us. Everywhere we went, people cleared out of our way.

It's possible that we smelled bad.

But it didn't really matter to us.

We were walking on clouds. We were in such a good mood, so happy and so smiley, laughing and dancing and telling jokes and singing songs.

Nineteen days!
Nineteen crazy days!
Happy nineteen-day anniversary!

Eventually, the sun set and a cold wind blew through the city.

Our fleece refugee jackets were back at Jim and Nancy's house, trapped in the washing machine.

"Hey, let's go buy some jackets," Emily said. "We're going to need to buy replacement jackets when we get home anyhow, so let's buy something nice while we're here."

"Nice." I said. "Souvenir jackets. I love it."

"And then for the rest of our lives," Emily went on, "whenever we wear these jackets, we'll think back to our shipwreck honeymoon."

We walked from shop to shop, trying on every jacket we could find, in every shop, while the passersby stared at us and wondered what gutter we had crawled out of.

"Hello, do you speak English?" Emily asked a group of sales girls at one of the shops. We had found a particularly kickass pair of jackets from a Japanese brand name. These were very funky jackets.

"Yes, a little," said one of the girls. The rest of the sales clerks in the shop turned to watch us.

"Do you have this jacket in a slightly bigger size?" Emily asked.

The shop girl helped Emily find the right size jacket and when we were completely happy with our choices, Emily asked "Would it be possible to ask for a discount on these jackets? We lost our own jackets in the Costa Concordia shipwreck."

"No no. Sorry." said the shop girl. "Both jackets, total is 450 euros."

"Oh okay," said Emily. "But did you see the news about the shipwreck? We were on that ship when it sunk."

"Oh, yes. Very good." the shop girl replied.

281

She had no idea what we were talking about.

"There was a big ship." Emily pantomimed, waving her arms around in the air and pretending to be a boat. "And it hit the rocks." She made a crashing sound, and then pointed at herself and me. "And we were on that boat."

The shop girl looked annoyed and indifferent.

And then suddenly, she figured it out, and her eyes widened.

"Oh no... The two of you... You were on sinking ship?"

"Yes yes yes. We lost all of our clothes," Emily told her again.

The shop girl put her hand over her mouth and rushed back to the counter for a calculator. "Yes, I can sell you these... These both jackets... For 350 euros."

She laughed nervously.

"Thank you," Emily said. "That's very generous of you."

"Yes, of course," said the shop girl, "Normal is 450. But I can sell to you for 350."

We spent the last of our money on those jackets. The cash John and Apple had saved from the sinking ship was gone now.

The other kids working at the shop came around to see what was going on — they had seen their friend suddenly electrified into action after talking to us — and Emily and I spent the next twenty minutes telling them the most exciting bits of our story. They listened in rapt attention and when we had finished, they wished us well on our way.

We walked back out into the night, pulling our new jackets tight and zipping them and unzipping them and enjoying the zippiness of a brand new jacket. We still looked like refugees with our ridiculous sweatpants, but now at least we had nice jackets.

This was our date night. This was our honeymoon evening date night cruising around and exploring Rome. We passed through many of the same places we had been before just a few days ago, but now we literally saw them all in a different light.

Street light, and lamp light, and neon light.

The worst part about seeing Europe from a cruise ship is that you spend your afternoons walking through the cities (usually during the local siesta hours, when everything is closed), and by nighttime when the city comes to life, you're already back on the cruise ship eating "luxury" cuisine thawed out in a microwave oven.

Now we were finally getting to see Rome at night, and it was gorgeous. All around us, the streets were full of people, strolling arm-in-arm with their lovers or carousing boisterously with a group of friends; this is how Rome comes to life.

At some point, we realized we had no idea where we were. It was the Klonopin. In our drug-induced haze, we had wandered aimlessly for two hours through the streets of Rome, and now we couldn't figure out how to get back to Jim and Nancy's house.

Emily called Nancy, and described the street corner where we were standing. Nancy figured out where we were and gave us some basic instructions for finding our way down to the *Piazza Venezia*.

"I'll pick you up at the statue of Vittorio Emanuele in a half hour," she said.

We followed her directions, stopping again along the way to look at the fountains (though we didn't want to risk returning to Rome prematurely again, so we didn't toss any coins this time), then we strolled down the *Via del Corso*, looking in the windows of all the little shops and rubbing shoulders with the increasingly-dense group of Romans in front of the *Palazzo Chigi*, a stately white building with the Italian and European Union flags hanging above the entryway.

This is the official residence of the Italian prime minister, Silvio Berlusconi.

Then we noticed some of the people on the streets were holding signs. Big signs. Protest signs. One of them said:

MARIO MONTI SCIALLA!

But we couldn't venture a guess about what that might mean. We had somehow walked into this huge gathering, this river of people, marching and demonstrating out in the public square. Nearby, someone else held a sign reading:

TASSISTI NAPOLETANI dicono
NO alla LIBERALIZZAZIONE dei TAXI

And then another:

LAVORO DURO... PROVARE PER CREDERE

283

And another:

IL MIO TAXI... NON SI TOCCA!

We couldn't really read any of these signs, but we saw the word "TAXI" often enough to guess that maybe this was the public demonstration to go along with the taxi drivers' strike we had heard about from the hotel concierge a few days ago.

At the center of the group, a man in a black overcoat and a crimson necktie held a megaphone up to his mouth and delivered a speech to the gathered masses. Everyone in the crowd looked like a cab driver; these were middle-aged men, with square shoulders and square chins, and gray hair on their temples. The ones without picket signs in their hands folded their arms across their chests, but when the man with the megaphone spoke, their raised their fists into the air.

These were times of fiscal austerity in Italy, the government reducing its services to the people in order to pay down its debts to the big institutional creditors, at the insistence of the European Central Bank.

Emily and I pressed through the crowd, pushing our way between the congregating masses, trying to find our way to the *Piazza Venezia*, another hundred meters or so down the *Via del Corso* from the epicenter of the protest.

When we finally reached the other side, near the statue of Vittorio Emanuele, Nancy picked us up and whisked us off to dinner. I looked back down the street as we drove away, watching the mass of people with their picket signs and megaphones, and I wondered whether the big institutions would listen to them.

We met Jim at a quaint little neighborhood restaurant, where the wait staff knew Jim and Nancy by name, and they welcomed Emily and me with open arms. The hours rolled past, as we ate and ate and ate drank and ate and drank. The food was even better than the wine, which is saying quite a lot.

But the company was even better. Jim and Nancy had become our family.

55

The next morning, we borrowed a little green backpack and a tiny black duffel bag from Jim, and we packed up all of our meager possessions. In the backpack, we had our temporary passports, and a stack of about twenty-five papers. Our humble little green iPad had grown into a quite a stack! Phone numbers, documents, notes from the psychiatrist telling us about acute stress disorder and post-traumatic stress disorder, and instructing us to find a cognitive behavioral therapist as soon as possible.

In the duffel bag, we carried our meager little collection of refugee clothes. Jim and Nancy had finally managed to liberate our laundry from the ravenous jaws of the washing machine, so we could finally wear some of our own clothes.

I was wearing the same tee shirt and jeans I had worn during the evacuation. Emily was in the same outfit she had worn too, as we both let go of the rope and jumped into the lifeboat.

No life jackets, though.

So the duffel bag only held the few odd scraps of refugee clothing we had gotten from the relief workers, and the five-dollar sweatpants we bought at the Chinese discount store. There couldn't have been more than three pounds of luggage.

"How are your kids?" Nancy asked me, as she drove us to the airport, Emily and I both riding in the back-seat of the SUV so that we could sit together.

"I actually haven't talked to them yet," I said. "But I asked my brother to check in with their mom and see how they're doing. If they don't know anything about the shipwreck — if they haven't seen the capsized ship on TV yet and they don't know that Emily and I were involved — then I'd rather just wait until we get home, and I can tell them about it in a non-scary way, after the whole thing is finished. Telling them about the situation while it's still unfolding seems a little too scary."

"I think that's a good idea," said Nancy. "But kids have their own way of dealing with fear. Sometimes, they can be very sophisticated about it. You might be surprised. When Eero was just seven years old, he spilled out some uncharacteristic wisdom over an after-school snack one day."

"Which one is Eero?" I asked.

"You haven't met him. He's nineteen years old now," Nancy replied. "Anyhow, he was sitting at the kitchen table, just drinking his juice box like an ordinary little kid, and out of nowhere he says, 'All the humans in the world have all the knowledge they need when they're born,' which is a pretty sophisticated concept for a seven year old. So I said, 'Eero, that's a very interesting thought.' But he wasn't finished. He went on to say, 'When they're afraid, sometimes they can't get to their knowledge.'"

"Wow!" I said. "That's very perceptive."

"He sounds like a very special kid," added Emily.

"I know, right?" Nancy nodded her head and glanced back at us through the rear-view mirror. "But then he polished off the rest of his snack and ran out the door to dig up some beetles out in the garden. I just sat there for a second, you know? Just marveling at this brilliant child... A keen observer, for sure, but not interested in following the herd... A compassionate heart taking his cues from nature."

"Snack-time must be a very philosophical event in your household," I said.

We got out of the car at terminal five. Nancy wished us well and gave us each a big hug.

"Take care, you guys!" she said. "It hasn't even been a week, but I already feel like I've known you for so long."

"You too," said Emily. "I feel like we've known you forever."

"Thanks for all you've done for us," I said. "I can't express how grateful we are for your kindness."

Nancy beamed, and I saw the same look on her face as I had seen in the innkeeper of Giglio.

"I just have one final piece of advice," she said. "If you're looking for justice at the end of all this, good luck... But if you're looking for *meaning*, you might just find something."

286

* * *

At the check-in desk, somehow, the staff was already expecting us. They knew our names before we walked in the door, they knew we were on our way home from the shipwreck, and they knew we'd be exhausted and frazzled.

There were four Italian women working at the counter when we walked in, and we were the only customers, so all four of them tended to me and Emily. They fawned on us, asking all sorts of questions about our story.

"Were you scared?"

"Did you think you were going to die?"

"You didn't know how far you were away from shore?"

They gasped and put their hands on their cheeks and they cursed the captain and told us to please come back to Italy again someday. It's a wonderful country, so full of beauty and love and food. We should come back again and maybe we wouldn't be so unlucky next time.

"But why did you not go home two days ago?" asked one of the women from at the counter. "Everyone else went home before, did they not?"

"Yeah, they did," said Emily. "But we wanted to stay for another few days, and do some paperwork. File a police report. That sort of thing."

"Ah, good good," said the woman. She had bright blue eyes and a smile like an elf. The name tag on her blouse identified her as Lorenda. "You got help from the embassy, of course?"

"Funny you should mention that," I said.

And then, of course, Emily and I told her and all her friends the whole story about the embassies.

It didn't take much to get us going. Anybody willing to sit and listen through every minute detail could pretty much count on hearing our life stories, if they just took a moment to ask. We wanted to tell our story so badly, we would tell literally anybody.

But this woman at the ticket counter was especially interested in our story about getting turned away from the embassies.

"You know, from every other country, we are seeing the ambassadors," she said.

"They are finding all the shipwreck people from their own countries, and bringing them to the airport, and making sure everyone is on their way home."

"Really?" Emily asked. "You saw the other ambassadors? Here at the airport?"

"Yes yes yes. First, from Australia, all the way back on Saturday. Right after the crash. Even before twenty-four hours have passed, they have already brought all their people to the airport. Just like that."

"I can't believe it," said Emily. "The two biggest countries in the world, Benji."

"I know."

"The United States and China. It figures. So big and so rich," Emily continued.

"And they just left us to fend for ourselves."

Lorenda continued. "After Australia, then all the other countries too. England and Ireland. Who else?" she tapped her foot and turned toward the other girls at the desk.

"Spain… Japan…", together they tried to remember all the countries that had gone out of their way to mobilize some logistical support for their citizens.

"There was group from South Korea. And Argentina, and I think a few more too." she ran her fingers through her hair. "But I don't remember everything. Maybe that's all."

I could imagine what it must have looked like, with all those ambassadors leading their citizens through the airport terminal. At the front of the pack, somebody with an official-looking hat, waving a badge and telling somebody to "take extra special care of this group. We're bringing them home."

But the only one taking care of us, in this case, was our travel agent. He must have been the one who called the airline and informed them of our arrival. Once again, it was the individuals — the little people—who went out of their way to lend us a helping hand. The big corporations and the big governments couldn't bother to acknowledge our existence, but individual folks just like us bent over backwards to be nice.

And on that note, the nice women at the United check-in counter gave us a pair of passes to the VIP lounge and arranged to upgrade our seats to first class. I asked for Lorenda's contact info — in case we needed more information from her later — and then I added her deets to the green paper iPad.

"Oh, one last thing," I asked. "Do you have a pen you don't mind giving away? And maybe a pad of paper? I'd like to write down some notes on the flight."

Lorenda hesitated. "I think I can find something. Just a moment."

She disappeared for a few minutes and then returned with a bag from a stationary store nearby in the terminal. She hadn't been able to find a pad of paper, so she had gone ahead and bought one for us.

We hugged her.

As soon as we boarded the plane, I started writing. I wrote five or six pages of notes before editing those notes down into an outline and fleshing out the outline into a short essay.

An open letter to Secretary of State Hillary Clinton, regarding the United States Embassy in Rome.

Even if the TV news people didn't have the attention span to tell our story, and even if Good Morning America refused to discuss the institutional failures at the root of this story, surely the *New York Times* would pick up the story and help us tell the unvarnished truth.

I scratched out the paragraphs by hand, filling page after page, scribbling in the margins, writing and rewriting the drafts until my wrists cramped:

We are survivors of the Costa Concordia cruise ship disaster.

We were on our honeymoon when, in the wee hours of Friday night, after the hull breached and all the working lifeboats had been deployed, we accepted the truth that we would probably not survive. We kissed each other and said our final goodbyes, clinging precariously to an improvised rope ladder halfway down the hull of the ship.

As we've recently learned, the captain abandoned us, leaving the ship while we still hung there with our family, shivering and terrified, wondering whether anyone would help us.

Our harrowing experience aboard the ship has been well-reported over the past few days, and I'm proud to do all I can to continue making sure that story is told thoroughly and accurately.

But the story of abandonment, neglect, and indifference doesn't stop there.

For now, I'll skip a few details about the ferries that transported us back to the mainland and the buses that dumped us at hotels in Rome without first telling us where we were going or informing the hotel staff to expect our arrival.

It took 33 hours from the time of the accident until we were able to speak face-to-face with a Costa representative to ask for assistance. They abandoned us too.

In the meantime, we turned to the American embassy for help, calling the embassy's emergency number at about 3 o'clock on Saturday afternoon.

"We are survivors from the Costa Concordia. Can you help us?"

More than 100 American citizens were on that boat. None of us had eaten a meal for at least 16 hours. None of us had changed clothes since the evacuation, and a few people still had wet clothing and shoes from swimming to the shore. No one had undergone a physical or psychological exam. With no passports, no phones, no money, no local friends, no Italian language skills, and no idea how we'd get home, we asked for help from our country.

"That's not our job. We're very short-staffed, and this is a holiday weekend."

Cold comfort for those of us with nowhere else to turn.

According to U.S. Airways Passenger Service Supervisor Loredana Ippoliti, the Australian embassy gathered their citizens and brought them to the airport by Saturday morning, quickly evacuating them from the country and bringing them safely home to their loved ones.

Ambassadors from England, Ireland, Spain, Japan, South Korea, and Argentina (among others) swiftly mobilized their own teams — often personally accompanying the team — to find citizens from their own countries and bring them home.

By contrast, where was the American Ambassador?

The American Embassy had low-level staff on hand to process passport paperwork. And those guys worked hard to help us get new travel documents. But the high-level consular officials — those with the power to mobilize food, clothing, lodging, transportation, and medical attention — were completely absent throughout the whole ordeal.

Just like Costa Cruises failed to protect their passengers in the hour of their greatest need, the U.S. State Department failed to protect its citizens. Whether out of incompetence or indifference, we were abandoned.

And that is shameful.

It had taken nearly three hours to write, especially with all the little tweaks, but I was very pleased with how it turned out. I folded the paper and put it away. Into the backpack with all the other important papers. Emailing my op-ed to the *New York Times* editorial desk would be one of the first things I would do when we finally got home.

* * *

We slept a little while and watched a movie. Afterwards, some of the flight attendants came by for a chat.

"You must have been so scared!"

"I can't believe that the captain just abandoned ship like that! What a horrible person!"

"How did you know where to find a rope?"

They asked us questions about the lifeboats and the captain and the rope-ladder, and they asked if we would ever go on another cruise again. We said we might go cruising again someday, though maybe not on such a huge boat.

And maybe not in Italy.

"Can I give you a hug? I know if it was me, I would definitely need a hug."

So the flight attendants gave us each a hug. And while they were there, we told them our entire story. We talked to them for fifteen minutes. Or twenty. Or thirty. I don't really know, but eventually, there were three women gathered around our seats, listening to our barely-coherent ramblings.

And because they listened, we talked. And talked and talked and talked. Because they cared what we had to say, we couldn't stop talking. Most of the passengers didn't glance back at us. When we started talking, they turned up the volume on their iPods and buried their faces in their SkyMall magazines.

"I know it's not much," said one of the flight attendants, "but we all wanted to give you something. This is the only American money we have." She gave me a small handful of cash. Thirty dollars.

I wanted to refuse. It wasn't necessary. We truly didn't need their money. But each of these women had such a look of pure compassion. They wanted so badly to help us somehow.

Accepting a kind gesture is almost as difficult as offering a kind gesture, but I swallowed my pride and held out my hand.

"Thank you."

PART FIVE

56

My mom flew to Boston.

"You guys need somebody to cook you food." I could hear her smiling over the phone. A vaguely uneasy smile with little worry-lines around the edges. "And to bake you some cookies."

My mom is in my top five list of most favorite people ever. She's four feet and eleven inches tall and weighs no more than a hundred and two pounds. When I was in high school, she was sometimes mistaken as my older sister. She's a sucker for anything cute — especially babies and kittens and teddy bears — and she always makes quilts for the new mothers in her church congregation.

Besides cooking for us, she drove us all around town, helping us run a million errands and replace all the necessary items that had gone down with the ship.

First of all, we had lost our car keys in the shipwreck, as well as both of our drivers licenses, so we were temporarily immobile. Before doing anything, we had to have a locksmith make replacement keys.

Then my mom drove us around all day, taking us to the bank to replace our debit cards and to the mall to replace our lost wardrobe full of clothing. We had taken all of our favorite shirts and pants and dresses and shoes and underwear with us on our honeymoon, and now the only clothes we had left were faded, old, and threadbare, or a little too tight. So we spent the morning shopping.

Emily was starting to lose her voice — probably from all the shouting we had done during the evacuation — and as a professional singer, this was especially terrifying. Her whole upper register was thinning out, becoming breathy and scratchy.

So she scheduled an appointment with a specialist at the Mass General Hospital Voice Center, who put a camera down her throat and looked closely at her vocal cords on a big-screen TV.

"I can see some swelling and some redness here. There's definitely been some inflammation of the vocal folds," said the doctor. "But that's completely normal, based on your situation."

Emily nodded her head.

There was a fiber-optic cable and a miniature camera apparatus stuffed into her nose, through her nasal cavity, and down into her throat. So she couldn't talk.

"In stressful situations like this," the doctor continued, "the vocal folds often suffer minor stress injuries. I've seen it many times myself, when a patient experiences a traumatic or stressful event. Shouting or crying can put strain on the blood vessels in the throat. Sometimes there's bleeding."

As he spoke, he pointed to the screen.

"But now I want you to imagine how the rest of your body responds. Think about how you get butterflies in your stomach when you're feeling scared or nervous or how your eyes involuntarily produce tears when you're sad. Your body has been through a jarring, stressful situation, and your fight-or-flight mechanisms are all out of balance. Your muscles are tense — including the muscles in your larynx — and that tension can cause your vocal folds to grind against each other. And your parasympathetic nervous system, which controls your digestive processes, has been knocked out of calibration, and you're producing too much stomach acid, which can lead to heartburn. Acid reflux. And when that stomach acid comes up into your throat, it irritates the tissues in your larynx, exacerbating the injuries and preventing them from healing."

Emily nodded her head. I stroked the back of her hand with my index finger.

"Emily, you have some minor injuries, and you've lost part of your voice. I know it's stressful and that your voice is essential for your career, but you're going to recover. You should regain your full vocal register within a few weeks, as long as you get some rest and don't put too much strain on your vocal folds."

Now the doctor turned away from the screen and faced us.

"You know, I've always been fascinated by the human voice. That's why I chose this field, I suppose." His fingers moved delicately, as he pulled the fiber-optic cable back up and out of Emily's nose. He had performed this maneuver many times. "The vocal cords are the only organs in our bodies capable of expressing the full range of human emotions. Not even our faces or our hands. Did you know there are five times as many nerve endings in the vocal cords as there are in the hands?"

Emily and I shook our heads as the doctor sat down on a rolling stool in front of the examination table.

"Of course, we can express *some* emotions with our body language, or with our eyes or our facial expressions. But whenever we're overcome with joy or sadness or terror, the fullest expression of those feelings comes from our voices. Nothing else even comes close."

Emily nodded and smiled. "Thank you."

The doctor stood back up and pulled the latex gloves from his hands with a snap. "You're going to be just fine, Emily. Rest for a few weeks, and you'll get those high notes back."

* * *

It took more than three hours to get all of our paperwork sorted out at the DMV, since Emily's drivers license had been issued in Florida, and since she's a citizen of Hong Kong, and since both of us lost our passports in the shipwreck, and our temporary emergency one-time-use passports were no longer valid.

While we waited — through multiple phone calls and emails and faxes, so that the people at the DMV could figure out our situation — my phone rang.

"Hello, I'm looking for Benji Smith," said the voice on the phone. "I'm an associate producer with Anderson Cooper 360, and we're interested in potentially booking you and your wife for an interview on tonight's show."

"Yeah, this is Benji," I said, maneuvering my way out the front door of the DMV and looking for a quiet place to talk. "I'd be happy to help. Emily and I really care about this story, and we want to make sure it's told well."

"That's great. Thank you so much, Mr. Smith," she said. "I know you've been through a lot, and you've probably told this story a million times, but would you mind just taking me through the events, as you remember them? Starting with the moment you realized something had gone wrong on the ship."

I took a deep breath.

And then I talked for a half hour or so.

By this point, we had talked to so many TV news producers and told our story so many times, it was starting to feel like a recurring dream.

Every conversation started out with an associate producer apologizing for contacting us at this stressful time and asking if we'd be willing to spend just a few minutes being interviewed for their show. We would always respond by thanking them for their sympathy and saying that we'd be happy to appear on their show because we truly believed in the significance of these events, and that we wanted to make sure that the story was told right. The producer would vigorously agree with us about the importance of the story and the sacred stolid duty of the press in telling that story.

This is what journalism is all about!

We would speak truth to power!

Nothing could stop the fourth estate!

"All right, Mr. Smith. I have all the information I need now. What I'd like to do next is arrange for you to have a conversation with the segment producer and talk about the specifics of your interview."

This is how it always went.

The first conversation was always with a low-level producer, prepping the story for a segment producer, the person responsible for actually producing the individual three-to-five-minute interview segment. When the segment producer called, I would have to tell the whole story all over again.

"Mr. Smith, it's so good to finally talk to you. I really appreciate your time," said the segment producer. "I hate to ask you to relive all those traumatic events, but can you walk me through everything that happened to you and your family? This was your honeymoon, right?"

So I told the story again.

Sinking ship. Life jackets. Muster stations. Lifeboat failures. Saying goodbye and preparing to die. Climbing the rope ladder. Waiting three hours. Waving at helicopters. Shouting at Coast Guard boats. Getting rescued. Wandering onto Giglio Island. Shitting in the bushes. Shivering in the Hotel Bahamas. Chaos at the marina. Being herded like cattle onto a ferry boat. Squeezing onto a bus with no idea where we were going. Getting dumped at a hotel with no explanation. Asking the U.S. Embassy for help with transportation or food or shelter or clothing or money or some way to get home safely, and getting nothing. *Nothing.* Being shamed by the Chinese Embassy for showing up at their doorstep dirty and desperate and helpless, while they were trying to host a black-tie event with dignitaries arriving in their black Mercedes, and waiting on the other side of the street so that nobody would have to look at us and then trying to file a police report while the officers of the Italian Police laughed at us and told us to go home.

These were the details of our story, the nitty-gritty nasty details. Just like we had told them over and over again to the journalists in Rome, we recited them again and again to the producers and reporters back home.

I finished the story and looked at the clock. Another hour had passed.

"That's a remarkable story, Mr. Smith. It's just incredible what you and your wife went through," said the segment producer. "If you're willing to come into the studio tonight, I'd like to arrange a live interview with Anderson Cooper."

I took a breath and wiped the sweat off my forehead. "Yeah, absolutely. I'll be there."

The producer thanked me for all the time I had spent so far, helping them understand the details of the story. "And, Mr. Smith, I hope it doesn't sound like I'm bragging when I say that AC360 is going to be an ideal platform for telling this story. When there's an important story to tell, it's hard to get better than Anderson Cooper."

It was almost 5 o'clock when I hung up the phone. I needed to be at the Boston studio by 6:30.

Our drivers licenses were finally ready, and we rushed back home so that I could have enough time to change clothes and maybe take a shower before the interview. It was 5:45 when I walked out the front door, and just a moment later my phone rang. It was the segment producer from CNN.

"I'm really sorry to have to do this to you, Mr. Smith. But

we're going to have to postpone your interview with AC360"

There was a breathlessness in her voice.

"Newt Gingrich just won the South Carolina primary, so that's going to be the focus of our show tonight."

* * *

"Daddy!" said Macy. "We're so happy to see you!"

"Yeah," said Owen, his forehead scrunched and his eyebrows folded down in concern. "We're really glad you didn't get killed."

Emily and I had set up a video-chat. This was the first time we had talked to my kids since the shipwreck, and I had been feeling especially anxious about it. I was afraid they would be scared or anxious — or maybe I was afraid that they would see how scared and anxious Emily and I both still felt — but I hoped they wouldn't be too freaked out.

When they answered the call, Owen and Macy stood right up against the webcam, their foreheads bright with the glow of the screen illuminating their faces. Julie stood in the background holding Chloe's hand.

"Daddy Benji!" said Chloe, squinting through her thick glasses and smiling her big goofy smile. "We are talking to Daddy Benji and Aunt Emily."

Life can be confusing for a kid. My brother is also married to a woman named Emily, and Chloe hadn't yet figured out the difference between them. But after a few moments of explanation, Chloe tilted her head and blinked her eyes and said "Daddy Benji and *Mommy* Emily."

Nice.

"Did you see us on the news?" I asked the other two kids.

"Well, we didn't see *you* on the news," said Owen, "but we saw the ship. We saw the Costa Concordia, all tipped over onto its side. It's the biggest shipwreck I've ever seen!"

"Were you scared?" asked Emily.

"No, we weren't scared!" said Macy, her eyes icy blue with excitement. "We saw it on TV. We saw the ship sinking, and… and we said *wow that's so cool.* And then we said *That's our dad on that ship! And our new mom too!*"

"Well, I think we should come out to see you," I said. "After an experience like this one, I just want to wrap my arms

300

around you guys and squeeze you until your guts come out."

"Ewwwww," said Owen. "That's gross!"

"Maybe sometime in March or April," I continued. "we can come out there to hang out with you guys, and you can finally meet Emily face-to-face. And then maybe we'll take you snowboarding… If you're lucky…"

Owen and Macy literally jumped up and down with excitement.

57

The *New York Times* never replied.

I emailed them again, reminding them that this had been a significant world event and that I had a unique vantage point. I told them I would wait one more day to hear from them before sending the op-ed to other newspapers.

They still didn't respond.

So I contacted the op-ed editor at the *Boston Globe*, who returned my call the next day and expressed some interest in my op-ed.

"But I'd like you to do some additional reporting," she said.

"But I'm not a reporter," I replied.

"I know. I understand that, Mr. Smith," she said. "But your article is too short for publication. And you haven't reported anything from the other side of the story. Can you try to include something from the embassy's perspective? Maybe try to get a quote from the ambassador?"

"Are you kidding me?" I asked. "If I knew how to talk to the ambassador, I would never have been in this position in the first place!"

The next day, I tried looking through the Embassy's website, trying to find somebody I could call for a quote. But the embassy doesn't list the names of actual people. And what was I going to ask them anyhow? What would I say when they picked up the phone? As I learned just a few days ago, the people answering the phone at the U.S. Embassy won't even divulge their *names*.

I emailed the *Globe* again, asking for help from a reporter. But nobody ever wrote me back. So my op-ed never got published.

I wrote an email back to the editor:

Hi, I just wanted to touch base with you again and let you know that I'm not going to be able to follow-up on the additional reporting you requested for this op-ed. I really don't even know where to begin.

I'd be happy to work with a professional reporter to shed light on this story from my vantage point, but I'm just a citizen and don't know how to properly follow up on this story with the kind of journalistic rigor it deserves.

In fact, the whole reason I decided to approach the Globe with this op-ed was because it seemed like the embassy was essentially opaque (except for providing basic bureaucratic services). If anyone at the embassy is capable of (or authorized to) mobilize an emergency-response team, that person has hidden well enough that 120 American citizens couldn't find them, even after a major catastrophe. And after the fact, I can't figure out how to approach that person to request a comment.

Let me know what you think.

Thanks again for returning my calls and engaging with me.

She never returned my calls or engaged with me again after that.

I wish I could tell you why the *Boston Globe* lost interest in this story. I wish I could find out why the *New York Times* never expressed any interest to begin with.

I wish I could do some additional reporting.

I wish I could get a big scoop and find out why every news outlet seemed so apathetic about the story of the U.S. Embassy being so apathetic about the cruise line being so utterly apathetic about the shipwreck.

58

The nightmares started almost immediately.

Sometimes Emily and I are back on the ship. We're alone and it's the middle of the night, and the whole world is toppling over to one side. We're walking on the walls and then we're walking on the ceilings and then we're running, and we're climbing down ropes and jumping off balconies and sometimes we're swimming.

Sometimes the ship keeps sinking and we get stuck in a stairwell and the water rushes in and sucks us under and pulls us down and we hold our breaths for as long as we can until.

In my dreams, Emily dies.

Every time.

Sometimes I die with her, and sometimes I watch her disappear into the water without me.

Most of the dreams aren't actually even on the ship.

Emily and I are at the airport. We can't find our flight. We've been down through every gate, in every terminal, but we can't find our plane anywhere. If we don't find the right gate soon, the plane will leave without us, and we'll be trapped in Rome.

As we move through the airport, it seems to be getting bigger and bigger. The moving sidewalks move faster. The terminals wind around in loops and bends. Our phones don't work. There's no internet.

Emily sits at a table in the airport food court, face in her hands and crying. We'll never get out of here, she says. We're going to miss our flight and how will we get home? And we don't have any money and how will we eat?

I tell her it'll be okay. I'm going to find a phone and call my little brother Michael, and he'll come find us. Then we'll be okay.

Emily says not to take too long. She'll just wait for me here at this table.

So I go down the hall and past a bookstore and take the escalator through the coffee shop and between two x-ray machines and around a corner and into a souvenir shop and then back into another hallway, where an electric car whizzes past me on the left with its yellow light blinking and a sharp electric beep beep beeping. And I can't find a phone anywhere.

Maybe I should just turn around and go back to the food court and tell Emily maybe there just aren't any phones in this airport.

And maybe I would, and maybe then she'd think of something else, but when I turn around and try to retrace my steps, nothing is familiar.

I walk past old heavy tables covered in dark velvet fabrics and glass cases full of gold watches. Brass fixtures on mahogany cabinets and high ceilings with crystal chandeliers and lamps with bulbs shaped like flickering flames.

How did I get into a department store, and where is Emily?

I'm lost.

Or she's lost.

And we're trapped here.

I'm running, sprinting through the department store. A salesman in a three-piece suit and wire-rim spectacles raises his arm and calls out to me, but when he opens his mouth, there's no sound. Only the rustling of heavy fabrics and the scrape of coat hangers.

Everywhere I turn, the tables seem closer together and the cabinets seem shorter, with more and more items packed into the shelves. I'm squeezing through corridors packed with hat-boxes and walking sticks and horse figurines and pocket-watches.

Finally, the hallway comes to an end, terminating in a hodgepodge of stained glass windows on the walls and ceiling.

One of those windows is near the ground, made of dark blue and green glass, and through that window, I can see Emily. I'm looking down at her from above. She's still sitting at the table in the food court, in a room down below where I am now. My little brother Michael is standing there beside her, with his hand on her shoulder while she cries.

I tap the window, but she doesn't hear me, and she doesn't

look up to see me.

I keep tapping, harder and harder. Banging. But she doesn't know I'm here.

I'm lost.

And she's lost.

The glass goes dark, and I know I'll never see her again.

I reached over to the space next to me and found Emily by my side. It was morning. I pulled her body close and fell asleep again with my head on her shoulder.

A dream is a dress-rehearsal for the dangers we might face in life. In dreams, we practice not dying. But sometimes we don't succeed.

Some other night, in some other dream, Emily and I are walking through the park when we find a tall tree with a broad trunk and a huge canopy of green leafy branches. I give her a boost and she climbs up onto a low-hanging branch.

As soon as she stabilizes herself, she reaches down and pulls me up onto the branch next to her.

Bit by bit, we climb up deeper and deeper into the tree. After a few hours, we find a plywood trap-door above our heads and open it to find ourselves inside a monumental treehouse.

The walls of the treehouse stretch upward for hundreds of feet above us. You could fit a whole football field in here. Or a city.

In every direction, people carry hammers and screwdrivers and duct tape and wooden beams and conduit. Every direction we look, structures are being erected. Ropes and pulleys are hoisting supplies to upper levels, where more workers are cutting and joining, welding and gluing and tying. Building.

This whole treehouse is a scaffolding of interconnected compartments, with ladders and ropes and pulleys connecting tiny rooms across vast expanses of open space. It's like a beehive of independent architects, each buzzing along alone or in pairs to hammer together this massive structure.

Suddenly, something isn't right.

Emily is gone.

I turn around, but she isn't there.

Frozen is a panic, I cast my eyes all over the room, looking for her among the faces of the architects and the builders. What will I do if I can't find her?

And then finally, there she is.

Standing in a circle of people, talking and laughing. When she smiles, her eyes squint closed and she throws her head backward, laughing with her whole body. The people standing next to her can feel the warmth and joy radiating from her smile.

I've never been so relieved to see her. Never so full of happiness.

But then she loses her balance.

At the height of her laughter, with her head tilted backward and her hands in the air, she leans a little bit too far backward and loses her balance.

And falls.

Behind her, the open trap-door gapes. It doesn't even try to catch her.

And she falls.

Between the branches.

Hundreds of feet, until I can't see her anymore.

She's gone.

I cried out... and the sound of my cry woke me.

It was the middle of the night, and Emily was still sleeping. My heart was racing, pumping adrenaline throughout my body.

I kissed her cheek and put my head on her pillow, trying to sleep again. Tossing and turning while the hot vivid memory of the dream crackled and burned in my head.

Over and over again, we dreamed horrible dreams.

We didn't always remember the details, but we woke up exhausted and knew that we had spend our resting hours chasing through a dreamland full of winding hallways and tilting walls, getting lost down windy hallways in enormous buildings. And boats. Capsized and lost. Trapped in a flooded room.

Drowning.

Separated.

Night after night.

59

After a few days, I went back to work.

By this point, I had already burned through an entire year of vacation days, which was especially bad because this was a brand new job — I had only just started working there two weeks before leaving for the cruise — and I didn't want them to regret hiring me.

I had been recruited to be the team-lead in charge of developing a search engine for a new travel-inspiration website called *Hopper*.

Yeah... travel.

The company was originally founded in Montreal, but when they started expanding their technical team, they wanted to hire from the Harvard/MIT talent-pool. So they opened up an office in the Boston area. My first day on the job had been back in mid-December, the week before Christmas. I had spent two days visiting Montreal, getting to know the rest of the team — about twenty people — before coming back to Boston and opening up our new office. And then, with only two more weeks on the job, I left for my honeymoon on the Costa Concordia.

But now that I was back, those first few weeks of work felt like they had happened a hundred years ago, in a different lifetime. My memory of the trip to Montreal flickered in my head like an old 8-millimeter home movie from my childhood. A distant nostalgic memory, from back in the pre-shipwreck word where I was a normal person and hadn't yet gotten swept up into a whole new obsession.

So.

On a particularly cold January morning, I put on my gloves and trudged through the wind, taking the subway to South

Station, and then clenching my jacket around my body for the ten minute walk to my office in the Seaport District.

It was a decrepit old factory building, refurbished (but just barely) into an office space. Yes, technically, we had hardwood floors. But the planks didn't quite fit together, and the surface was pimpled with the jutting heads of rusty nails. An yes, we had exposed duct-work, but the ancient heating system created a never-ending racket of noise, sputtering and clanking and banging all day long. Wind drafted through the cracks around the edges of the window panes.

This was just our temporary space while a real estate agent searched for our permanent location. And for now, I was the only employee in Boston anyhow, so I sat by myself in this space — in my solitary chair at the room's lone table — and tried to work.

For the next eight hours, I sat alone in that room and studied the computer code I would be working on. This project was going to be pretty complicated, and I wanted to understand how everything worked so that I could start focusing on my parts.

A computer program is a lot like a blueprint for a sophisticated machine. For example, the schematics of a car show how the electrical system powers the fuel injectors, which interact with the engine, turning the gears in the transmission and sending torque down through the drive-shaft, and on and on and on. Likewise, a computer program has thousands of different systems and subsystems, millions of specialized objects sending messages back and forth according to a dense programming language with an arcane vocabulary.

The Hopper data center in Montreal has a 100 servers — organized into an 800-core computational cluster — responsible for crawling the web and finding travel-related blogs and websites. Whenever those systems find interesting information about *Bermuda* or *New York City* or the *Taj Mahal* or the *Jukkasjärvi Ice Hotel* in Sweden, they process the text and the images and they add that item into our hierarchical ontological geospatial model of the world. The team in Montreal created the data pipeline and the infrastructure.

My job was to build a travel search engine on top of the mountain of data they collected.

Presumably so that some other unsuspecting couple could book their own Mediterranean cruise honeymoon.

I rubbed my temples and looked down at the tiny laptop screen in front of me.

I clicked open a web browser and searched.

costa concordia news

I clicked into an article from the Daily Telegraph:

Young Peruvian waitress Erika Fani Soriamolina, whose body was recovered from the shipwrecked Costa Concordia off the Tuscan island of Giglio, has been hailed a heroine. Her body was found by divers on the sixth deck of the vessel wearing the ship's uniform but no life jacket.

Witnesses said Soriamolina had helped dozens of terrified passengers into lifeboats on the night of the disaster before giving the life jacket to an elderly man.

A tourism graduate, Soriamolina was working on only her third cruise on the Costa Concordia.

Her name sounded strangely familiar, though I wasn't sure why, and for a moment I wondered whether we had known her. But then suddenly, the details all came rushing back to me.

Erika was the *waitress*! The one who had double-charged us for a bottle of wine on the day before the shipwreck! Now it all made sense: it had only been her third week aboard the cruise ship, so she was still learning how to do her job, and her English was still a little rusty. We had called her manager and probably gotten her into trouble.

But now she was dead.

I read through the news story again and again: She had been helping people. She had given away her own life jacket. She was a hero.

I squeezed my eyes shut against an onslaught of tears. Why hadn't we been more *patient* with her? Why hadn't we been more *kind*? What was *wrong* with us?

I took a deep breath and looked at the clock.

Two hours had passed.

I felt anxious.

I hadn't done any real work yet today.

Ten times a day, I would find myself back online, reading more news reports about the shipwreck, more salacious details about the captain and his mistress, more updates about the search-and-rescue efforts. On and on and on…

Something in my brain had switched off. Every time I tried to focus on my work, I got lost in the cavernous complexity of the project.

I just couldn't wrap my head around it. And to make matters worse, I couldn't even muster up the enthusiasm to care anymore. I couldn't find the energy to overcome my confusion.

I hate this.
I don't want to do this anymore.

I thought back to my college days, where I studied theatre. I had been an actor, a director, a playwright. I wrote something almost every day. I stood on stage and told stories. I taught myself to draw and to paint. In my former life, I had been a passionate, creative person. Using voices and bodies, light and sound and shadow to create imaginary worlds and populate them with characters and conflict. And from that conflict, weaving a latticework of themes and meanings.

That's all I really wanted to be doing right now.

Sitting in this sad little room and trying to comprehend a tangle of interlocking software components, I felt brittle and bereft, incompetent and despondent.

I couldn't keep my mind on my work for more than a few minutes at a time.

But every day, I rode the same train to that same empty office and sat in the same chair, reading the same code and feeling the same crushing burdens of emptiness and inadequacy.

I don't know how to do this.
I'm not smart enough to take this job.

And whenever the anxiety overwhelmed me, I would take a quarter-dose of Klonopin to calm down. But although the drug softened the edges of the anxiety and put solid ground

311

beneath my feet, it also put my mind into a haze where creativity was impossible.

My feeble attempts at comprehension had failed, and my motivation to persevere had vanished.

So I just sat in the chair.

Every day.

60

Emily got back to work too.

After visiting the voice doctor and confirming that there were no major long-term injuries to her vocal cords, she started scheduling rehearsals and confirming the upcoming travel dates for her touring schedule.

After just two weeks home, she was already on the road again, performing in Illinois and then Arizona and Maryland, and then back to Arizona again. Between each of the out-of-town gigs, there were a few shows back home in Boston.

But after every concert, she would come back to me with shoulders hanging low and a shaky lower-lip.

"I don't know why I even bother singing," she said one day. "Every gig is exactly the same. We sing music from a bunch of dead composers that nobody's ever heard of, and the musicians spend all their time worrying about 'historical authenticity' or some other pretentious bullshit... And... and it doesn't *mean* anything. The whole thing is pointless and stupid, and I hate it. I don't even like the music anymore."

I shuddered. "Really? Are you sure it's not just the PTSD talking? I thought you loved this music."

She scowled at me.

"No, I don't think it's that." She looked down at her feet. "I just don't want to do it anymore. I don't want to sing these songs. I don't want to do it. I just... It's..."

I sat down next to her as her voice trailed off. There wasn't really anything to say. We sat and stared at her feet and listened to the sound of our own breath.

"I don't want to do anything," she said. "I don't want to do anything."

I nodded my head.

That's exactly what it was.

I didn't want to do anything either.

But then... If neither of us wanted to do anything, why were both of us so full of energy? Why did we have this unstoppable nervous energy bubbling and boiling inside of us?

While I sat at my sad little desk and cast an apathetic eye over a daily deluge of emails and conference calls and planning meetings, Emily dove deeper into an increasingly frenzied routine. She planned programs and rehearsed. She booked travel and transcribed manuscripts and auditioned new collaborators and translated from French and German and Spanish and Italian into English and learned to play the frame-drum and the psaltery and the riq and the hammered dulcimer.

She worked and worked and worked and worked.

And then she came home frustrated and exhausted and cursed by ambivalence, bruised by the sudden disconnection from the soul of the music and promising to quit performing forever.

"Maybe I just want to get a membership at the YMCA and swim laps in the pool every day," she said, almost in a whisper. "You can't join a swim team if you're on the road performing every week, and I've always wanted to join a swim team. Maybe I'll quit singing entirely."

But then, three weeks after the shipwreck, she got back on a plane again and traveled to Arizona for a gig, singing the Brahms Requiem with a full orchestra. Before leaving Boston, the director of the group called and asked if she would mind dedicating the upcoming concert to the memory of the people who died on the Costa Concordia.

"I would be honored," Emily replied.

* * *

When Emily got to Arizona, she was welcomed with open arms into the local community. The local FOX news station aired a story about the show, their headline reading: *Costa Concordia cruise ship survivor visits Tucson.*

On top of that, the concert organizers had arranged for a half-hour Q&A Session before the concert, where Emily could take questions about the shipwreck from curious audience members.

314

"I don't know if I can do it!" Emily called me as soon as she heard about it, frantic and horrified at the prospect. "I think I'm going to throw up."

"It'll be okay," I said. "Just tell them you can't answer any questions. It's *way* too soon for that. But maybe you can say a few words at the beginning of the concert. Something nice. Like... how grateful you are to be alive and how happy are to be there performing this beautiful piece of music in memory of the people who lost their lives in this horrible catastrophe. Something like that..."

"Actually, maybe I could just talk about the music," mused Emily, her voice suddenly much less anxious. "Do you know anything about the Brahms Requiem?"

"Nothing," I replied.

"A *requiem* is a mass for the dead," she explained. "It's a song of mourning that we sing for the repose of departed souls."

"Oh wow," I said. "Now it makes much more sense why they would dedicate this concert to the shipwreck victims."

"Exactly," said Emily. "And this is probably the most beautiful requiem I know. When Brahms wrote it, he didn't follow the usual Catholic tradition. He didn't use the traditional Latin scriptures about the salvation of souls in purgatory. Instead, the whole thing is a blessing for the living, for those who have lost their loved ones. It's in German, but I have a translation here... Hang on a second... Okay, now just listen to these passages from the first movement..."

She recited the words to me:

Blessed are they that mourn:
for they shall be comforted.
They that sow in tears
shall reap in joy.
They go forth and weep,
and bear precious seed,
and shall come again with rejoicing
bringing their sheaves with them.

"I just love the message it sends: when we sow tears of sorrow, we will reap joy," she said, her voice starting to shake a little. I could hear the rustling of paper through the phone as she looked through her sheet music two thousand miles away from me. "It's true, though, isn't it? When we mourn, we're remembering everything that made us happy about that person and we're saying goodbye. And then when we're finished mourning, we can find new happiness and joy knowing that we honored all the happiness that came before."

"You're really good at this," I said.

"The next section is even better," she continued, "I just love this imagery..."

For all flesh is like grass,
and all its glory like the flower of grass.
The grass withers,
and the flower falls...

61

Within just a few days of the shipwreck, Representative John Mica — a Republican from Florida — called a hearing for *A Review of Cruise Ship Safety and Lessons Learned From the Costa Concordia Accident*. In fact, the hearing was announced to the public on January 18th, the same day Emily and I arrived back home in Boston, five days after the accident.

We read the announcement online, during our daily obsessive news-googling sessions where we read every possible fact we could find about the shipwreck, clicking the *refresh* button every five minutes to see if the search and rescue teams had located any more bodies or if the any new scandalous details about the captain had surfaced.

Anyhow, the congressional hearing was scheduled for the 29th of February, just one day after Emily would be performing in the Washington D.C. area.

She immediately called the representative's office.

"Hello, my name is Emily Lau," she said. "I'm a survivor of the Costa Concordia shipwreck and I'm calling about the congressional hearing on cruise ship safety coming up next month."

"Well, thank you for calling," the staffer on the phone replied. "The hearing is open to the public, so you're welcome to attend and observe."

"Actually, I'd like to testify in the hearing," said Emily. "My husband and I almost died on that boat, and we'd like to tell our story to Congress. We couldn't even get off the cruise ship because our lifeboat was broken, and then we held onto a rope for three hours waiting for someone to help us. If this is a hearing about cruise ship safety, there isn't *anybody* better to testify than us."

"Where are you calling from?" asked the staffer. "Are you in Representative Mica's district?"

"No," said Emily. "I'm calling from Boston, but I can arrange my own transportation and lodging. I'll be in the D.C. area already that week on business, and I can make myself available the entire day of the…"

The staffer cut her off mid-sentence. "I'm sorry, but we already have all the witnesses we need for this hearing."

We were stunned.

We had been angry when the Italian police told us to go away. We had been shocked by the apathy of the U.S. Embassy and disgusted by the cruelty of the Chinese Embassy. We felt burned by the TV news media, and we couldn't help but notice the shadows from a cloud of vulture-like attorneys circling us overhead.

But we hadn't expected this from the U.S. Congress.

A few weeks later, on the afternoon before the day of the hearing, I got a phone call from a producer at *CBS News*.

"Hello, Mr. Smith," she said. "First of all, I just want to tell you how glad we are here at CBS News that you and your wife are both home safe and sound."

"Thanks," I replied. "What can I do for you?"

"Well, you may have heard something about the House of Representatives holding a hearing tomorrow morning about cruise ship safety, based on lessons learned from the Costa Concordia accident."

"Yeah," I replied. "I've heard about it."

"Good. Well tomorrow, we're going to air a segment during *CBS This Morning* focusing on the passenger reaction to that hearing, and we wanted to know if you'd be willing to appear as an interview guest on that program."

"Yes. Yes, absolutely," I said, unable to mask my enthusiasm. "You have no idea how much we would like to talk about this hearing on your show. We would be delighted."

"That's great!" she said. "And if there any particular issues you'd like to hear discussed in this hearing, we'd be especially interested in hearing about those issues during our interview."

"As a matter of fact," I said. "My wife and I were hoping to testify in this hearing. We called Representative Mica's office and volunteered to be witnesses, but they refused to let us testify."

"Really?" said the producer. I could hear the sudden sound of rustling of papers on her desk through the phone receiver. "Tell me more about that."

I told her the whole story, with all the crazy details about the cruise company and the Italian police and the embassies, and now the U.S. Congress too.

"That's an incredible story, Mr. Smith," she said, when I finished. "We'd love for you and your wife to come out to our studio this evening and tape an interview for broadcast tomorrow morning."

So Emily and I drove out to a studio about an hour from our house in Cambridge. We spent about a half hour setting up for the interview — putting microphone wires up through our shirts and satellite thingamajigs into our ears — and then another hour talking to the morning-show host.

But the host of the show kept asking the same questions that every other reporter had already asked us a million times over the past three weeks. She asked us what was going through our minds at the moment the ship hit the rocks. She asked us to describe our dramatic escape climbing down the rope. She asked us how we felt about the captain and how it felt to be back home again.

We were pissed. This is not what we came here to talk about.

"Well, Benji and Emily, we'd like to thank you for talking to us this morning," said the voice over the satellite feed. "The two of you have been through quite an amazing experience, and we're glad you made it home."

"I'm sorry," I said. "We only agreed to this interview because we thought we were going to talk about the congressional hearings tomorrow. I thought we were going to talk about Congress refusing to hear our testimony."

"Of course, Mr. Smith," said the producer. Not the same producer I had spoken to this afternoon. Some other producer. Somebody new. "If you'd like to talk about Congress, we can keep going for a few more minutes."

For the next five minutes or so, the host asked a few quick questions about the congressional hearing. But I could tell from the tone of her voice that she had lost interest. The story was already in the can.

So we weren't too shocked the next morning to discover that our interview had been edited down to a few sound-bites

— no more than thirty seconds of audio — with no mention of Congress refusing to hear our testimony.

* * *

At about the same time, I had a long phone conversation with Bryan Burrough, an investigative journalist working on a feature-length story (*ten thousand words!*, everyone kept telling me) about the Concordia shipwreck.

I told him everything I knew.

"This is going to be a big story," he said, "Thanks for all the information you've given me. You've been very helpful."

"Great," I said. "And please, *please* include the details about the embassy and the congressional hearing. We've talked to dozens of different reporters, and nobody has been willing to report on those aspects of the story — seriously, *nobody* — and I don't know why."

"Okay," he replied. "I'll do my best."

After our conversation, we exchanged emails for a few weeks as he continued working on his story and needed help clarifying certain details about the story. The next week, *Vanity Fair* sent a team of photographers — four people — up from New York to Boston to take our picture. And then, during the week before publication, a *Vanity Fair* fact-checker called and spent another hour on the phone with me, double-checking all the information I had given Bryan.

But when the magazine appeared on shelves two months later, there was no mention of the embassy or the congressional hearing.

Not one word.

* * *

Divers found more bodies yesterday.

Four people had been trapped inside an elevator when the ship sank. When the water flooded the elevator shaft, those people drowned. In the dark.

It's hard for me to imagine anything quite so horrible.

In other news, they found traces of cocaine in the captain's hair. Not in his bloodstream, though. But I guess that's the last we'll hear of that.

* * *

I'm not a conspiracy theorist or some kind of nutcase. I don't have a natural mistrust of the "media."

At the beginning of this disaster, in the days immediately following the shipwreck, Emily and I regarded the members of the media as journalists we could trust.

I don't have a working theory that explains the systemic failure of every media organization to report all the important facts of this story. It doesn't make sense to me that all these journalists — some of them with decades of experience digging up the hard-hitting facts and speaking truth to power — would keep editing away the parts of our story that truly matter.

I can't explain it.

When Sándor Fehér (the violinist) and Erika Soriamolina (the waitress) gave away their own life jackets and ultimately lost their lives to help passengers escape the sinking ship, they didn't do so as Costa employees. They did so as human beings.

When Paolo Fanciulli let 500 cold shivering strangers with no money into his hotel and emptied his cabinets to give them food and drink, he didn't do so as the proprietor of the Hotel Bahamas. He did so as a neighbor and a friend.

When Jim and Nancy took us into their home and fed us, and let us wear their clothes, and took us to the doctor, they didn't do so because we were the friend-of-a-friend-of-a-friend. They did it because we're all just *people*.

But when the Embassies couldn't be bothered to help us with money or clothes or food or transportation, the reason they didn't help is because we're a bunch of nobodies. We're not the President or the CEO or the Secretary Of Anything. We're nobodies.

When the big fancy TV networks send their diamond studded producers to ask us "how it felt" when we lost everything, only to jump back on their jets home to New York City and leave us behind to fend for ourselves, the reason they do so is because we're nobodies.

They don't care what happens to us. They want to put our story on their show so that they can sell more laundry detergent and Infiniti luxury sedans.

When Congress calls a hearing on cruise ship safety, and

the Representative in charge refuses to hear our testimony, we think somebody in the media ought to be interested in telling that story.

But if we *do* tell that story, and a national news show already has it on *tape*, and they've told us how *horrible* and *shocking* the whole this is... but then they edit those details out *anyhow*...

The only conclusion I can come to is that these journalists must be suffering from the same disease as the other big institutions: they're so caught up in the romance of the elites — so completely captured by the tentacles of the great vampire squids of power and money and influence — that they've just lost interest in the plight of the nobodies... There's just no other way to interpret it.

I guess it's not very exciting to report a story where a bunch of nobodies get quietly swept under the rug. That's not *news*.

62

I have never spoken directly to a lawyer.

Early on, Emily started acting as our collective mouthpiece. She's a very canny observer of people, and I completely trust her opinion of any person. If Emily says a person is trustworthy, then I completely trust her opinion. She knows how people work. She understands people's intentions and objectives, and she gives incredible advice about dealing with tricky social situations.

So Emily is in charge of vetting lawyers.

And lots of lawyers approached us. Seriously. Lots of them.

They called us. They emailed us. They googled us and Facebooked us. They sent us postcards in the mail.

Some of them were slick used-car-salesmen types. And some of them were New York City Johnny Cochran types. Some of them were from small family partnerships, and some of them approached us from huge international firms with thousands of partners and offices in Boston, Miami, New York, London, and Rome.

And while this fleet of attorneys approached us, they also approached all the other passengers from the United States, Canada, and England (passengers from other countries don't really sue, for some reason).

At first, all of the different lawyers pursued their cases with equal vigor, grabbing up as many potential plaintiffs as they could. Some firms ended up with only a single client. Some of them got ten or twenty or thirty clients.

After that first round of client-grabbing, everyone waited a few months to see what would happen next. They filed bits of preliminary paperwork in all the relevant jurisdictions, but mostly nothing happened.

Wait.

And see.

After a few months, some of the lawyers lost interest, deciding that the case wasn't worth much to them. With only a single client, it doesn't make much sense to pursue such a complicated case. A case that could take years to go through the court systems all over the world, and cost millions of dollars in research and preparation and overhead and travel.

So those lawyers started giving their clients subtle hints to drop their cases or take a settlement. But rather than being frank with their clients, they just started slacking off, hoping the clients would just go away. Maybe they made lowball predictions about odds of winning so that their clients would get frustrated and go away.

And as soon as those first lawyers started disappearing from the landscape, the rest of the attorneys scavenged the refugee clients into their own cases, collecting as many new clients as possible.

It's got to be said that — as a survivor of a shipwreck where the captain abandoned ship and our home country shrugged their shoulders in indifference — it really stings to have your own lawyer abandoning the case.

Eventually, a few of the remaining lawyers had accumulated all of the survivors into a few sizable cohorts. The number of potential plaintiffs made the numbers worthwhile. The lawyer we have right now seems like a pretty decent guy, but like I said, I don't know much about lawyers, and I don't know much about this case.

I know that the jurisdiction issues are really tricky and that the terms and conditions of our ticket basically take away all of our rights. I hope the case goes forward and that we prevail and that we are paid a fair and reasonable settlement.

But that raises a very interesting question.

What is a fair and reasonable settlement anyhow?

We're not greedy. We don't expect to get rich from this. But we don't want to be taken advantage of. And we don't want the people who put our lives at risk to evade taking responsibility.

So we don't want too much. But we don't want too little either.

What's the sweet spot?

In the first few days after the shipwreck, we were notified

by Costa's representatives that we would each get a reimbursement of our ticket cost, plus eleven thousand euros (about $14,000 in US dollars) to cover the cost of our lost belongings, medical care, and psychological trauma. If we accepted their offer, we would be ineligible for any future settlement.

We thought about it.

We considered the cost of our lost clothes, shoes, jackets, cameras, phones, luggage, jewelry, souvenirs, and on and on and on.

We lost our video camera, with some of the original wedding footage we had just shot two weeks before. We lost our original marriage license, and a hand-carved wooden comb that I had bought for Emily in a thousand-year-old water village near Shanghai.

We don't know how to properly account for the monetary value of all the stuff we lost, let alone the non-monetary sentimental value.

On the other hand, some of my tee-shirts are old. My pants were frayed around the edges. Should the shareholders of Carnival Corporation and its subsidiaries and their shareholders have to pay the full retail price to replace my old socks?

Costa offered to provide psychological counseling to us. We decided not to accept that offer either. It isn't very comforting to place your trust in someone with a history of abandoning you. And anyhow, they had a huge vested interest in making sure that a therapist of their choice quickly declare us all-better.

But anyhow, I still haven't figured out the answer to the original question: what is a fair price? If we had to someday decide whether or not to accept a new settlement offer, we had to have some idea in our minds about what amounts we would be willing to accept.

Maybe we would never accept any dollar amount. Maybe we would only be satisfied with a full apology and statement of guilt from the captain of the ship and the executive officers of Carnival and Costa. Maybe we'd only be happy if the CEO was personally handcuffed and frog-marched out his front door and into solitary confinement for the rest of his life.

We wanted them to know that they couldn't just sink us in the sea or dump us on the street. We wanted them to know that the world wasn't their fucking playground. They couldn't risk the lives of thousands of people just to cover their own asses.

We wanted them to suffer the consequences of their actions. We wanted it to sting a little bit.

But is this story really new? Isn't it the same thing over and over again with big faceless companies and big faceless governments. We give way too much trust to fancy psychopaths and turn the other cheek when they stick their blood-funnel into our throats and suck out our life-savings. We look the other way when they sink their cruise ships or leech benzene into the drinking water or when their oil-rigs explode or they bankrupt the whole world economy. Again.

In the end, they'll try to pay everybody a few bucks without admitting any wrongdoing, and they live another day to perpetrate the whole scam over and over again while people suffer all around them.

If we let these people stay in charge of our countries and our money and our food and our laws and our guns and our oceans and our mines, eventually, they are going to destroy the world. They're going to take all the good bits for themselves, leaving us with only the burning garbage, and they'll make us their slaves in the process.

We didn't want to let that happen. We would reject the settlement and take Costa to court, for the principle, not for the money. We wanted to punish them. We wanted them to feel the sting for once.

But a corporation isn't a person. A corporation is just an imaginary creature made out of money and held together by laws. And the only way you can injure a corporation is by depriving it of money.

So how much is our suffering worth? How much money would Carnival have to lose before the structure of the company would even tremble?

I don't know.

But here's a number I actually do know:

The Costa Concordia was insured by for 405 million euros ($513 million US dollars). That's just for the loss of the ship. I don't know how much of that money will be spent on the salvage operation, but I guess it's probably a lot.

I think the lost lives and the suffering of the passengers is worth at least as much as the ship itself. So it seems fair to me that the victims (the passengers and the non-nautical crew) deserve a lump sum somewhere in the neighborhood of $500 million.

With 4,200 people aboard the ship, if we split the settlement evenly, we'd each end up with about $120,000.

The families of the people who died probably deserve a bigger slice of the pie. And people like Patrick and Elizabeth, anybody who had to swim to shore, also probably deserves a bigger settlement.

If a judge determines that Emily and I only deserve a hundred bucks and a six-pack of beer for our troubles, that's fine by me. I trust a neutral judge to decide upon a fair settlement, even if I believe taking the cash from Costa would be akin to accepting hush-hush money.

So that's my reasoning. That's what I think would be fair.

Maybe the lawsuit will fall apart, and we'll end up getting nothing. Our chances of succeeding in court are very slim, in my opinion.

Whenever I think about attorneys and judges and court systems, I'm reminded of the last thing Nancy said to us before we got on the plane home:

If you're looking for justice at the end of all this, good luck... But if you're looking for meaning, you might just find something.

63

"I keep getting sick," said Emily. "I have acid reflux all the time, and I keep catching colds. I never used to get sick like this before…"

"That's just your body's natural reaction to stress," said the therapist.

"But it's been a long time," Emily replied, "and I should be getting better by now, right? The shipwreck was three months ago."

"Your body doesn't know that," said the therapist. "You might know in your mind that the accident was three months ago, but you have all these stress hormones in your body *now*. So as far as your *body* is concerned, the disaster is still happening."

"But how can I convince my body that the trauma is over?" Emily asked.

The therapist replied with a question of her own:

"I don't know. Is it really over?"

* * *

When we first got home from the shipwreck — within a day or two of getting back to Boston — Emily called the head of the psychiatry department at Massachusetts General Hospital and asked for help finding a doctor. We had heard too many horror stories of people vanishing down the rabbit-hole of PTSD, spending decades battling against phantoms from the past, and we were terrified of slipping down into that abyss.

"I need a recommendation," she said. "My husband and I were passengers on the Costa Concordia when it sank last week, and we're afraid of developing PTSD. We need help. Can you give me the name of the best trauma therapist in Boston?"

That's how we got in touch with Dr. Luana Marques, a senior clinical psychologist at the *MGH Center for Anxiety and Traumatic Stress Disorders* program, and an Assistant Professor of Psychiatry at Harvard Medical School.

* * *

During our first session with Dr. Marques — as we sat drinking hot lemon tea on the overstuffed couch in her office — we told the doctor that we had come up with some ideas on our own for how to cope with the stress and anxiety.

"Very good," she said. "Tell me what you've come up with."

"Well, first of all," I said, " Neither of us want to be separated from each other. And since I'm pretty much alone in my office all day, we thought it would make sense for me to set up an extra table so that Emily can sit next to me while we work."

"And I think I'm going to cancel all my upcoming concerts," said Emily. "I hate the music, and I hate everybody I'm working with. I hate travelling and being away from Benji every day, and I don't even know if I want to make music anymore."

"Well," said Dr. Marques. "I'm glad to see that the two of you are thinking a lot about developing new coping skills, but I'm going to suggest a slightly different approach, okay?"

Emily and I nodded our heads and scooted to the edge of the couch.

"First of all, let's not make any drastic changes," she said. "Not yet anyhow. Don't quit your jobs or move to a new city or turn your lives upside-down with unnecessary changes. You might decide to make some of those changes over the coming months. But there's no rush. For now, let's just keep things as stable as possible, okay?"

"Okay," we said.

"Benji, I also think it would be a bad idea for you to bring Emily to work with you," said Dr. Marques. "It's normal and healthy for you to spend some time apart every day, and I think going to work is a good example of that. Maybe you can eat lunch together or go for a walk if you need to see each other. But you should both be able to cope without each other's presence for eight hours."

"Okay," I took a deep breath. "I think we can do that."

"Now I'm also going to give you some homework assignments, and I want you to take these very seriously."

We listened closely.

"First things first," said Dr. Marques. "I want you to eat healthy food. Three or four nutritious meals every day. Your brain needs a lot of fuel right now, so let's make sure it's good."

"That's our first homework assignment?" asked Emily. "To eat good food?"

"Yep," said Dr. Marques with a smile. "Pretty easy, huh?"

"The therapist in Rome said exactly the same thing," I added.

"Well, it sounds like he really knows what he's talking about," she replied. "Maybe he also told you to get a good night's sleep every night?"

I nodded. "Yes, he did."

"Good. Because that's your second homework assignment," she said. "At least seven hours of sleep every night. Eight, if you can."

"Okay, I think we can do that too," said Emily. "You give the easiest homework, Dr. Marques. I think we're going to ace this class."

"I hope you do," said the doctor. "But I have one more assignment for you, and this one is a bit more difficult. I'd like you to schedule some time each day — maybe just an hour or so — where you don't talk about the shipwreck or read the news. Plan an hour every day to get engaged in other activities that you both enjoy. Kind of like a little window back into normal life."

* * *

One day a few weeks after the shipwreck, Emily's friend Al — a rocket scientist who works for NASA — called to check up on us and make sure we were doing all right. Emily told him the whole story and he followed along in rapt attention.

"Wasn't there even a drill?" he asked. "Aren't all cruise ships required to put the passengers through a safety drill before they leave port?"

"Nope," Emily replied. "We had been on the cruise ship for four days, and there never was a drill."

Al shook his head and sighed.

Emily shrugged. "Well, I guess there's no drill in life either."

But Al cocked his head over to one side and said, "At NASA, we do drills all the time. For every mission, we have to think of all the worst-case scenarios and develop an emergency protocol for everything. And then when we've got all those protocols nailed down, we run drills together, over and over again. That's why they're called *drills*, you know? Because we're trying to drill all these emergency responses into our brains."

"Oh yeah," said Emily. "I never thought of that."

"So anyhow, we have to drill all the scenarios, you know? Some scenarios have solutions to the problems. The astronauts can fix the vehicle and land safely, and everything works out fine. And we practice that in our drills. But some of the other scenarios present a no-win situation, and we have to practice those too. In those cases, sometimes the best scenario is that you kill all the crew and crash the vehicle into the sea. Sometimes that's the *best* outcome, but we still have to run those drills. And you always follow the protocol."

Emily thought for a moment.

"I guess that's what we're doing right now," she said. "We're just following the protocol: Go back to work. Travel for a gig. Laugh at someone's joke. Go to work. Try to keep smiling. That's the protocol. Sometimes it doesn't feel natural, but we're trying to fake it for a while to see if we can get back into the groove of our lives again."

64

On our second visit, Dr. Marques asked if we had been doing our homework — my wife is a valedictorian, so yes, of course we had been doing our homework — and then she gave us a questionnaire to complete:

Do you avoid being reminded of the experience by staying away from certain places, people or activities?

Have you lost interest in activities that were once important or enjoyable?

Have you begun to feel more distant or isolated from other people?

Do you find it hard to feel love or affection for other people?

Have you begun to feel that there is no point in planning for the future?

Have you had more trouble than usual falling or staying asleep?

Do you become jumpy or easily startled by ordinary noise or movements?

After each question, we were asked to write ALWAYS, OFTEN, SOMETIMES, or NEVER.

The only difficult part about answering these questions was deciding between SOMETIMES and OFTEN. When we finished writing, we gave our pages back to the doctor.

She glanced through our responses and tallied up the results in her head.

"Both of you have moderate acute stress disorder," she said, "which is pretty much what I expected to see from you at this point. So there are no surprises there... And since you've both been so good at doing your homework, I want to talk with you a little bit today about where we want to take this therapy."

Emily and I held hands, sitting on the puffy couch with our paper cups of hot lemon tea while the doctor continued her explanation.

"I want you both to think about what the accident *means* to you in your life," she said. "As human beings, we live our lives searching for patterns and meanings in everything. We build a narrative about ourselves and about the world, and whenever some new event challenges our understanding, then we're forced to adjust our narrative to compensate for the new information. That's true for all the mundane events in our lives, but it's especially true for the traumatic events. So we need to find out... What does this accident mean to each of you? How does it fit into your personal narrative?"

I blinked my eyes.

What did the shipwreck *mean* to me?

I had no idea.

* * *

At first, I blustered at the very premise of the doctor's question.

The shipwreck didn't *mean* anything.

It was just an accident.

Shit happens, right?

When I was a kid — raised in a faithful Mormon household — I belonged to a community where everything had a meaning. God played an active role in our lives, sending us coded messages every day to teach us kindness and humility and devotion. Each day, we would think about the events of our lives and ask ourselves what God was trying to teach us.

According to Mormon doctrine, nearly everyone goes to heaven, but Mormon theology actually includes lots of different levels within heaven. There are lesser kingdoms and greater kingdoms within the grand kingdom of heaven. Each of those kingdoms is a classroom where we learn better how to become more like God.

At the very highest levels, those of us who learn best to emulate God's love and mercy and kindness will become gods ourselves. Since God's power comes from his perfection, when we achieve the same perfection as God, we naturally take upon ourselves the same powers and responsibilities that He holds.

In fact, Mormons believe that's how God became God in the first place. He was a person just like us, worshiping His own god. But after He died — because He was a such a good person — He kept advancing in love and knowledge and power and kindness until eventually, He became a God too and populated the Earth with all of His spirit children. This planet is just one in an endless succession of other planets where humans are born and grow and ripen into godhood.

Mormons believe that godhood is just the final stage of the human lifecycle. Like caterpillars become butterflies or tadpoles become frogs, so too do humans become gods.

There's an elegance and symmetry to it that truly appeals to me.

Of course, I don't actually *believe* in any of it. Even if I think the stories are beautiful, I don't think they're true. To me, it's just painfully obvious that there's no such thing as ghosts or gods or magic.

But Mormons see magic everywhere. They see tiny miracles happening around them all the time. When you wear those Mormon-colored glasses, it's hard not to believe that God has a personal plan for each and every one of us. A detailed plan, including where and when each of us will be born, who our parents will be, and what opportunities will present themselves in our lives. It's not fate, *per se*; it's just how all our lives would ideally unfold, if we were all in tune enough with God.

His plan includes details about our relationships (especially our marriages) and our children, our careers and our travels, our tragedies and our triumphs. When we live our lives according to his plan, God can wave away the obstacles in our paths and we can achieve our fullest potential.

The thing that makes us human is that we have a choice.

Having a choice is what makes us unique in the universe. It's what makes us different from the animals. It's what separates us from the trees and the rocks and the sun and the moon.

Everything else in the universe obeys the commandments of God without question. God commands the sun to shine, so it does. God commands the Earth to orbit the sun, and it obeys. He commands monkeys to monkey-around, and they do their duty.

Obedience is the primary force that holds the universe together. God commands particles to have mass and energy and gravity and magnetism. He commands water to freeze at a certain temperature and light to travel at a certain speed. According to Mormon theology, the laws of physics are basically the same as the ten commandments; the only difference is that we humans have a choice to disobey.

Of course, God can change His commands at any time. He can command the laws of gravity to be temporarily suspended. He command spirits back into dead bodies. He can command the waters of the sea to retreat or the Sun to turn black.

To a Mormon, miracles don't contradict science. God invented science, and He can invent a different kind of miracle-science whenever He wants. The universe will bend to His will.

Only man can defy God.

And the only reason we can defy God is because He created us to have *will*, just like He has will. Obedience is the process of changing our own will to conform with the will of God. And the purpose of our lives on Earth is to learn how to make God's will our own.

Obedience is, therefore, the most important element of Mormon law.

It's more important than kindness or generosity or love or forgiveness. Sure, we're supposed to do all those other things, and the ultimate purpose of all the commandments is to teach us how to be more like God. But the reason we do them is because God said so, and we trust him to mold and shape our will to be more like his own.

So anyhow, these were the thoughts going through my mind when I considered Dr. Marques's question — *what did the shipwreck mean?* — and tried to answer it for myself.

Mormons have a framework for answering questions about existential meaning. But what did I have? In my world, without a cosmic central-planner, how could I possibly answer that question? What did the shipwreck *mean*?

The more I thought about it, the more it stressed me out.

It didn't mean anything, and I didn't want it to mean anything.

* * *

"I've decided to write a book," I told Dr. Marques during one of our one-on-one sessions.

For the most part, Emily and I had been attending our therapy sessions together, but Dr. Marques suggested meeting separately a few times, so that she could focus on us each individually instead of always as a couple.

"Why?" she asked. "Why do you want to write a book? What does it mean to you?"

I scratched my head. "I don't know. I mean... isn't it obvious? We have a story to tell, and we've tried to tell our story so many times, but nobody ever listens to us. They take our story, and they edit down into sound-bites, and they ignore all the important parts."

"So?" she asked, shrugging her shoulders.

"So... if we tell this story ourselves, then finally the whole truth will be out there."

"The *whole* truth?" she asked. "Wow, that must be a pretty big book."

"Well, not the whole truth," I replied. "It's just *our* story, obviously. But we're contributing that story into the public commons. You know... for the betterment of society."

"So you're writing this book as a public service?" she asked, raising her eyebrows. "How noble of you!"

"It's an important story," I said.

"Why?" she asked again. "Why is this an important story?"

I sighed, trying to collect my thoughts.

Why was it so hard to answer these basic questions?

"It's an important story because... Thirty-two people died for no good reason. And the institutions entrusted to care for us all failed: the cruise company, the Italian police, the American and Chinese Embassies, the United States Congress..."

I trailed off into silence. The words coming out of my mouth were starting to feel empty and repetitive. I felt like a caricature of myself. I mean, I knew these things were important, right?

336

But now I was just reciting a speech rather than actually speaking from the heart. Why was this so hard?

"Let me ask you a different question," said Dr. Marques, her voice both soft and strong. "What does it *feel like* when you write?"

I closed my eyes and tried to remember what it had felt like the night before, as I hunched over a keyboard and wrote the first scattered bits and pieces that would eventually become this book.

"It's hard to write anything," I said. "Every time I sit down at the computer and stare at the blank page, I feel lost. I don't know where to start, and I don't know if I can do it. But I feel like, if I don't write this down myself, the world will basically just forget this event. A year from now, will anybody still remember? I'm afraid I'm already starting to forget it myself."

"What have you forgotten?" she asked.

"Little things... Like... I forget what it smelled like on the fourth deck while we waited to board the lifeboats. Was it salty like the sea? Or did the smell of fear overpower the salty air? And how long did we stand on the deck before we finally got into a lifeboat? I don't know. I don't remember."

"Do you want to forget?" she asked.

"I want to forget the fear." I answered. "I want to forget the terror. I want to forget the feeling I felt when Emily and I said goodbye, and the thought that both of us might die out there in the cold."

"Sometimes, forgetting is the mechanism our brain uses to help us remember," said the doctor.

I nodded. "I want to remember the people we met. I want to remember the innkeeper, and I want to remember Jim and Nancy. I want to remember the kindness of strangers. I feel like I need to write something important about all the lessons we learned through this experience. But what if I don't have anything important to say? What if everything I say is shallow and trite and obvious?"

"Who are you writing this book for?" she asked.

"I guess I'm writing it for me," I replied.

"Why? Why would you write a book for yourself? What does this story *mean* to you?" she asked again.

"I don't know yet," I said. "But I know I have to write it."

"Have you ever written anything before?" she asked.

"Actually, yeah. I've been writing all my life," I replied. "I started writing short stories and poetry when I was a little kid. My dad even helped me submit one of my books to a publisher when I was in fourth grade."

"Sounds like you have a pretty good dad," she said.

"Yeah, he's a good guy. My parents have always been very supportive," I nodded with a smile. "So that's how I got started writing. And I loved it so much… There's nothing in the world more satisfying than building something beautiful — singing a song or painting a picture or telling a story — and then when I went to college, I studied playwriting. I was hoping to be a screenwriter someday."

"What happened to that dream?" she asked.

"I put that dream on hold a long time ago…" I said. "Back when the twins were born, I put all my writing ambitions on the back burner. I was scared about the uncertainty of a career in the arts, and I knew I'd probably make better money working as a computer programmer."

"Do you ever wish you could suddenly change your destiny?" she asked. "Do you wish you could snap your fingers and return to the arts?"

"I think about it all the time," I replied. "For the past ten years, I've been daydreaming about it every day."

"So what does this book *mean* to you?" she asked again.

"This book is my big chance to change my life," I said, my eyes filling with tears. "This is my chance to come back to the kind of work I love the most. I've been waiting ten years for a chance like this."

"Okay," said Dr. Marques. "If that's what this *book* means to you, then what does the *shipwreck* mean to you?"

By this point, the tears were streaming down my cheeks.

"I don't know. I don't know," I sobbed. "I think about all the people — tens of thousands, if you count the passengers and the crew plus their families and friends — whose lives were turned upside down by this disaster. Thirty-two people died out there… How can I take all this suffering and just treat it like an opportunity for me to write a book? Isn't that just the worst kind of selfishness?"

"I don't know. What kind of book are you writing?" she asked. "Are you going to write the kind of book that exploits their suffering?"

"No," I replied. "I want to write a book that honors their memory. I want to write a book that brings them joy. I want to write a book that *means something*."

"What does it mean to you?" she asked again.

"It means… we can do *anything*," I said. "It means, even in the worst of circumstances, we can still find peace and beauty and truth. It means we can overcome adversity. Even when our ship sinks into the sea, and all seems lost, when our hearts are heavy with sadness and our minds are burdened with anxiety… we can either view that moment as a devastating loss or as an opportunity to create something wonderful and share it with the world. The sheer joy of *creation* can uplift our spirits more than almost anything."

Dr. Marques smiled.

"Go write that book."

65

That was it for me. That was the end of therapy.

And I knew exactly what I had to do: I had to go write this book.

I would take my crazy energy and convert it into creative energy until the crazy energy dried up, leaving nothing behind but the instinct to create. I didn't know if the book would be any good or if anybody would read it. But for the next ten months, I would spend every day writing and rewriting, scratching my head and trying to figure out how to tell the story.

Meanwhile, Emily wasn't quite finished with her therapy. She had withdrawn from her social life and had been spending most of her days at home alone in the house, wrapped in a blanket and watching TV. She still went to rehearsals and flew out to gigs, but she became socially withdrawn and it seemed like the joy had drained from all her former passions.

At first, she stopped going to therapy with me too. Both of us presumed that we had recovered from our trauma, and we resumed our former lives. But in my case, I dove into the writing process, spending hundreds of hours untangling the tentacles of this story and putting words down on pages. Emily hadn't gone through that process, so her mind was still tangled in knots, and she... well, she got stuck.

And now that she was stuck, she didn't want to have coffee with her friends in the afternoons or go out to dinner with her colleagues after a gig. She just wanted to see me. I was the only person in the world who she felt like she could trust, and she didn't want to spend time with anybody else. *Why bother with them anyhow?*

"I'm not getting better," she said to me one day.

I put my arm around her and touched the back of her ear. She looked down at the floor and held back the tears.

"You can go back to therapy again," I said.

But she didn't want to go back to therapy. She was supposed to be better by now, right? She was supposed to be happy to be alive and grateful for each new day. But every day felt bleaker than the one before, and she didn't know why. She didn't want to admit defeat, and she felt like a failure for failing to spring back into life with the same gusto as before. She didn't know what to do, and she didn't know why she couldn't do it.

"And it will cost too much money anyhow," she said. "It's four hundred dollars per session, and she doesn't take health insurance."

But I insisted she go back. There is no medical bill so high that I'm willing to give up my wife's happiness. I would rather go into lifelong debt than see her sanity deteriorate.

So she went back to therapy.

* * *

"I don't understand why I'm still so angry and sad," said Emily. "I should be fine by now."

"Well, I don't know why you're angry or why you're sad, but I know we can find out why," said the doctor. "I'm going to ask you to tell your whole story, from the beginning of the shipwreck to the end. I want you tell me all the details — as much as you can remember about everything that happened — and I'm going to record the whole story. It will probably take us a few sessions to get through the whole thing, but when we're done, I'll give you a recording you can take home. I'll ask you to listen to that recording over and over and over again. When you're at home alone during the day and Benji is at work, just listen to these recording and think about how they make you feel. After that, we'll use our sessions to talk about those feelings and hone in on the specific triggers of your anger and sadness. It's kind of like using an x-ray to find an injury, if you think about it."

I wasn't there, so I didn't hear the stories she told. And I never listened to any of the recordings, so I can't say exactly what transpired during those sessions. But I know during that time, that the life and light and happiness came back into Emily's face. I think she forgave the world for its imperfections, and in the process maybe forgave some of her own.

But there was one thing in particular that emerged near the end of these final weeks of therapy. She kept thinking about a moment back on the night of the shipwreck, in the wee hours of the morning, after we had finally been rescued and taken back to Giglio Island. In the wee hours of the morning, under the gathering twilight of dawn, as we sat on the floor of the Hotel Bahamas — surrounded by a dramatis personae of wide-eyed castaways — Emily had looked around and found all the rest of us sleeping.

For just ten or fifteen minutes, all the rest of us drifted off into slumber, leaving Emily behind.

All alone.

"I was so mad at them," she said. "And I know it sounds stupid, but I just felt like it wasn't *fair* for them to be sleeping when I was still awake, planning and plotting and obsessing about how to get everyone home safely. I wanted to sleep too, you know? But I couldn't, because my brain just wouldn't stop shouting at me. And then… when everybody was asleep, I felt so lonely. Not just because they were asleep, but because maybe I was the only one who was so messed up inside that I couldn't even fall asleep."

"Actually, sleep is a coping mechanism," said Dr. Marques. "Most people who manage to get some sleep within 24 hours of a traumatic event are able to recover much more quickly than if they hadn't slept. In these cases, sleeping is actually a *stress response*, with therapeutic benefits. So if you didn't get any sleep that night, it makes sense that you're still carrying around more negative feelings with you. But it's not a sign of weakness, and you shouldn't feel bad that your body and your brain had a different response. But don't be angry at them for sleeping either. They were just doing what their bodies told them to do."

We didn't realize it at the time, but Emily was embarking upon the same course of treatment as I had begun myself. Both of us recorded our stories — me on paper, and she on tape — but the real healing for both of us came from listening.

When she went back and listened to her own words in that recording, I like to think she experienced something similar to what I felt as I went back and rewrote these chapters, crafting the language until it felt authentic. It's not just that we were looking for the words to accurately represent our emotions, but also to clarify who we wanted to become on the other side.

And that's how Emily stopped going to therapy too.

Dr. Marques told her to come back anytime if she ever needed to talk.

66

Every night, I sat on the couch with a computer on my lap, tapping away at the keys.

And every night, Emily sat next to me — the glow of a laptop screen illuminating her face — writing music and recording bits and pieces of songs. As soon as we got home from the shipwreck, Emily had been talking about recording an album of new music inspired by the shipwreck, but now she was hard at work, actually making it happen.

"You know, I've always wanted to write this music," she said. "This is the music that was always inside me, from even before the shipwreck. But I've always been such a perfectionist — like, a *crippling* perfectionist — and I never felt like my life was profound enough to write any profound music about anything. That's the thing about classically-trained musicians... Improvisation is risky and scary, and we have this crazy idea that all of the really *good* music was written by dead guys five hundred years ago with dramatic important lives. And our job is just to perform it — and *interpret* it — with as much virtuosity as possible... We're taught to be technicians almost more than we're taught to be musicians."

"So, what changed?" I asked.

"I guess, after the shipwreck," she said, "there's not really anything left to be afraid of anymore. For a while, I was still stuck back on the ship. Like my brain hadn't ever gotten off... But once I figured out the reasons why I was still so sad and angry — and when the therapist helped me overcome all those issues — now I actually wonder how I could ever have been so scared of really *making* music. And once I wasn't afraid anymore to tell people how I really feel, it opened up the light inside of me that said: share this music with people."

"Do you remember what the voice doctor said?" she continued. "The vocal cords are the most expressive organ in the human body. And there are emotions we can only express with our voices. That's what I want to do with this music."

So Emily wrote her music, and I wrote my book.

We're not sure whether the projects healed us or whether the healing enabled us to finish our projects. But this is how we've taken a catastrophe and folded it back into the fabric of our lives.

67

One afternoon, long before we started dating, Emily and I ate lunch at a Thai restaurant across the street from our house. We were getting to know each other and talking about our childhood years. I told Emily what it had been like growing up in a Mormon family, and she told me about growing up in a typical Hong Kong family, as the only daughter of two musicians. But I was particularly interested in one unusual story she told me about going to kindergarten in Hong Kong.

The elementary schools in Hong Kong are all paid for by the government, but many of them are staffed and operated by religious organizations, most of them Christian churches. Emily went to a Protestant kindergarten and a Roman Catholic elementary school, where she learned all of the prayers by heart, as well as all the fundamental principles of Chinese philosophy.

"If you think you know the Tao, then that is not the Tao," she said. "We used to say it every morning when we got to school."

"So what is that?" I asked. "Is that from Taoism?"

"Yeah, but that's only part of why we learn it. It's really just a part of a the whole tapestry of Chinese ideas, including Confucianism and Buddhism and Taoism, not to mention Christianity and British imperialism and capitalism. Hong Kong is a real melting pot of ideas. We learned the *Tao Te Ching* at the same time as we learned Grimm's Fairy Tales and Hans Christian Andersen."

"How old were you when you learned that?"

"Five years old," she replied. "Kindergarten."

My eyes lit up. I could just imagine a class full of five-year-olds in 1989 or 1990. Little Chinese girls with pigtails and red ribbons, sitting in rows in their Catholic school classroom, repeating in unison "The Tao is not the Tao."

"Wow," I blinked. "That's a pretty advanced concept for a little kid."

"Not really," she shrugged. "That's just an ordinary part of everyday life in Hong Kong."

"Did you even know what you were saying?" I asked. "Why do they teach about the Tao so early?"

"No, actually. I had no idea what I was saying." she said. "But it seemed like a cool idea at the time, and it planted a seed that I eventually understood much later."

Just like American culture has embedded within it the idea of meritocracy and entrepreneurship and Christianity all rolled into a conglomerate Americanism religion, the same thing is true in Hong Kong: before learning anything about math or science, or really how to even read and write, they're learning about ambiguity. They're learning to question certainty.

In American culture, philosophical ideas *compete* with one another, but in Chinese culture, ideas are made for mixing. Because ideas themselves are ephemeral.

If you think you understand, you do not understand.

68

A few months after the shipwreck, Emily and I flew to Washington to see my kids. Although Emily had talked to them on the phone and video-chatted with them over Skype, this was the first time they would meet each other face-to-face.

As we pulled up in front of their house and parked the car, the kids' faces appeared in the window and their eyes sparkled when they saw Emily.

The main event that weekend would be a day spent at Snoqualmie Summit, a few hours outside of Seattle, where I would spend a day teaching Owen and Macy to snowboard. But with Chloe's cerebral palsy, she's not really much of a snowboarder.

We took her swimming instead, at a huge indoor pool with a big water slide. Because that's what Chloe likes :)

When we got inside the swimming center, I helped Chloe change into her swimming suit and slid her water wings — a pair of plastic inflatable floats — up onto her arms near her shoulders. She was so excited, she couldn't contain it anymore. She flapped her arms up and down like a happy little penguin and looked up at me, her eyes a little bit crossed, and said "let's go swimming, daddy."

Then I strapped on her styrofoam life jacket — she had always worn this whenever she went swimming, since long before Emily and I ever set foot on a cruise ship together — and buckled the straps before we walked to the water's edge.

We slid down the slide five times. And then we splashed around in the pool until closing time, Chloe clinging to my body with her arms and legs like a koala bear cub. Emily swam with Owen and Macy, and together the five of us laughed and played and hugged.

The next day, we drove up into the mountains. It was late in the season, and the snow would be melting soon.

Macy picked up snowboarding effortlessly, especially for a seven year old. When we got to the top of the hill, she would race down the slope as fast as she could fly. But since she didn't know how to turn (or stop), she would tumble dramatically into a snowdrift, sending a plume of upturned crystalline dust into the air.

"Are you alright down there?" I would ask.

"I'm fine!"

"Do you need any help?" I would call down to her.

"No!"

And then she would untangle her arms and legs on her own, grunting and heaving until she got back up onto her feet again, finding her balance, and then suddenly swooshing into motion again, slicing through the snow at maximum velocity before losing control and crashing into the snow again. All day long, she crashed and got back up and crashed and got back up. Again and again.

But Owen is a bit of a worrier. He worries about losing his balance. He worries that the snow might be too slippery or that his boots might not be quite tight enough. Most of all, he worries that he'll fall down and hurt himself, which makes him clench his shoulders, which makes him lose his balance, which makes him fall down. Of course. And then he's so shaken up and upset by falling that he loses even more confidence, which throws him even further off-balance. He's so sweet and sensitive and caring, but worry is his downfall.

To help him overcome those worries, I rode along with him, my knees behind his knees and my hands on his waist. He could feel the way my hips turned and the way I balanced my body as I steered us through the turns. Pretty soon, I could feel his shoulders unclench. My presence there gave him confidence and steadied him. And when he felt steady enough, I loosened my grip and let him ride on his own.

It took him a moment to realize I wasn't there anymore, but when he turned to see me, he didn't panic. Instead, he threw his hands up in the air and shouted, "Yes yes yes!" as he broke away from me and rode down to the base of the hill on his own.

* * *

After saying goodbye to the kids and leaving Seattle, Emily and I travelled to San Francisco for a few days and had a do-over honeymoon.

We spent a couple of days in San Francisco itself, walking through the Mission District and admiring Dave Eggers' pirate shop and eating sushi. It was the weekend of the pride parade, and the city was full of life and energy, and we loved every moment of it. Then we spent a day driving through Napa Valley and enjoying the local restaurants with fresh-picked vegetables from organic gardens and wine from the vineyard's own cellar.

But our real destination on this trip was Harbin Hot Springs.

* * *

You can hear the sound of water everywhere.

Harbin Hot Springs is actually one of the oldest nonprofit resorts in California. The hillside is dotted with springs, some of them hot from a deep volcanic furnace and some of them cold from shallower aquifers. And for hundreds of years the people living nearby — natives or settlers or modern Americans — have ascribed healing properties to the waters from those springs.

The first incarnation of the resort was built in 1870, and over the next hundred and forty years, it's been a hotel, a hunting lodge, a boxing camp, a free-form university, and I think also a hippie commune. But the central attraction has always been the springs themselves, trickling down the rolling foothills and forming pools where travellers would soak their weary bones.

These days, the flow and temperature of water is carefully controlled by mixing the output of the hottest springs and the coldest springs, and then piping it into a collection of five different pools in the main area, as well as a variety of other smaller pools in the camping areas or near the lodges. You can pitch your own tent, or you can stay in one of the big canvas tents or cabins that are permanently erected on the property. I'm not sure why, but all of them are in the shape of huge circular domes. Like geodesic igloos, or lunar encampments from the future.

Ever since the early 1970s, the resort has been operated as a nonprofit retreat, deep in the woods and off the beaten path, about two hours north of San Francisco.

And the San Francisco vibe is all over the place. I almost think of Harbin as being the temple for San Franciscanism — a mecca of hippies connecting with their universe using whatever ancient traditional symbols they can find: burning sage, statues of Buddhas, dream-catchers, and stone altars and arches. Down the hill from the pools and past the lodge, there's a great circular temple where they offer yoga classes and meditation sessions.

The place is operated by a staff of about a hundred permanent residents. They earn a fair wage for performing the duties of the resort — cooking or cleaning or working in the massage studio or balancing the checkbook — and then in return, they pay a fair price for their food and shelter and community. Some of the residents have lived at Harbin for more than twenty years.

Emily and I had already registered for a one-hour *watsu* session in a pool near the domes, so we checked in at the front desk and then found our way up to the watsu pool. The word "watsu" is actually a portmanteau of the words "water" and "shiatsu," but the experience is a bit more unusual than what you'd expect. It's not really anything like getting a shiatsu massage.

"The first thing we're going to do," said the therapist as she stood facing me, chest-deep in a pool of warm water, "is attach these floats to your ankles and wrists. Then I want you to close your eyes and lean your head back and relax. I'll do everything else."

When she finished rigging my limbs with soft foam buoys, she hooked her arms beneath my shoulders and began to spin my body around hers in a slow outward spiral, stretching my muscles and tilting my head slightly back and opening up my chest toward the sky. Then, in one seamless motion, she released my right shoulder and reached for my left knee, using my momentum through the water to reposition herself at my side, guiding and gliding my body like a dolphin. With my eyes closed and the gurgling sound of water bubbling around my ears, I felt like I had been transported to another dimension.

For the next hour, my mind disconnected from the real world around me and then eventually from the thoughts of my inner world, until the only thing left was the sensation of exis-

351

tence and the dual joys of warmth and movement. This must be what fish feel like when they dance.

The whole time, Emily was in the pool nearby, experiencing the same cozy swirling and stretching, her therapist moving her through a variety of poses like an undersea marionette with invisible strings.

Eventually, the hour elapsed, and we emerged from the trance feeling lively and refreshed and particularly hungry.

We ate a hearty late-afternoon lunch: thick chunks of organic chicken and slices of fresh mango stewed in a rich yellow curry sauce, over a bed of brown rice, with fresh apple juice on the side. When we finished eating, we licked our fingers clean.

From there, we climbed up the hill to the main area with the five spring-water pools. There were fifty or sixty people soaking in the pools or sunning themselves on the wooden deck or walking the stone steps through the trees to the upper pool.

Nearly everyone was nude. This wasn't a nudist resort *per se*, but the pools are all part of a clothing-optional area, and very few guests choose to avail themselves of that option.

Emily and I put down our things on a bench near the deck. She flashed me a wry smile and a wink as she unbuttoned her shirt. I smiled and winked back. Then both of us shed our clothes, baring ourselves to the elements and to each other and to the dozens of strangers all around us.

The pools are temperature-regulated according to the goldilocks principle: some of them are hot and some are cold, but one of the pools is *juuuuuust* right. And of course, the hottest and coldest pools are both designed to be barely tolerable, at the furthest ends of the human temperature spectrum. Naturally, one of the most popular activities here is to move back and forth between those two extreme pools, enjoying the heart-stopping moment of shock when going directly from the hot pool into the cold pool, or vice versa.

The middle-temperature pool is a heart-shaped basin lined with blue porcelain tile, designated as a place for socializing. A dozen or so people floated around the edges, their heads sticking up out of the water as they whispered quietly to one another, sometimes softly laughing.

Emily and I stepped into the pool and smiled at the other people already there. They said hello and smiled back. Something about this situation felt exceptionally good: all of these strangers gathered together, each of us naked and vulnerable and weightless in the water. I felt a sense of trust in this space; it was baked into the tiles and dissolved in the water, like a trace mineral coming up from the bedrock and through the aquifer.

I wondered where this water went when it drained from these pools. Did it flow from here down into a babbling mountain creek? Did the creek join with others to form a stream and feed a river? Where would the water go when it left here?

Then we noticed that even this pool was fed by a trickle of hot steaming water, emanating from one of the pools above. We rose from this pool, our bodies dripping wet, and walked up through the rocks into a stone building fed by the hottest of the hot springs.

A sign hung overhead: *Silence please. This is a contemplative space.*

We slipped into the water as quickly as possible, without stopping to think about the sudden scalding sensation on our skin. Within moments, the heat would become overwhelming.

There were only a few people in here, most of them with their eyes closed and breathing deeply. The only other sound in the room was the soft splash as someone slid into the pool or emerged from the water, climbing the stone steps near the entryway. Fresh hot water poured in through a slot in the wall, straight from its underground source and onto our flesh.

In my mind now, I imagined this water flowing down into a great mighty river — rushing and roaring into a valley far below — quenching the thirst of the people and their crops and their animals.

I looked around at the other visitors here, soaking at the very source of that great river. With our costumes cast away, here we were just *people*, enjoying a simple elemental pleasure together.

When we could no longer withstand the heat, we left that stone room and dipped ourselves into the coldest pool. A thousand tiny excruciating pinpricks erupted all over our skin. It was like being wrapped in a blanket of frozen daggers, the shock strong enough to knock the wind out of us and deprive us of breath. I submerged my head beneath the water for a second — just long enough to wet my hair and face — and then pulled myself up out of the pool, my naked body now covered in goose-flesh but feeling so vibrant and so alive.

We spent a few hours there, resting and relaxing in the warm pool between alternating turns teasing our senses with blistering heat and frigid cold.

"I can't remember when I felt so alive," I told Emily.

"I know," she said, as we toweled off and got dressed again. "This is a special place."

In the early evening, we went down to the temple and joined a group of residents and guests for an hour making music together, sitting on pillows in a circle at the center of the wide circular room. Some of the people in the group were skilled musicians, but most of us just followed our instincts, making joyful sounds with our voices and our hands, singing and clapping and banging on drums. Nobody gave any instructions or passed out any sheet music, and nobody needed it anyhow. Without coordinating anything at all, we formed a collective voice... and our common song rose up into the evening air.

This was the sound of life.

When the song subsided, we put away the drums and stacked up the pillows.

"Let's go back up to the water," I said to Emily, taking her hand and leading her out the door of the temple, back up the hill toward the five pools.

The sun had set while we had been inside making music, and now the nighttime sky was decorated with the dazzling ornamentation of ten thousand constellations twinkling overhead.

We stopped in our tracks.

Emily looked up and whispered, "the stars are so beautiful tonight."

We stood there awhile, looking up at the heavens and thinking about our life together, overcome with gladness and gratitude.

THE END

Thanks

I'll try to keep this short and sweet.

I'd like to say thank you to my dear wife, Emily, who was by my side at every moment of this wild odyssey. I couldn't imagine being on this journey without her.

We were also blessed to travel with some of our favorite people in the world. Thanks John and Apple, for taking this crazy trip with us, and for introducing us to Erik and Chui Lin.

Emily and I would like to express our most heartfelt gratitude to Nancy Boyd and Jim Zingeser who gave us a place to stay in Rome, taking us into the bosom of their home and making us part of their family. We will never forget such kindness and generosity.

Naturally, we're grateful to Daryn Tufts and Cam Deaver and Sean Kaplan, for using the magic of Facebook to find Jim and Nancy for us.

We'd also like to thank Jamie Walker for nurturing us through our first major media appearance and proving to us that some journalists out there truly care about the subjects of their reporting. We've met a handful of other journalists with the same kind of dedication and heart, but none who exemplified those qualities quite as thoroughly as Jamie.

Special thanks to Paolo Fanciulli, for opening the doors of the Hotel Bahamas to hundreds of desperate strangers and emptying his cupboards for all of us. We're likewise thankful to the management and staff of the Airport Mariott Hotel Roma who put a roof over our heads and food in our bellies, with no advanced warning that a hundred castaways would be dumped on their doorstep.

Of course, we wouldn't be where we are today without the expert touch of Dr. Luana Marques, who helped us recover our sanity after this trauma and taught us to make something meaningful from it.

I'd like to thank my co-workers at Hopper for being so understanding of my first few frazzled months back on the job, as well as all of Emily's musical collaborators for their patience while she got back in the groove again.

I'm also very grateful to my editor, James Dargan, for believing in this project so fully and for helping me find the words to tell this story.

We can't say "thank you" enough to all the other generous people at home and abroad who took care of us: Rod Fernandez, from AffordableTours.com, for flying us home; Dr. Mark Palermo, in Rome, for listening to our fresh traumatic rantings and helping us put a name to our "electric-spaghetti" emotions; the members of the Italian Coast Guard and the search and rescue teams who risked their own health and safety to come to the rescue; the aide workers and EMTs who brought food and warm socks and medical attention; the kind people in the congregation of the Trinity Episcopal Cathedral in Miami, who wired us cash when we got back to Boston and helped us replace our lost clothes and luggage.

There are many many others who helped us along the way — dozens, if not hundreds — who are missing from this list, including so many of the passengers and crew of the Costa Concordia who bravely offered help to those in need. Thanks for your unsung help, and I wish I had enough room here to thank everyone personally.

Finally, Emily and I would like to express our deepest condolences to the families and friends of the thirty-two people who lost their lives in this catastrophe. We think about them often, and their memory has fueled the fire of our passion to tell this story. We're so sorry for your loss, and we hope this story honors their memory.

One More Thing

A book without readers is an empty, hollow, lifeless thing, so I'd like to offer a huge heartfelt thanks to *you* for reading this book. I hope you'll keep in touch. Come swing by my website and say hello anytime:

www.benjismith.net/thanks-for-reading

Writing this book has really meant a lot to me — honestly, it's been just as much of a life-changing experience as the shipwreck itself — but I also hope it'll be the first of many.

At my website, there's a sign-up form where you can register for my newsletter, and I'll email you with info about the next book when it's ready for publication.

But in the mean time, I hope you'll also check out Emily's album, *Isle of Lucidity*, a beautiful and haunting collection of original compositions inspired by the shipwreck events:

www.emily-lau.com/isle-of-lucidity

The music on this album was all written and recorded during the same nine-month period when I wrote this book. So you can think of the two works as companion pieces, telling the same story but with entirely different building-blocks.

You can download a digital copy from the iTunes music store, or you can buy an actual compact disc at CDBaby.com or Amazon.com.

CPSIA information can be obtained at www.ICGtesting.com
Printed in the USA
LVOW130238230513

335164LV00001B/2/P